TRAINING IN CHRISTIANITY

TRAINING IN CHRISTIANITY

AND THE

EDIFYING DISCOURSE

WHICH 'ACCOMPANIED' IT

BY

SØREN KIERKEGAARD

TRANSLATED

WITH AN INTRODUCTION AND NOTES

BY

WALTER LOWRIE, D.D.

PRINCETON
PRINCETON UNIVERSITY PRESS

First published in Great Britain, 1941

Reprinted by offset in the United States of America, 1944

ISBN 0-691-01959-2

First Princeton Paperback printing, 1967
Third printing, 1972

PREFACE

THIS volume, and another of equal size which I propose to bring out on the same date, contain between them six works which originally were published separately, but which now are all of them, with exception of the last 'Discourse', comprised in vol. xii of the Danish edition of Kierkegaard's *Collected Works*. This present volume contains only two of these works: the longest of them all, *Training in Christianity* and the 'Edifying Discourse' which accompanied it. The other volume contains *Two Discourses at the Communion on Fridays*, the two longer works, *For Self-Examination* and *Judge for Yourselves!*, and concludes with the 'Edifying Discourse' entitled *The Unchangeableness of God*, which was published in 1855, in the midst of the open attack upon the Established Church, but which had been written in 1851 and was actually preached on May 18th of that year.

These works were written in the order in which they here appear, and they are the last works Kierkegaard wrote—the last at least which properly belong to what he called his 'authorship', for the newspaper articles and pamphlets, which were issued so rapidly and in such abundance during the last eight months of his life (chiefly in 1855) when he was engaged in the open attack, did not in his eyes belong to the category of literature: he accounted them rather a *deed*, a deed in the doing of which he died. This attack was preceded by a pause of approximately three years during which he published nothing. The period we are here concerned with was limited vaguely on one side by this pause, but very precisely on the other by a profound experience of the forgiveness of sin which prompted him to exclaim, 'My whole nature is changed. I must speak'—meaning, as the sequel shows, that now for the first time he *could* speak out, utter his mind *directly*, without needing to employ the device of 'indirect communication'. The date of this experience was April 19th (Wednesday in Holy Week), 1848. In this experience he was so radically changed that all of the works he produced after this date bear a distinctive, an unmistakable stamp.

In the division of labour, which is clearly necessary in the translation of S. K.'s numerous works, I have made myself responsible for all the works of this period, with exception of *The Sickness unto Death*, which has been translated by Mr. Payne and will soon be published along with Mr. Dru's translation of *The Concept of Dread*, an earlier work which is closely associated with this, not only by its theme, but also by the fact that S. K. describes both books as 'psychological'. I have already published Kierkegaard's intimate self-revelation, *The Point of View*, together with the other documents which properly go with it. I was in haste to produce this, so that it may be available as a guide to the earlier works which have already been published in English or are about to be. And I am in haste also to publish the volumes now being issued, containing the last and most decisive expressions of S. K.'s Christian convictions. Hence I translated them promptly, and now that they are translated I publish them—without waiting to produce, as I intend to do, translations of the earlier 'Discourses' of this period (*Christian Discourses*, the Discourses about the Lilies and the Birds, and the Discourses about 'The High Priest', &c., as well as the Discourses about *The Works of Love* which belong to the end of the preceding period).

But although my impatience has led me to put the last first, I am not unmindful of the 'difficulty' to which Professor Swenson rather anxiously called my attention, remarking that '*Training in Christianity* and the subsequent quasi-polemical discourses are very strong meat, not just adapted for babes. To introduce these discourses of Kierkegaard to an unprepared public, and one which is so far from having any very concrete religious education as our public in America, either experimentally or ideologically, is certainly putting the blunt end of the wedge in first, and may cause misunderstanding.' This is true, it may cause a little misunderstanding, and many who do not misunderstand may be offended—and yet a man so 'unprepared' as Georg Brandes, a Jewish free-thinker, said of the *Training in Christianity*, 'I consider this book one of his most admirable writings, and it is a work above all distinguished for acuteness of thinking and love of the truth. He who cannot find time to read many of the works of Kierkegaard's last period must at least read this book thoroughly. In it he will find Kierkegaard's whole train of thought and his most profound feeling.' And I have in mind also a remark made to me some years ago by Professor Geismar, to the effect that the

book entitled *For Self-Examination*, because it is the clearest, had
best be put first before a reader who wants to know what was
essential in S. K.'s thought. This remark, as it seems to me,
applies with no less force to *Training in Christianity* and to *Judge
for Yourselves!* and with even greater force to the Discourses
which are distributed in these two volumes of mine.

So I do not hesitate to publish now these latest works, which
are so clear and definite in their aim that they may serve to define
the tendency and purpose of the earlier, the strictly pseudonymous
works which seem to leave the either/or undecided, which are so
delightful to the reader, but are so ambiguous, so full of mystification, so baffling. Moreover, being a serious person in a serious
calling, one of the 'parsons' so roughly treated in these last works,
it is a matter of course that I should devote my effort to rendering
these most serious books accessible, leaving the philosophical
works to Swenson as Professor of Philosophy, and to more aesthetic
persons the 'aesthetical' works. It is not my fault if by prodigious industry and by reason of leisure from other tasks I have got
a little ahead of the procession.

In fact I am not far ahead of it. It is amazing how much has
been published in the space of two years. My biographical
sketch of S. K. in a sense opened the way. In a sense it was the
thin edge of the wedge. But this big book was preceded by Mr.
Dru's translation of Haecker's admirable little book, and by the
publication of Professor Geismar's lectures in America. Professor
Swenson's translation of the *Philosophic Fragments* had already
appeared, and I have no doubt that before these present volumes
are published his prodigious labour of translating the *Unscientific
Postscript* will be completed. In the mean time, Mr. Dru has
published his *Selections from the Journal* in a big volume which is
more adequate than the German edition, he is working on *The
Concept of Dread*, and translations of *Fear and Trembling* and *The
Present Age* have appeared beside my own translation of *The Point
of View*. Slighter things of and about S. K. have been appearing unexpectedly in various quarters during the last couple of
years. Professor Steere of Haverford College was at work for
some time translating one of the most important of S. K.'s 'Discourses', and was working as hard to find a publisher—when to
his chagrin the same thing was published in London by Daniel,
in a translation by Aldworth and Ferrie—a book of 180 pp.

entitled *Purify Your Hearts!* Professor Steere properly punctuated
the significance of this fact when he said to me, 'There are more
hens sitting on these eggs than we have any notion of'. Mr. Dru's
translation of *The Concept of Dread* will soon be published at the
same time as Mr. Payne's translation of *The Sickness unto Death*.
From this it will be seen that nothing of importance in S. K.'s
prodigious 'authorship' remains unaccounted for except the
Eighteen Edifying Discourses, *Prefaces*, and *Stages on Life's Road*
—and at both ends of the 'authorship' (but outside of it according
to S. K.'s reckoning) his dissertation on *The Concept of Irony*, and
the brief and pungent articles of the open attack, which all united
make a big volume. It seems probable therefore that within so
brief a period as five years the whole of S. K.'s works will be made
available in English.

This result seems nearly incredible when I reflect that only a
short while ago, when I had come back to America as an apostle
of European culture and published in 1932, in a little book on
The Theology of Crisis, a brief bibliography of Kierkegaardian
books in German, I called attention to our complete lack of such
a literature and concluded with a challenge which was perhaps too
trenchant, or perhaps too querulous: 'For what reason have we
so many universities? Is it to ensure that studious youth shall be
shielded from contact with contemporary thought?' This was
printed in type so small that I hoped no one would notice it, but
I was reminded of it lately by seeing it quoted in a review of
Swenson's translation of the *Fragments*. The progress made since
that date is not only far beyond my hope but beyond my understanding. Not long ago Henry Leach, editor of the *Forum*, and at
that time President of the American–Scandinavian Foundation,
dramatically apostrophized me in a public place as the man responsible for all this—'by making everybody mad'. Still I do not
understand how it all came about. For though I must suppose
that Mr. Leach's injurious qualification was true—or at least that
I had made him mad, unintentionally and unwittingly—it is not
true that I am responsible for what came about, except in the
sense that a man is responsible for an explosion when a mine is
already charged and he sets fire to the fuse. In England Mr.
Alexander Dru was pressing the cause as earnestly as I was, and
over here Professor Swenson was ready to devote his life to it.
Humanly speaking, this amazing result is attributable to the

Oxford University Press, which, first of all in the person of Mr. Charles Williams, became interested, then concerned, and then excited, about the enterprise of publishing S. K.'s works. It undertook to do what no commercial press would ever undertake, thus filling, not 'a long felt want', but a long unfelt want, not (as S. K. would say) providing 'what the public demands', but what the public needs.

If this enterprise had been initiated with a clear prevision that it would result in the publication of S. K.'s Collected Works, an effort might perhaps have been made to publish these many books in the order in which they were written, or at least to conform to the criterion so ardently defended by S. K. in *The Point of View*, that 'the aesthetical' should come first, as it actually did in his 'authorship'. This, however, is a thesis which, stoutly as it was defended by S. K. (in defence of himself and what he had actually done), seems far from plausible in view of the fact that the earlier writings, instead of enticing men to follow the author into more serious fields, rendered them incapable of understanding or believing that he was really a serious man when he reached the point of uttering his most serious call. Hence the infinite pains he was put to when, in the *Point of View*, he sought to prove that from the very first his writings aimed at 'the religious', that from first to last he was a religious writer—a proposition which (to borrow an expression from Jeremy Taylor) 'had more truth than evidence on its side'. At all events, it has not been possible to conform to this criterion. And, in my opinion, it is not a matter of primary importance in what order S. K.'s works are published in English—more especially since they are all to be published within a short space of time. It is important only to avoid the gross affront to S. K. which was perpetrated long ago in Germany and in Italy by publishing *first*, in an anticlerical or anti-Christian interest, the open attack upon the Church, when the readers had no way of knowing (as one can know from the volumes which are here introduced) in what a profoundly Christian interest the attack was launched—and the no less gross affront which has been perpetrated in several languages (and lately in English) by publishing *first* 'The Diary of the Seducer', torn from its context in *Either/Or* (where it is justified by its position as a foil to the serious consideration of the meaning and importance of marriage) and presented in a salacious interest.

This Preface has perhaps been exorbitantly prolonged because the publication of S. K.'s works has reached a point where a survey of the whole enterprise is in place. I would prolong it still further by a reflection upon the perplexities encountered in so simple a task as the publication of another man's works.

I planned at first to publish in one big volume all the works now contained in these two volumes of moderate size. But I yielded readily to the desire of the publisher to present them in two volumes—and to Mr. Dru's vivacious protest that already the Danish editors had buried S. K. by uniting in large volumes the many works which he had published separately and (with but two exceptions) in small volumes. I yielded gladly, for no one is more eager than I to see these works published at such a price that the readers who might be expected to profit from them most may not, by the cost, be deterred from buying them. So the works I here comment upon are now issued in two volumes, and no one is constrained to buy more than one of them.

Nevertheless I would call attention to the extraordinary unity which pervades these six works. The reader will perceive that they properly belong together, insisting as they do upon the same themes and written as they are in the same style of 'direct communication'—the 'Discourses' no less than the longer works. Indeed, the longer works are assimilated to the Discourses by the fact that they comment formally and exclusively upon Scriptural texts, and by the constant personal address in the second person *singular*, which was so characteristic of S. K.'s aim to reach 'the single individual', 'my hearer', 'my reader', that I have felt compelled to use the singular forms of address, which are unfamiliar to us except in the Bible, instead of the familiar forms of the plural. The reader, in fact, cannot help feeling that what is said here is addressed to him individually, and it is difficult for the 'Christian' to extricate himself gracefully from this embarrassing situation when everything that is said is so directly and persuasively deduced from the New Testament. S. K.'s open attack upon the Established Church was so terrible and so unanswerable because there too he spoke with the New Testament in his hand, constantly referring to chapter and verse.

Had I united all these several works in one volume it would have been necessary to invent a title for the collection, and I could think of no title so appropriate as 'Kierkegaard's Serious Call'.

This, of course, was meant to recall the title of William Law's most famous book, *A Serious Call to a Devout and Holy Life*. Although there is no need now for a collective title, I would call attention to the striking likeness which exists between Kierkegaard in his last manner and Law in his first, before he became a mystic and put himself at a remote distance from S. K. And yet there are striking differences. It might well enough be said that S. K.'s serious call was to 'a devout and holy life', and yet such terms might be misleading, might be understood to mean no more than the 'hidden inwardness' which S. K. in this period disparaged, insisting instead upon the unequivocal duty of imitating Christ by actually following Him, with the inevitable consequence of suffering. His therefore was a serious call to suffering in likeness with Christ. From the very beginning of this period he resolutely discarded the 'unity of jest and earnest' which was characteristic of the pseudonyms in general, and here we have hardly a glimpse of the humour and poetry which lend so much charm to his earlier works. It is most evidently a *serious* call he now utters, and sometimes (like Law—and like Bunyan) he appears grim. Thirty years ago Professor William Palmer, writing an introduction to *Liberal and Mystical Writings of William Law*, said disparagingly of *A Serious Call*, that 'it is striking and terrible, if one is of Law's mind when he wrote it; and it may be amusing if one is not'. For my part, however I may contrive to shield myself against the force of S. K.'s serious call, I should not like to be the man who finds it amusing. There is no evidence that Law ever came to regard his earlier work as amusing, even when he had found refuge in mysticism from 'all that is stirring and terrible' in it. S. K., even when he was writing the stirring and terrible, found his refuge in 'grace', notwithstanding that he regarded all these writings as addressed principally to himself.

And here is another example of the perplexities which even a mere editor encounters. I had innocently proposed to adorn the large volume I had in mind with a frontispiece reproducing a photograph of the well-known statue of Christ by Thorwaldsen which is erected above the altar in the Cathedral Church of Copenhagen, where the statues of the Twelve Apostles (virile pagan figures!) are ranged on either side of the nave. This proposal provoked an indignant and horrified protest from Professor Swenson, who could point to a passage in *Training in*

Christianity (pp. 283 ff.) which is the most trenchant attack ever made upon Christian art, or rather upon the vain attempt to depict Christ in art. I confess that I read this passage with profound sympathy. Iconoclasm has been a recurrent phenomenon in the Church, and probably never was without justification. In the Eastern Church it got no farther than the abolition of 'graven images'. In Protestantism, especially in the Reformed branch, it was far more thoroughgoing. And now, when art seems to be on the point of paganizing Protestantism, S. K.'s passionate protest deserves to be heeded. And yet I did not yield to Swenson. The last words of the passage he triumphantly cited, a passage which apparently is so absolute, compel us to remember how dialectical S. K.'s positions were. It is not impossible that at one moment he derived inspiration from this statue, and the next moment decried fiercely the attempt to depict Christ. There is much to be said for this view. Almost every Sunday S. K. sat in the cathedral, listening to Mynster's sermons—and thinking his own thoughts, which he jotted down regularly in his Journal. And several times he stood in front of this statue to deliver one of his 'edifying discourses'. In one of the two *Christian Discourses* which were actually delivered in the cathedral on the occasion of a Friday Communion, he alluded, apparently, to this figure, perhaps even pointing to it, when he said: 'But thou knowest, my hearer, who the Inviter is, and thou hast followed the invitation to attach thyself more closely to Him. Behold He spreadeth out His arms and says, "Come hither, come hither unto *me*, all ye that labour and are heavy laden", behold, He invites thee to His bosom!' We do not know exactly when this discourse was delivered, but it was published on March 6th, 1848, and presumably it was on April 18th of the same year that he made three entries in the Journal, registering his purpose to write 'seven discourses' upon the theme which is inscribed in bold letters upon the base of the statue: COME UNTO ME. We see this resolution carried into effect in Part Three of *Training in Christianity*. Inasmuch as the 18th of April was Tuesday in Holy Week, S. K. presumably was in the cathedral and drew inspiration, if not from the sermon, at least from the statue. Moreover, since these are the entries immediately preceding the record of the profound religious experience of Wednesday, the inspiration he drew from the statue was presumably not unconnected with what may be called his third conversion. In *Training in Christianity* (p. 14) he refers again, presumably, to this statue, as if it were visible to the reader: 'The Invitation opens the Inviter's arms, and there He stands, an everlasting picture.' This argument is of a piece with the 'psychological microscopy' which P. A. Heiberg applied to S. K., and I cautiously use the word 'presumably' because no other writer, so far as I know, has noticed S. K.'s interest in Thorwaldsen's statue.

With such considerations to support me, I stubbornly resisted Professor Swenson's attack; but when Mr. Dru assailed me from behind with the indignant assertion that this statue 'is not art' (though he admitted reluctantly that S. K. was perverse enough to admire Thorwaldsen as an artist), and when my wife gave succour to my enemies—I had to yield. The story I tell here is therefore neither apology nor defence, but only a reminiscence of defeat, which may serve at the most to throw a little light upon S. K. This picture, however, shall be inserted in my own copy of this volume.

Nothing more remains to be said in this long preface, except that I have accompanied both of these volumes with such notes as may be wanted by readers who are not deeply acquainted with S. K.'s life and works. I am indebted to the Danish editors—or rather to the sole survivor of them, Dr. H. O. Lange—for permission to reproduce the notes which refer to Scandinavian literature. I have not thought it necessary to give the source of scriptural references as often as these editors do. As a matter of fact, the allusions to the New Testament are far more numerous than they have found it convenient to note. I have indicated them sufficiently by translating them in the familiar words of our version.

WALTER LOWRIE

PRINCETON

June 10th, 1938*

* This date indicates that the Preface was written almost three years before this book is actually published. After all, respect for Professor Swenson's scruple moved me to postpone the publication of this book until I had translated the milder Discourses contained in he volume entitled *Christian Discourses*, which was published in December of 1939. Nevertheless I prefer to leave the original Preface unchanged, as an historical document which bears witness to hopes which reasonably were entertained before the war. By the war the situation had been greatly changed. The

English collaborators have been drafted for sterner labours. I wonder that the Oxford University Press has had the courage to carry on. And in America the most indispensable worker in this field, Professor David F. Swenson, has been taken away by death. Upon me has devolved the task of completing his translation of the *Concluding Postscript*, which will be published by the Princeton University Press early in the coming year; and by that press there will be published at about the same time as this volume my translation of the *Stages on Life's Way*. I have also translated *The Sickness unto Death*, being encouraged to do so by the fact that Professor Swenson had begun it. In collaboration with the Rev. John M. Jensen I am translating *Repetition*, and I understand that Mrs. Swenson will see to it that the work her husband began on *Either/Or* will be carried to completion. It needs to be observed that the footnotes in this volume which are indicated by an asterisk are by the author, the others by the translator.

August 18, 1940

CONTENTS

A GENERAL INTRODUCTION

BY THE TRANSLATOR

GENERAL INTRODUCTION

A BOOK of mine on *Kierkegaard*, a very big book, which was published in 1938 by the Oxford University Press, contains two chapters ('Back to Christianity' and 'Venturing Far Out') which are specifically an introduction to the works comprised in this volume and a far more adequate introduction than I can furnish here. Because my book is big and costly I cannot assume that it is available to every reader of this translation, and yet the mere fact that it exists justifies me in making this introduction brief. Some time ago Admiral Mahan fired a shot which was heard around the world, when he demonstrated the strategical importance of 'a fleet in being', wherever it might be located; and here I reflect upon the importance of a book in being.

It has been pointed out in the Preface that the six works comprised in this and the companion volume (and five more of like character which are not comprised in it) belong to a distinctive period in S. K.'s life which began with the Easter experience of 1848, and that the writings of this period differ from all that went before, not only because of the concentration upon Christian themes, but also because of the directness of speech. The pseudonyms, which were so characteristic of the 'method of indirect communication', were all but abandoned, essentially abandoned. The continuity of these later works with the earlier production can be most clearly traced in the religious 'Discourses', which were never pseudonymous, and which 'accompanied' the pseudonymous works from the very beginning. In them we can mark a gradual development, from what is called in the *Postscript* 'religion A' ('religion in the sphere of immanence'), to 'religion B' ('religion in the sphere of transcendence')—that is, to the distinctively Christian categories. It will be noticed that all of the works in this volume formally resemble the 'Discourses' in the fact that they are based upon scriptural texts; but it is evident enough that they are not sermons which could be 'delivered' or were designed for delivery—not even three of the four which are here called 'Discourses'. In another instance S. K. points to the difference observable in the few 'Discourses' which were designed for delivery and actually were delivered. Although the

'Discourses' from first to last were published over S.K.'s name and undoubtedly reflect his personal beliefs, I have the impression that in the earlier period they regularly lagged behind the religious stage he had actually attained at the moment of writing, whereas in the pseudonymous works he was not restrained by diffidence or modesty from asserting positions somewhat in advance of his positive and secure attainment at the moment. He himself said of the *Postscript* that it represented a 'deliberation', and he said of all the pseudonymous works that they were his own schooling in Christianity. What he called his 'authorship' (which began with *Either/Or* and ended with the works here published) was a movement, a development, in a definite direction: 'Away from the aesthetical!'—'Away from speculation!'—'Back to Christianity!' Considering that it was all comprised within the brief period of eight years, it was a very rapid movement. He could well say that his position was that of a bird in flight. In the Preface to one of his Discourses at the Communion he said, 'The movement aptly terminates here at the foot of the altar'. In this volume we are dealing with the concluding stage.

And yet it must not be supposed that the themes which we encounter here are new. References to thoughts developed in the earlier works are here so frequent that I have not essayed to indicate them all in the footnotes. The pseudonyms, in fact, said the same things, but they said them in so different a way, and, alas, they said so much more, that S. K. finally felt obliged to warn his readers not to ascribe to him anything the pseudonyms had said. This imposes upon us great caution in interpreting S. K. by his earlier works, whereas we can be confident that everything we find in these last works gives exact expression to his thought and faith. They present to us the essential Kierkegaard. This, however, cannot be said of his last productions, the brief and pungent articles which constituted the newspaper and pamphleteering attack upon the Established Church. For there, naturally enough, he had little or nothing to say about fundamental Christian doctrines, but concentrated attention upon the abuses which he sought to reform, and for tactical reasons, as he confesses, he did not scruple to employ exaggeration.

True as it is that S. K.'s interest at this time was concentrated upon the most decisive Christian categories, there is one publication which stands out as a marked exception. It is entitled *The*

Crisis and a Crisis in the Life of an Actress, and it was an aesthetic appraisement of a distinguished actress. It gave pleasure in high circles, for she had become the wife of J. L. Heiberg, the arbiter of literary taste in Denmark. Although S. K.'s conscience pricked him terribly for publishing a work so out of keeping with the interests which absorbed him at that time, he was glad later to be able to point to it as a proof that he was not an author who had become religious only when advancing age had dulled his aesthetic sensibility.

No sooner had S. K. acquired the freedom to speak out than he felt the necessity of speaking out about himself with the aim of throwing light upon the earlier writings which he had perversely involved in so much mystification. This resulted in *The Point of View for My Work as an Author.* Though it is not complete enough to be called a biography, it is the most exquisitely biographical thing he wrote outside of his Journal. He had no difficulty in writing it, for in the Journal he had a hundred times more matter than he had use for here. But when it came to publishing he drew back. He was deterred more especially by the unusual scruple, 'whether a man has a right to let people know how good he is'. He finally decided to call this work 'an accounting', 'a report to history', and leave it to be published after his death. He eventually published, however, an impersonal abstract from it, entitled *About My Work as an Author.* And at this time he had the courage to publish an abstract of 'The Book on Adler', a book which he had taken the pains to rewrite three times without getting to the point of publishing it. This was called *Two Minor Ethico-Religious Treatises,* and the subjects discussed were: 'Whether a man has a right to let himself be put to death for the truth', and 'The Difference between a Genius and an Apostle'. Nothing could sound less personal than this, and yet these two themes were his deepest personal concern. The first of these essays, translated by Mr. Dru, was published after my translation of *The Point of View.*

Neither did he find any trouble in writing *Training in Christianity* in the most outspoken terms of rebuke; but when it came to publishing . . . ! The difficulty in this case was of a different sort: so far from disclosing to others how good he was, he might seem in this book to require others to be good when he was not, or to claim to be better than he actually was; and he could be sure that his summons, 'Back to Christianity!' and his description of the book as 'an endeavour to introduce Christianity into Christendom' would be resented as an attack upon the Established Church and would perhaps preclude the possibility of obtaining a benefice when his dwindling fortune was exhausted. It meant (to use his own figure of speech) 'venturing far out', like a lonely swimmer who floats 'above 70,000 fathoms of water', so far out that 'God can get hold of him' and there is no possibility of returning to the secure conditions of life on dry land. He had not yet acquired such a degree of heroism. Two years earlier he had been fearful about publishing *The Works of Love*, lest it gave offence to Bishop Mynster and others by its implied renunciation of the Lutheran dogma, 'by faith *alone*'. More recently he had had qualms about publishing *The Sickness unto Death*, notwithstanding that its principal offence was treating seriously the Christian doctrine of sin. His reluctance was finally overcome when he was smarting under an affront he had received from Mynster. 'Now let him have it', he said to himself as he handed the manuscript to the printer. It was ascribed to the pseudonym Anti-Climacus, but it was so far from being pseudonymous that he sent a copy, as he was accustomed to do with all his works, to the Bishop—and he was thankful that no complaint was made of it.

But *Training in Christianity* presented a far more serious case. In spite of the Moral and the Preface, it was clearly enough an attack upon 'established Christendom'. The open attack of 1855, in the midst of which S. K. died, contained nothing substantially new, nothing that had not been at least adumbrated in this book. No wonder then that the debate about publishing it was long and agonizing. At the moment when he had decided to publish it Chancellor Olsen, father of his one-time fiancée, died. That was a new complication, for the death of this irreconcilable enemy suggested the possibility of a friendly *rapprochement* to Regina, who was then happily married—and such a book as this might blast the hope. On the night when he received this news and was thrown by it into an agony of indecision, the debate was decided by an auditory hallucination in which contending voices were distinctly *heard* but hardly understood. S. K. was enough of a psychologist to ascribe both voices to his subliminal self, yet the experience was so terrible that it decided him to publish.

Although this book was written with the intention of publishing it over his own name, it was ascribed to Anti-Climacus, with the name of S. Kierkegaard on the title-page as editor. There is something childish in the glee he felt in the discovery of the pseudonym Anti-Climacus. It seemed to him to resolve the difficulty, although no one was left in the least doubt who the author was. The new pseudonym was reminiscent of Johannes Climacus, the reputed author of the *Scraps* and the *Postscript*, who was exceptionally competent to expound what Christianity is, but confessed of himself that he was not a Christian. Anti-Climacus, as the name implies, is the exact opposite of this: he is a Christian in a superlative degree—to a degree, S. K. thought, almost repulsive, almost demoniacal.

In 1848 (before he had written *For Self-Examination* and *Judge for Yourselves!*) S. K. thought of publishing *The Sickness unto Death* and *Training in Christianity* in one volume, which was to have had as its title 'The Collected Works of Completion'—or, as he thought later, 'of Consummation'. He hesitated between these two words (*Fuldendelsen* and *Fuldbringelsen*, cf. IX. A 390) because each emphasized in a different way the thought he wished to express: the former suggested more clearly that this was the *end* of his work as an author; the latter, that these last works were the consummation of his whole effort. At that time he proposed as a sub-title:

An Endeavour to Introduce Christianity into Christendom

By way of atoning for so presumptuous a statement he proposed to print at the bottom of the page:

A Poetical Endeavour—without Authority

'Without authority' was S. K.'s category as a writer. He would persuade by the truth alone. He was neither a parson nor a professor. In all his works (and not only in the work which in this volume is so entitled) he virtually said to the reader, Judge for yourself! This title expressed the feeling that he himself was only a very ordinary sort of Christian. For the reader of to-day the pathos of the work lies in the fact that he actually became such a Christian as he here depicts, a Christian who stood ready to sacrifice everything for Christ and did in fact die in performing the task he believed was laid upon him.

So the book was published—and, strange as it may seem, it made hardly any impression. The public was not prepared to believe that the author of *Either/Or* was a serious man. And, strange as it may seem, S. K. was glad that it made no impression, that it was neither denounced by the ecclesiastical authorities, nor criticized by the religious press. Later he expressed the opinion that it ought to have been publicly denounced—or else accepted and acted upon. But for the moment he was grateful for the respite, for at least a temporary exemption from the necessity of opening a sharper attack. The fact, however, that so strong a rebuke produced so little impression must have made him aware that the attack, when it had to come, must in the face of such deafness of hearing be as loud and shrill and piercing as it actually was five years later. It might, I should think, make us aware also that a less violent reproach of existent evils in Christendom had no chance to be heard. If the attack 'had to come'—for in the Preface and the Moral this book held out an olive branch, an invitation to the Church to make, through the constituted authorities, and more particularly through Bishop Mynster as Primate, a formal admission that the Christianity it exemplified was not true Christianity but a compromise with the world. S. K. naively hoped for such an admission, for he thought it must be apparent that the Church could justify itself in no other way.

But one man there was who understood this book, and understood it as an attack upon the Establishment, which (as S. K. said) he 'deified'. That man was Bishop Mynster. His son-in-law, Pastor Pauli, reported to S. K., 'The Bishop is very angry, his words were these, as soon as he came into the sitting-room the first day [after receiving the book from S. K.]: "The book has greatly embittered me. It is a profane game played with holy things".' He charged Pauli to report this to S. K., and 'Let him come up here at once to visit me, and I shall tell him that myself'. Thereupon S. K. remarked in his Journal, 'He has practically given the book its passport, and me with it'. Nevertheless (as the Journal reports), 'The following morning I went to him. . . . I began at once in this wise; "Today I have come on a particular business. Pastor Pauli told me yesterday that you have a mind to see me at once and to reprimand me for my last book. I beg you to regard it as a new expression of the deference I have always shown you, that as soon as I am informed of this I instantly make my appearance." . . . He replied, "No, I have no right to reprimand you. I have told you before that I have no objection to every bird singing with its own beak." Then he added: "People are free to say what they will about me." . . . I begged him to tell me if I had in any way offended him by publishing such a book. Then he answered, "Yes, I really believe it will not do any good." With this reply I was contented, it was kindly and personal. There was nothing remarkable about the rest of the conversation, except that at the beginning he said, "Yes, one half of the book is an attack upon Martensen,[1] and the other half on me;" and later we talked about a passage in the "Reflections", which he considered coined for him.'

We are apprised by this that S. K. was not vainly beating the air, that the corruptions of Christian thought he so vehemently attacked were common in Christendom and were exemplified by the two most influential religious leaders in Denmark, and that so religious a man as Mynster was 'greatly embittered' by a book which, if it is bitter to us, is bitter only because it stresses so insistently the most decisive Christian categories.

Training in Christianity, written for the most part in 1848, was not published until September 27, 1850. But when his next book, *For Self-Examination*, was finished, S. K. seems to have felt no difficulty about publishing it promptly, and it appeared on September 10th, 1851, over his own name, without the fiction of a pseudonym. In the mean time the breach with Mynster had widened, so that he felt less distress at offending him. Moreover, he had acquired boldness to venture farther out. This book is as decisively Christian as its predecessor, and for that reason just as exasperating, although it is not so polemical against anyone or anything in particular—'only infinitely polemical', as S. K. said on one occasion.

Judge for Yourselves! was written shortly after this, with the evident intent of publishing it immediately; for the sub-title, *For Self-Examination—Recommended to this Age*, expressly recalls the title of the previous work, and it is designated, moreover, as 'Second Series'. There is no record of any debate, or any hesitancy, about publishing it; and yet it was not published in S. K.'s lifetime. In fact, it was not published till twenty-one years after his death, having been held back by the grim hostility of his brother, Bishop Peter Kierkegaard, who had possession of his

---

[1] The Professor of Theology, who succeeded Mynster as Bishop, and against whom in the first instance the attack of 1855 was directed.

papers and was doubtless of Mynster's opinion that 'such a book will not do any good'. The story is a pitiful one, and yet it shows that as between that age and this there is a difference which is not altogether to our disadvantage; for if we are no better, at least we are not so unwilling to be told that we are bad. Why S. K. himself did not publish it remains something of a mystery. As I am not a professor, I need not pretend to see more deeply into the millstone than others. I suspect that the tone of it may have seemed too strong for the period which preceded the open attack, which he was both impatient and reluctant to begin; and that when he was in the midst of the conflict the tone seemed not strong enough. Yet in the midst of the conflict *Training in Christianity* appeared in a second edition, which still contained the Preface 'thrice repeated' and the Moral; but in the newspaper broadside which appeared at the same time S. K. formally withdrew them. He explained that the book was republished in its original form because he regarded it as an historical document, but that if it were being published now for the first time it would have been altered in the following particulars: 'It would not have been by a pseudonym but by me, and the Preface thrice repeated would have been omitted, and consequently also the Moral to Part I'. This retraction concerns me personally, for I find comfort in the Preface and the Moral. S. K. explains in this context that in the Preface and the Moral he had treated 'grace' as if it were available not only for the forgiveness of sins past but also 'as a sort of dispensation from the actual following of Christ and the actual exertion of being a Christian'. I think he puts the case against himself too strongly. I would say rather that the Preface and the Moral, which offer the grace I so much need, might too easily be twisted into an indulgence or dispensation. This means, as S. K. often affirmed, that 'it is so frightfully easy to fool God'.

Of all S. K.'s works, those composed between 1848 and 1852 seem to me the most likely to 'do good', Bishop Mynster's opinion to the contrary notwithstanding. They are free from the exaggeration which mars for us the effect of his pamphleteering attack, however necessary it may have been in its time; and they represent the real Kierkegaard more truly than do any of the pseudonymous works, even if they do not represent him so completely, with the poetical and humorous embellishments which make the earlier works so delightful. At all events, they 'do good' to me, and I hope that some individual reader may find them as profitable. It seems as if they were written expressly for me, yet I know that they were not written for me exclusively, but for 'that individual', whoever he may be.

WALTER LOWRIE

TRAINING IN CHRISTIANITY

by
ANTI-CLIMACUS

Parts I, II, III

Edited

by

S. Kierkegaard

Copenhagen 1850

CONTENTS

'COME HITHER, ALL YE THAT LABOUR AND ARE HEAVY LADEN, I WILL GIVE YOU REST.'

For Revival and Increase of Inwardness.

Part I

Part II

'BLESSED IS HE WHOSOEVER IS NOT OFFENDED IN ME.'

A Biblical Exposition and a Christian Definition of Concepts.

Thoughts which determine the meaning of 'the offence' strictly so called.

Part III

FROM ON HIGH HE WILL DRAW ALL MEN UNTO HIMSELF

'COME HITHER, ALL YE THAT LABOUR AND ARE HEAVY
LADEN, I WILL GIVE YOU REST.'

For Revival and Increase of Inwardness

By
Anti-Climacus

PROCUL, O PROCUL
ESTE PROFANI

EDITOR'S PREFACE

[i.e. S. K.'s]

In this little book, which originated in the year 1848, the requirement for being a Christian is strained by the pseudonym to the highest pitch of ideality.

Yet indeed the requirement ought to be uttered, plainly set forth, and heard. There must be no abatement of the requirement, not to speak of the suppression of it—instead of making admission and acknowledgement on one's own behalf.[1]

The requirement must be heard; and I understand what is said as addressed solely to me[2]—that I might learn not only to take refuge in 'grace', but to take refuge in such a way as to make use of 'grace'.

S. K.

[1] The admission, namely, that one, alas, is not fulfilling the requirement. This is the 'admission' S. K. was from this time on constantly urging the Church to make through its chief bishop, the acknowledgement that it was not a fair exponent of Christianity, but a compromise with worldliness. This would at least be 'honesty', and that, he thought, was the only way to justify the Church so long as it remains as it is. On his own behalf he made this admission again and again, not only privately in his journals, but publicly in his Works, that he was not yet truly a Christian but only in process of becoming one.

[2] One will be more irritated than edified by the pungent reflections of this book if one will not take S. K. at his word when he affirms that he regards them as addressed primarily to himself, does not recognize how poignantly they wounded him, and does not know how salutary his wounds proved to be at the last.

INVOCATION

IT is eighteen hundred years and more since Jesus Christ walked here on earth. But this is not an event like other events which, only when they are bygone, pass over into history, and then as events long bygone, pass over into forgetfulness. No, His presence here on earth never becomes a bygone event, and never becomes more and more bygone—in case faith is to be found on earth. And if not, then indeed at that very instant it is a long, long time since He lived. But so long as there is a believer, such a one must, in order to become such, have been, and as a believer must continue to be, just as contemporary with His presence on earth as were those [first] contemporaries.[1] This contemporaneousness is the condition of faith, and more closely defined it is faith.

O Lord Jesus Christ, would that we also might be contemporary with Thee, see Thee in Thy true form and in the actual environment in which Thou didst walk here on earth; not in the form in which an empty and meaningless tradition, or a thoughtless and superstitious, or a gossipy historical tradition, has deformed Thee; for it is not in the form of abasement the believer sees Thee, and it cannot possibly be in the form of glory, in which no man has yet seen Thee. Would that we might see Thee as Thou art and wast and wilt be until Thy return in glory, see Thee as the sign of offence and the object of faith, the lowly man, and yet the Saviour and Redeemer of the race, who out of love came to earth in order to seek the lost, in order to suffer and to die, and yet sorely troubled as Thou wast, alas, at every step Thou didst take upon earth, every time Thou didst stretch out Thy hand to perform signs and wonders, and every time, without moving a hand, Thou didst suffer defencelessly the opposition of men—again and again Thou wast constrained to repeat: Blessed is he whosoever is not offended in Me. Would that we might see Thee thus, and then that for all this we might not be offended in Thee.

[1] Contemporaneousness with Christ is from this time forth an emphatic and persistent theme of S. K.'s. What he means by it is nowhere so clearly expressed as here. Cf. the *Fragments*, caps iv and v. In *The Instant* this thought is again pungently pressed.

Come hither to me, all ye that labour and are heavy laden, I will give
you rest

OH! Wonderful, wonderful! That the one who has help to give is the one who says, Come hither! What love is this! There is love in the act of a man who is able to help and does help him who begs for help. But for one to offer help! and to offer it to all! Yes, and precisely to all such as can do nothing to help in return! To offer it—no, to shout it out, as if the Helper were the one who needed help, as if in fact He who is able and willing to help all was Himself in a sense a needy one, in that He feels an urge, and consequently need to help, need of the sufferer in order to help him!

I

'Come hither!'—There is nothing wonderful in the fact that when one is in danger and in need of help, perhaps of speedy, instant help, he shouts, 'Come hither!' Neither is it wonderful that a quack shouts out, 'Come hither! I heal all diseases.' Ah, in the instance of the quack there is only too much truth in the falsehood that the physician has need of the sick man. 'Come hither, all ye that can pay for healing at an exorbitant price—or at least for physic. Here is medicine for everybody . . . who can pay. Come hither, come hither!'

But commonly it is understood that one who is able to help must be sought out; and when one has found him, it may be difficult to gain access to him, one must perhaps implore him for a long time; and when one has implored him for a long time, he may perhaps at last be moved. That is, he sets a high value upon himself. And when sometimes he declines to receive any pay, or magnanimously relinquishes claim to it, this merely expresses the value he attaches to himself. He, on the other hand, who made the great self-surrender here surrenders himself anew. He Himself it is that seeks them that stand in need of help; it is He Himself that goes about and, calling them, almost beseeching them, says, 'Come hither!' He, the only one who is able to help, and to help with the one thing needful, to save from the sickness which in the truest sense is mortal, does not wait for people to come to Him, but He comes of His own accord, uncalled for— for He indeed it is that calls them, that offers help—and what help! That simple wise man, too, of ancient times[1] was just as infinitely right as the majority who do the opposite are wrong, in that he did not set a high value upon himself or his instruction though it is true that, in another sense, he thereby gave expression with a noble pride to the incommensurability of the pay. But he was not so deeply concerned through love to men that he begged anyone to come to him. And he behaved as he did—shall I say, in spite of the fact? or because?—he was not altogether certain what his help really amounted to. For the more certain one is

---

[1] Socrates, who took no fees for the instruction he imparted. S. K. was constantly engrossed by the figure of Socrates.

that his help is the only help, just so much more reason he has, humanly speaking, to make it dear; and the less certain he is, so much the more reason he has to offer with great alacrity such help as he disposes of, for the sake of accomplishing something at least. But He who calls Himself the Saviour, and knows Himself to be such, says with deep concern, 'Come hither'.

'Come hither *all* ye!'—Wonderful! For that one who perhaps is impotent to give help to a single soul—that he with lusty lungs should invite all is not so wonderful, human nature being what it is. But when one is perfectly certain that he can help; when one is willing, moreover, to devote oneself entirely to this cause and to make every sacrifice, it is usual, at least, to reserve the liberty of selecting the objects of one's care. However willing a person may be, still it is not everyone he would help, he would not sacrifice himself to that extent. But He, the only one who can truly help, the only one who can truly help all, and so the only one who truly can invite all, He stipulates no condition at all. This word which was as though coined for him from the foundation of the world he accordingly utters: 'Come hither all.' O, human self-sacrifice! even at thy fairest and noblest, when we admire thee most, there still is one act of sacrifice beyond thee, the sacrifice of every determinant of one's own ego, so that in the willingness to help there is not the least prejudice of partiality. What loving-kindness, thus to set no price upon oneself, entirely to forget oneself, to forget that it is he who helps, entirely blind to the question who it is one helps, seeing with infinite clearness only that it is a sufferer, whoever he may be; thus to will unconditionally to help all—alas, in this respect so different from us all!

'Come hither *to* me!'—Wonderful! For human compassion does indeed do something for them that labour and are heavy laden. One feeds the hungry, clothes the naked, gives alms, builds charitable institutions, and, if the compassion is more heartfelt, one also visits them that labour and are heavy laden. But to invite them to come to us, that is a thing that cannot be done; it would involve a change in all our household and manner of life. It is not possible while one is living in abundance, or at least in joy and gladness, to live and dwell together in the same house, in a common life and in daily intercourse, with the poor and wretched, with them that labour and are heavy laden. In order to be able to invite them thus one must live entirely in the same way, as poor as the poorest, as slightly regarded as the lowliest man of the people, familiar with life's sorrow and anguish, sharing completely the same conditions as they whom one invites to one's home, namely, they that labour and are heavy laden. If a man will invite the sufferer to come to him, he must either alter his condition in likeness to the sufferer's, or the sufferer's in likeness to his own. Otherwise the difference will be all the more glaring by reason of the contrast. And if a man will invite all sufferers to come to him (for with a single individual one can make an exception and alter his condition), it can be done in only one way, by altering one's own condition in likeness to theirs, if originally it was not adapted to this end, as was the case with Him who says, 'Come hither to me, all ye that labour and are heavy laden.' This He said, and they that lived with Him beheld, and lo! there is not the very least thing in His life which contradicts it. With the silent and veracious eloquence of deeds His life expresses, even if He had never given utterance to these words, 'Come hither to me, all ye that labour and are heavy laden.' He is true to His word, He is what He says, and in this sense also He is the Word.

'*All ye that labour and are heavy laden.*'—Wonderful! The only thing He is concerned about is that there might be a single one of those that labour and are heavy laden who failed to hear the invitation. As for the danger that too many might come, He had no fear of it. Oh, where heart-room is, there house-room always is to be found. But where was there ever heart-room if not in His heart? How the individual will understand the invitation He leaves to the individual himself. His conscience is clear: He has invited all them that labour and are heavy laden.

But what then is it to labour and to be heavy laden? Why does He not explain it more precisely, so that one may know exactly who it is He means? Why is He so laconic? O, thou petty man, He is so laconic in order not to be petty; thou illiberal man, He is so laconic in order not to be illiberal; it is the part of love (for 'love' is towards all) to prevent that there be a single person who is thrown into alarm by pondering whether he also is among the invited. And he who might require a closer definition—would he not be a self-loving person, reckoning that this ought especially to take care of his case and apply to him, without considering that the more of such closer and closer definitions there were, just so much the more inevitable that there must be individuals for whom it became more and more indefinite whether they are the invited. O, man, why doth thine eye look only to its own? Why is it evil because He is good? The invitation to all throws open the Inviter's arms, and there He stands, an everlasting picture.[1] So soon as the closer definition is introduced, which perhaps might help the individual to another sort of certainty, the Inviter has a different aspect, and there passes over Him as it were a fleeting shadow of change.

'I will give thee rest.'—Wonderful! For these words, 'Come hither to me', must thus be understood to mean, abide with me, I am that rest, or, to abide with me is rest. So it is not as in other instances, when the helper who says, 'Come hither', must there-upon say, 'Go hence again', declaring to each individual severally where the helper he needs is to be found, where there grows the pain-quenching herb which can heal him, or where the tranquil place is where he can cease from labour, or where is that happier region of the world where one is not heavy laden. No, He who opens His arms and invites all—oh, in case all, all they that labour and are heavy laden were to come to Him, He would embrace them in His arms and say, 'Abide with Me, for in abiding with Me there is rest.' The Helper is the help. Oh, wonderful! He who invites all and would help all has a way of treating the sick just as if it were intended for each several one, as if each patient He deals with were the only one. Commonly a physician must divide himself among his many patients, who, however many they are, are very far from being all. He prescribes the medicine, tells what is to be done, how it is to be used—and then he departs ... to another patient. Or else, in case the patient has come to see him, he lets him depart. The physician cannot remain sitting all the day long beside one patient, still less can he have all his

---

[1] Here (as also in one of his *Edifying Discourses* which he delivered within sight of it) S. K. is presumably thinking of Thorwaldsen's famous and noble representation of Christ, the statue with outspread arms which was placed over the altar of the cathedral in Copenhagen, where Bishop Mynster commonly preached and S. K. always went to hear him.

sick people in his own home and yet sit all the day long beside one patient . . . without neglecting the others. Hence in this case the helper and the help are not one and the same thing. The patient retains beside him all the day long the help which the physician prescribes, so as to use it constantly; whereas the physician sees him only now and then, and only now and then does he see the physician. But when the Helper is the help, He must remain with the patient all the day long, or the patient with Him. Oh, wonderful! that it is this very Helper who invites all!

II

*Come hither, all ye that labour and are heavy laden, I will give
you rest*

WHAT prodigious multiplicity, what almost boundless
diversity, amongst the people invited! For a man, even
a mere man, can well enough attempt to conceive of
some of the individual differences; but the Inviter must invite
all, yet every one severally as an individual.

So the invitation fares forth, along frequented roads and along
the solitary paths, along the most solitary, aye, where there is a
path so solitary that only one knows it, one single person, or no
one at all, so that there is only one footprint, that of the luckless
man who fled along that path with his misery, no other indication
whatsoever, and no indication that in following that path one
might return again. Even there the invitation penetrates, finding
its own way back easily and surely—most easily when it bears the
fugitive back with it to the Inviter. Come hither, all ye—and
thou, and thou . . . and thou, too, most solitary of all fugitives!

Thus the invitation fares forth, and wherever there is a parting
of the ways it stops and calls aloud. Like the trumpet-call of the
warrior which turns to all four quarters of the world, so the invitation resounds wherever there is a parting of the ways—and with
no uncertain sound (for who then would come?), but with the
unequivocal sureness of eternity.

It halts at the crossways, where suffering temporal and earthly
has planted its cross, and there it calls aloud. Come hither, all ye
poor and miserable, ye who in poverty must toil to ensure for
yourselves not a care-free but a toilsome future. Oh, bitter
contradiction—to have to toil to *attain* what one groans under,
what one *flees* from!—Ye who are despised and disdained, about
whose existence none is concerned, not a single one, not even so
much as for the beasts, which have a higher value!—Ye sick,
lame, deaf, blind, crippled, come hither!—Ye bed-ridden, yea,
come ye also hither! For the invitation makes bold to bid the bed-
ridden . . . come!—Ye lepers! For the invitation abolishes every
barrier of difference in order to bring all together. It proposes

to make amends for the inequalities chargeable to the difference which allots one a place as a ruler over millions, possessing all the favours of fortune, and relegates another to the desert. And why? (oh, the cruelty of it!) Because (oh, cruel human logic!), *because* he is miserable, indescribably miserable; consequently for this further reason, because he craves help, or at least compassion; and consequently for this further reason, because human compassion is a paltry invention, cruel where the need of compassion is most evident, and compassionate only where in a true sense it is not compassion!—Ye sick at heart, ye who only through pain learn to know that a man has a heart in a sense quite different from the heart of a beast, and learn what it means to suffer in that part, learn how it is that the physician may be right in declaring that one's heart is sound while nevertheless he is heart-sick. Ye whom unfaithfulness deceived, and then human sympathy (for human sympathy is seldom in delay) made a target for mockery.[1] All ye who have been discriminated against, wronged, offended, and ill-used; all ye noble ones who (as everybody can tell you) deservedly reap the reward of ingratitude. For why were ye foolish enough to be noble, why stupid enough to be kindly, disinterested, and faithful? All ye victims of cunning and deceit and backbiting and envy, whom baseness singled out and cowardice left in the lurch,[2] whether ye be sacrificed in remote and lonely places whither ye have crept away to die, or whether ye be trampled under foot by the thronging human crowd where no one inquires what right ye have on your side, no one inquires what wrong ye suffer, or where the smart of your suffering is, or how ye smart under it, while the throng, replete with animal health, tramples you in the dust[3]—come hither!

The invitation halts at the parting of the ways where death parts death from life. Come hither, all ye sorrowful, all ye that travail in vain and are sore troubled! For it is true that there is rest in the grave; but to sit beside a grave, to stand by a grave, or to

---

[1] For his own part S. K. found it hard to endure the sting of human sympathy, with its implication of *Schadenfreude,* and the humiliation of selfish compassion.

[2] This is an echo of S. K.'s own personal experience in connexion with the *Corsair,* of which he writes so much in the Journal.

[3] S. K. says in the Journal that he was being 'trampled to death by geese'— thinking of the popular ridicule he was exposed to as a consequence of the cartoons in the *Corsair.* He shuddered at the sheer 'animal health' of the 'louts' who derided him.

visit a grave, all that is not yet to lie in the grave; and to scan
again and again the production of one's own pen, which one
knows by heart, the inscription which one placed there oneself
and which the man himself can best understand, telling who lies
buried there—that, alas, is not to lie buried there oneself. In
the grave there is rest, but *beside* the grave there is no rest—the
meaning of it is: hitherto and no farther . . . then one can go home.
But often as you return to *that* grave, day after day, whether in
thought or on foot—one gets no farther, not one step from the
spot; and this is very exhausting, far from expressing rest. Come
ye therefore hither, here is the path along which one goes farther,
here is rest beside the grave, rest from the pain of loss, or rest in
the pain of loss—with Him who eternally reunites the separated,
more firmly than nature unites parents and children, children
and parents (alas, they were parted), more inwardly than the
priest unites husband and wife (alas, separation occurred), more
indissolubly than the bond of friendship unites friend with friend
(alas, that was dissolved). Separation everywhere forced its way
between, bringing sorrow and unrest; but here is rest!—Come
hither, ye whose abodes were assigned to you among the tombs,
ye who are accounted dead to human society, yet not missed and
not mourned—not buried, although dead, that is, belonging
neither to life not to death; ye, alas, to whom human society
cruelly closed its doors, and yet for whom no grave mercifully
opened—come ye then hither; here is rest and here is life!

  The invitation halts at the parting of the ways where the path
of sin deviates from the hedged road of innocence.—Oh, come
hither, ye are so near to Him; a single step on the other path, and
ye are so endlessly far from Him. It may well be, perhaps, that
ye have not felt as yet the need of rest and hardly understand what
it means; yet follow nevertheless the invitation, so that the Inviter
might save you *from* a state which only with great difficulty and
peril ye might be saved out of, so that as the saved ye might abide
with Him who is the Saviour of all men including the innocent.
For if it were possible that somewhere there might be found
innocence entirely unsullied, why should it not also require a
saviour who could preserve it safe from the evil one?—The
invitation halts at the parting of the ways where the path of sin
veers more deeply into sin. Come hither, all ye that have strayed
and lost your way, whatever your error and sin may have been,

whether it be one which in human eyes was more pardonable and
yet perhaps more dreadful, or one more dreadful in human eyes
and yet perhaps more pardonable, one which was revealed here
on earth, or one which is concealed here yet known in heaven[1]—
did ye find forgiveness here on earth and yet no rest in your
inward mind, or found ye no forgiveness because ye sought it not
or sought it in vain—oh, turn about and come hither, here is
rest!—The invitation halts at the parting of the ways where the
path of sin again veers, for the last time, and is lost to view . . .
in perdition. Oh, turn about, turn about, come hither! Shrink
not at the difficulty of the journey back,[2] however hard it be;
fear not the toilsome path of conversion, however laboriously it
leads to salvation, whereas sin with winged speed, with ever-
increasing velocity, leads onward . . . or downward, so easily, with
such indescribable ease, as easily indeed as when a horse, relieved
entirely of the strain of pulling, cannot with all his might bring
the wagon to a halt which thrusts him over into the abyss. Be not
in despair at every relapse, which the God of patience possesses
patience enough to forgive and which a sinner might well have
patience enough to be humbled under. Nay, fear nothing and
despair not. He who says, 'Come hither', is with you on your
way; from Him come help and forgiveness in the path of conversion which leads to Him; and with Him there is rest.

Come hither, all, all, all of you, with Him is rest, and He
makes no difficulties, He does but one thing, He opens his arms.
He will not first (as righteous people do, alas, even when they are
willing to help)—He will not first ask thee, 'Art thou not after all
to blame for thy misfortune? Hast thou in fact no cause for
self-reproach?' It is so easy, so human, to judge after the outward
appearance, after the result—when a person is a cripple, or
deformed, or has an unprepossessing appearance, to judge that
ergo he is a bad man; when a person fares badly in the world so
that he is brought to ruin or goes downhill, then to judge that *ergo*

[1] Anyone who knows S. K. will not fail to detect here (as in so many, many other
places in his works) a reflection of his intimate personal experience. One who ignores
it will find such a passage as this less moving, perhaps even banal.

[2] S. K., during his own laborious return from 'the path of perdition', remarked
that one was compelled to tread backwards the whole way one had gone, and he
remembered a fairy-tale which recounted that deliverance from an enchantment
wrought by a piece of music was possible only when one was able to play it backwards
without an error.

he is a vicious man. Oh, it is such an exquisite invention of cruel pleasure, to enhance the consciousness of one's own righteousness in contrast with a sufferer, by explaining that his suffering is God's condign punishment, so that one hardly even . . . dares to help him; or by challenging him with that condemning question which flatters one's own righteousness in the very act of helping him. But He will put no such questions to thee, He will not be thy benefactor in so cruel a fashion. If thou thyself art conscious of being a sinner, he will not inquire of thee about it, the bruised reed He will not further break, but he will raise thee up if thou wilt attach thyself to Him. He will not single thee out by contrast, holding thee apart from Him, so that thy sin will seem still more dreadful; He will grant thee a hiding-place within Him, and once hidden in Him he will hide thy sins. For He is the friend of sinners: When it is question of a sinner He does not merely stand still, open His arms and say, 'Come hither'; no, he stands there and waits, as the father of the lost son waited, rather He does not stand and wait, he goes forth to seek, as the shepherd sought the lost sheep, as the woman sought the lost coin. He goes—yet no, he has gone, but infinitely farther than any shepherd or any woman, He went, in sooth, the infinitely long way from being God to becoming man, and that way He went in search of sinners.

III

Come hither to me, all ye that labour and are heavy laden, I will give you rest

'C OME *hither!*' For He assumes that they that labour and are heavy laden feel the burden all too heavy, the labour heavy, and now stand in perplexity, heaving sighs—one glancing searchingly around to see if no help is to be found, another with eyes bent down upon the ground because he descried no comfort, a third gazing upward as though from heaven it still must come, but all of them seeking. Therefore He says, 'Come hither'. Him who has ceased to seek and to sorrow He does not invite.—'*Come hither!*' For He, the Inviter, knows it as a sign of true suffering that one goes apart to brood alone in disconsolate silence, lacking the courage to confide in anyone, not to say the confidence to hope for help. Alas, that demoniac was not the only person possessed by a dumb spirit.[1] Suffering which does not begin by making the sufferer dumb does not amount to much— no more than love which does not make the lover silent. Sufferers whose tongues run easily over the story of their sufferings neither labour nor are heavy laden. Lo! for this reason the Inviter dare not wait till they that labour and are heavy laden come to Him of their own accord: He Himself lovingly summons them. All His willingness to help would perhaps be no help at all if He did not utter this word and thereby take the first step. For in this summons, 'Come unto me', it is He in fact that comes to them. Oh, human compassion! Perhaps it may sometimes indicate praiseworthy self-restraint, perhaps also sometimes a genuine and heart-felt sympathy, when thou refrainest from questioning a man who, as may be surmised, is constantly brooding over a hidden suffering; yet how often it may be only worldly wisdom which has no desire to learn to know too much. Oh, human compassion, how often was it merely curiosity, not compassion, which prompted thee to venture to penetrate a sufferer's secret! And what a burden didst thou feel it to be—almost a punishment upon thy curiosity—when he followed thine invitation and came to

[1] Mk. 9: 17, 25.

thee! But He who utters this saving word, 'Come hither', was not deceived in Himself when He uttered the word, neither will He deceive thee when thou comest to Him to find rest by casting thy burden upon Him. He follows the prompting of His heart in uttering it, and His heart accompanies [follows] the word—follow then thou the word, and it will accompany [follow] thee back to His heart. It is a matter of course [*selvfølge*]; the one thing follows the other—oh, that thou wouldst follow the invitation.[1]—'*Come hither!*' For He assumes that they that labour and are heavy laden are so tired and exhausted, in a state of swoon, that they have forgotten again, as in a stupor, that there is comfort; or, alas, He knows that it is only too true that there is no comfort and help unless it is sought in Him; and so He has to call them to 'come hither'.

'*Come hither!*' For it is characteristic of every society that it possesses a token or a sign of some sort by which one who is a member can be recognized. When a young girl is adorned in a certain manner, one knows that she is on her way to a ball. Come hither, all ye that labour and are heavy laden.—'*Come hither!*' Thou dost not need to wear a distinctive outward and visible mark . . . come also with anointed head and a face newly washed,[2] if only thou dost inwardly labour and art heavy laden.

'*Come hither!*' Oh, stand not still, considering the matter. Consider rather, oh, consider that for every instant thou standest still after hearing the invitation, thou wilt in the next instant hear its call fainter and fainter, and thus be withdrawing to a distance though thou be standing at the same spot.—'*Come hither!*' Oh, however tired and weary thou art with thy labour, or with the long, long quest in search of help and salvation, although it seem to thee as if thou couldst not follow one step farther or hold out a moment longer without sinking to the ground—oh, but this one step more, and here is rest! '*Come hither!*' Ah, if there were only one so wretched that he could not come—a sigh is enough, to sigh for Him is also to come hither.

[1] In brackets I have sought to indicate that there is a play on words: 'follow', with its two meanings and its derivative.
[2] Mt. 6: 17.

THE OBSTACLE

Come hither unto me, all ye that labour and are heavy laden, I will give you rest.

Halt now! But what is there to impose a halt? That which in a single instant infinitely alters everything—so that, in reality, instead of getting a sight, as one might expect, of an interminable throng of such as labour and are heavy laden following the invitation, you behold in fact a sight which is exactly the opposite: an interminable throng of men who turn backward in flight and shudder, until in the scramble to get away they trample one another under foot; so that if from the result one were to infer what had been said, one must conclude that the words were, '*Procul, o procul este profani*', rather than, 'Come hither'. [The halt is imposed, finally] by something infinitely more important and infinitely more decisive: by the **Inviter.** Not as though He were not the man to do what He says, or not God to keep the promise He has made—no, in a sense very different from that.

[IN the sense, namely] that the Inviter is and insists upon being the definite historical person He was 1,800 years ago, and that as this definite person, living under the conditions He then lived under, He uttered those words of invitation.—He is not, and for nobody is He willing to be, one about whom we have learned to know something merely from history[1] (i.e. world-history, secular history, in contrast to sacred history); for from history we can learn to know nothing about Him, because there is absolutely nothing that can be 'known'[2] about Him.—He declines to be judged in a human way by the consequences of His life, that is to say, He is and would be the sign of offence[3] and the object of faith. To judge Him by the consequences of His life is mere mockery of God; for, seeing that He is God, His life (the life which he actually lived in time) is infinitely more decisively important than all the consequences of it in the course of history.

a

Who spoke these words of invitation?

The Inviter. Who is the Inviter? Jesus Christ. Which Jesus Christ? The Jesus Christ who sits in glory at the right hand of the Father? No. From the seat of His glory he has not spoken one word. Therefore it is Jesus Christ in His humiliation, in the state of humiliation, who spoke these words.

Is then Jesus Christ not always the same? Yes, He is the same yesterday and to-day, the same that 1,800 years ago humbled Himself and took upon Him the form of a servant, the Jesus

[1] In this paragraph, as in an overture, the principal themes of the whole work are suggested. It needs to be noted that they do not emerge here for the first time. They had been more fully elaborated in earlier works, although they are more tellingly presented here in the style of 'direct communication'. In this and in subsequent notes I refer to earlier works where these themes are more fully discussed. For the significance of history—and its irrelevance for faith—see e.g. the *Fragments*, cap. iv; *Postscript*, Part I, cap. i, § 1; Part II, Second Division, cap. iv, Section I, § 3.

[2] S. K.'s definition of faith was in part determined by its opposition to knowledge: e.g. *Postscript*, Part I, Cap. i, § 1.

[3] The 'offence' of Christianity is very emphatically dwelt upon later in this book, but it had already been considered in the *Fragments*, e.g. Cap. iii, Appendix.

Christ who uttered these words of invitation. In His coming again in glory He is again the same Jesus Christ; but this has not yet occurred.

Is He then not now in glory? Yes indeed; this the Christian *believes*. But it was in the state of humiliation He uttered these words; from the seat of His glory he has not uttered them. And about His coming again in glory nothing can be known; in the strictest sense, it can only be believed. But one cannot have become a Christian without having already come to Him in His estate of humiliation—without having come to Him, who is the sign of offence and the object of faith. In no other wise does He exist on earth, for it was only thus that He existed. That He shall come in glory is to be expected, but it can be expected and believed only by one who has attached himself and continues to hold fast to Him as He actually existed.

Jesus Christ is the same; but He lived 1,800 years ago in His humiliation and becomes changed first [for us] with His coming again. As yet He has not returned, so He remains still the lowly one about whom it is believed that He shall return in glory. What He said and taught, every word He has spoken, becomes *eo ipso* untrue when we make it appear as if it were Christ in glory who says it. No, *He* maintains silence, it is the *lowly one* who speaks. The interval (between His humiliation and His coming again in glory), which at this moment is about 1,800 years and may possibly be protracted to many times 1,800—this interval, rather, all that this interval makes of Him, secular history and Church history, with all the worldly information they furnish about Christ, about who Christ was, and consequently about who uttered these words, is a thing completely indifferent, neither here nor there, which merely distorts Him, and thereby renders these words of invitation untrue.

For it is untruth if I imaginatively ascribe to a man words which he never uttered, affirming that *he* said them. But it is also untruth if I imaginatively represent him as essentially different from what he was when he spake certain words. I say, 'essentially different', for a falsehood which has to do only with some accidental trait does not make it untrue that he said the thing.— And so, when God is pleased to walk here on earth in a strict incognito such as only an almighty being can assume, an incognito impenetrable to the most intimate observation, when it pleases

Him to come in the lowly form of a servant, to all appearance like any other man (and why He does it, with what purpose, He surely knows best; but whatever the reason or purpose may be, they testify that the incognito has some essential significance), when it pleases Him to come in this lowly form to teach men—and then somebody repeats exactly the words he uttered, but makes it appear as if it was God that said them, the thing becomes untrue, for it is untrue that He uttered these words.

b

Can one learn from history* anything about Christ?

No. Why not? Because one can 'know' nothing at all about 'Christ'; He is the paradox,[1] the object of faith, existing only for faith. But all historical communication is communication of 'knowledge', hence from history one can learn nothing about Christ. For if one learns little or much about Him, or anything at all, He [who is thus known] is not He who in truth He is, i.e. one learns to know nothing about Him, or one learns to know something incorrect about Him, one is deceived. History makes out Christ to be another than He truly is, and so one learns to know a lot about . . . Christ? No, not about Christ, for about Him nothing can be known, He can only be believed.

c

Can one prove from history that Christ was God?

Let me first put another question: Is it possible to conceive of a more foolish contradiction than that of wanting to **prove** (no matter for the present purpose whether it be from history or from anything else in the wide world one wants to *prove* it) that a definite individual man is God? That an individual man is God, declares himself to be God, is indeed the 'offence' κατ᾽ ἐξοχήν. But what is the offence, the offensive thing? What is at variance with (human) reason?[2] And such a thing as that one would attempt

---

* By 'history' is to be understood throughout profane history, world-history, history as ordinarily understood, in contrast to sacred history. S. K.

[1] The thought of the paradoxical character of Christianity, culminating in the paradox of the God-Man, appears first in the *Scraps* (cap. iii) and the *Postscript* (Part II, Second Division, cap. iv, section 4).

[2] The opposition between faith and the understanding (or reason) was sharply

to prove! But to 'prove' is to demonstrate something to be the rational reality it is. Can one demonstrate that to be a rational reality which is at variance with reason? Surely not, unless one would contradict oneself. One can 'prove' only that it is at variance with reason. The proofs which Scripture presents for Christ's divinity—His miracles, His Resurrection from the dead, His Ascension into heaven—are therefore only for faith, that is, they are not 'proofs', they have no intention of proving that all this agrees perfectly with reason; on the contrary they would prove that it conflicts with reason and therefore is an object of faith.

But to return to the proofs from history. Is it not 1,800 years since Christ lived, is not His name proclaimed and believed on throughout the whole world, has not His doctrine (Christianity) changed the face of the world, triumphantly permeated all relationships—and in this way has not history abundantly, and more than abundantly, established who He was, namely, that He was God? No, history has not established that, either abundantly or more than abundantly; that is something which history in all eternity cannot establish. So far, however, as the first assertion is concerned, it is sure enough that His name is proclaimed in all the world—whether it is believed on I will not decide. It is sure enough that Christianity has changed the face of the world, triumphantly permeated all relationships—so triumphantly that all now say that they are Christians.

But what does that prove? At the most it might prove that Jesus Christ was a great man, perhaps the greatest of all; but that He was . . . God—nay, stop there! The conclusion shall by God's help never be drawn.

If, in order to lead up to this conclusion, one begins with the assumption that Jesus Christ was a man, and then considers the history of the 1,800 years[1] (the consequences of His life), one may conclude, with an ascending superlative scale: great, greater, greatest, exceedingly and astonishingly the greatest man that ever lived.—If on the contrary one begins with the assumption (the assumption of faith) that He was God, one has thereby cancelled,

expressed in the *Scraps* (cap. iii, Appendix, and cap. iv, § 4) and the *Postscript* (Part II, Second Division, cap. 2 and cap. 5).

[1] The argument from the 1,800 years was demolished already in the *Postscript* (e.g. Part I, cap. 1, § 3) and S. K. returned to the assault in *The Instant*.

annulled, the 1,800 years as having nothing to do with the case, proving nothing *pro* nor *contra*, inasmuch as the certitude of faith is something infinitely higher.—And it is in one or the other of these ways one must begin. If one begins in the latter way, everything is as it should be.

If one begins in the first way, one cannot, without being guilty at one point or another of a μετάβασις εἰς ἄλλο γένος, arrive suddenly by an inference at the new quality . . . God; as if the consequence or consequences of . . . a man's life might suddenly furnish the proof that this man was God. If this could be done, then one might answer the following query: What consequences must there be, how great the effects produced, how many centuries must elapse, in order to establish a proof from the consequences of a man's life (this being the assumption) that he was God? Whether perhaps it might be said that in the year 300 Christ was not yet completely proved to be God, something approaching that having been attained, namely, that He was already a little more than the exceedingly, astonishingly greatest man that ever lived, but there still was need of several centuries more? If such be the case, the further consequence presumably follows, that they who lived in the year 300 did not regard Christ as God, and still less they who lived in the first century, whereas on the other hand the certitude that He is God increases regularly with each century, so in our time, the nineteenth century, it is greater than it had ever been before, a certitude in comparison with which the first centuries seem barely to have glimpsed His divinity. One may make answer to this or leave it alone—it makes no essential difference.

What can this mean? Is it possible that by contemplating the consequences of something as they unfold themselves more and more one might by a simple inference from them produce another quality different from that contained in the assumption?[1] Is it not a sign of insanity (supposing man in general to be sane) that the first proposition (the assumption with which one starts out)

---

[1] Brandes conjectured that if S. K. had lived in his time he might have been perverse enough to reject Darwin's celebrated theory of evolution. In fact, he did emphatically reject it in advance, as we see from this passage. Exactly the same argument was urged by Benjamin Warfield, who was my teacher of theology in 1890. In those days it was scoffed at or ignored, but in the end it brought *that* theory of evolution into disrepute.

is so far astray about what is what that it errs to the extent of a whole quality? And when one begins with this error, how shall one at any subsequent point be able to perceive the mistake and apprehend that one is dealing with another and an infinitely different quality? The print of a foot along a path is obviously a consequence of the fact that some creature has gone that way. I may now go on to suppose erroneously that it was, for example, a bird, but on closer inspection, pursuing the track farther, I convince myself that it must have been another sort of animal. Very well. But here we are far from having an infinite qualitative alteration. But can I, by a closer inspection of such a track, or by following it farther, reach at one point or another the conclusion: *ergo* it was a spirit that passed this way? A spirit which leaves no trace behind it! Just so it is with this thing of concluding from the consequences of an (assumed) human existence that *ergo* it was God. Do God and man resemble one another to such a degree, is there so slight a difference between them, that I (supposing I am not crazy) can begin with the assumption that Christ was a man? And, on the other hand, has not Christ Himself said that He was God? If God and man resemble one another to that degree, if they have that degree of kinship, and thus essentially are included in the same quality, the conclusion, '*ergo* it was God', is nevertheless humbug; for if God is nothing else but that, then God doesn't exist at all. But if God exists, and consequently is distinguished by an infinite difference of quality from all that it means to be a man, then neither can I nor anybody else, by beginning with the assumption that He was a man, arrive in all eternity at the conclusion, 'therefore it was God'. Everyone who has the least dialectical training can easily perceive that the whole argument about consequences is incommensurable with the decision of the question whether it is God, and that this decisive question is presented to man in an entirely different form: whether he will believe that He is what He said He was; or whether he will not believe.

Dialectically understood—that is, with the understanding that one gives himself time to understand it—this ought to be enough to throw a spike into the gears of that argument from the consequences of Christ's life: *ergo* He was God. But faith, in the province of its jurisdiction, raises a still more essential protest against every attempt to approach Christ by the help of what one happens to know of Him through history and the information history has preserved about the consequences of His life. Faith's contention is that this whole attempt is . . . *blasphemy*. Faith's contention is that the one and only proof which unbelief allowed to stand when it demolished all the other proofs of the truth of Christianity, the proof which unbelief itself discovered (yes, the situation is curiously complicated), which unbelief discovered, and discovered as a proof of the truth of Christianity (mighty good! Unbelief discovers proofs in defence of Christianity!), the proof which Christendom has since made so much ado about, the proof of the 1800 years—faith's contention is that this is . . . *blasphemy*.

In the case of a *man* it may justly enough be said that the consequences of his life are more important than his life. When a person then seeks to find out who Christ was, and essays to draw a logical conclusion from the consequences of His life—he makes Him out *eo ipso* to be a man, a man who like other men has to pass his examination in history, which, moreover, is in this instance just as mediocre an examiner as a seminarist is in Latin.[1]

But strange! People are eager by the help of history, by considering the consequences of His life, to reach by logical inference the *ergo, ergo* He was God—and faith's contention is exactly the opposite, that he who even begins with this syllogism begins with a blasphemy. The blasphemy does not appear already in the hypothetical assumption that He was a man. No, the blasphemy is what lies at the bottom of the whole undertaking, the thought without which one would never begin, the thought which therefore is entertained without the slightest doubt that it is applicable also to Christ, the thought that the consequences of His life are more important than His life—which effectively is to say that He was a mere man. One says hypothetically, Let us assume that Christ was a man; but at the bottom of this hypothesis (which is not yet blasphemy) lies the thesis that this notion (that the consequences of a man's life are more important than his life) applies also to Christ. If one does not assume this, one must admit that one's whole undertaking is nonsense. And since this admission must be made at the start, why begin at all? But if one makes the foregoing assumption and begins the argument, the blasphemy is fairly started. The more profoundly one con-

---

[1] S. K. must have reflected that he, even before he became a seminarist, was a teacher of Latin. He was always ready to satirize himself.

siders the consequences of His life (if it be with the aim of reaching a conclusion as to whether He was God), the more blasphemous one's undertaking is, and such it remains at every moment, as long as this consideration continues.

Curious coincidence! One would like to make it appear that if only the consequences of His life are justly considered and to due effect, one will surely arrive at this *ergo*—and faith condemns the very beginning of this attempt as a blasphemous mockery of God, and the continuation of it therefore as a crescendo of blasphemy.

'History', says faith, 'has nothing whatever to do with Christ. As applying to Him, we have only sacred history (qualitatively different from history in general), which recounts the story of His life under the conditions of His humiliation, and reports moreover that He himself said that He was God.[1] He is the paradox, which history can never digest or convert into a common syllogism. In His humiliation He is the same as in His exaltation—but the 1,800 years (or if there were 18,000 of them) have nothing whatever to do with the case. The brilliant consequences in world-history which wellnigh convince even a professor of history that He was God—these brilliant consequences are surely not His return in glory! But this is really about what they mean by it: it appears here again that they make out Christ to be a man whose return in glory can be nothing more than the consequences of His life in history—whereas Christ's return in glory is something entirely different, something that is believed. He humbled Himself and was swaddled in rags—He will come again in glory. But the brilliant consequences (especially upon closer inspection) turn out to be a shabby sort of glory, at all events entirely incongruous, about which faith never speaks when it speaks of His glory. So on earth He exists still in a state of humiliation, and thus He will continue to exist until (as one believes) He shall come again in glory. History may be a very reputable science, but it must not

---

[1] About this frequent assertion of S. K.'s I would say once for all that, however shocking it may be to modern ears, it does not essentially misrepresent even the Synoptic Gospels. It has been said that the result of the Unitarian controversy in America was a general agreement that 'the Bible is an orthodox book'. More recently the general recognition of the eschatological expectation of Jesus, and His self-chosen title, 'the Son of Man', indubitably implies the consciousness and the claim that essentially He was 'beyond man', possessing what S. K. calls another quality—an infinite qualitative difference.

become so conceited as to undertake to do what the Father is to do, to array Christ in glory, costuming Him in the brilliant robes of the consequences, as though that were the Second Advent. That in His humiliation He was God, that He will come again in glory—this is considerably beyond the comprehension of history, and only by a peerless lack of dialectic can it be got out of history, however peerless one's knowledge of history otherwise may be.'

Strange! and they want above all things to make use of history to prove that Christ was God.

d

Are the consequences of Christ's life more important than His life?

No, by no means, quite the contrary—if this were so, Christ was merely a man.

There is surely nothing noteworthy in the fact that a man lived; millions upon millions of them of course have lived. If this fact is to become noteworthy, the man's life must acquire some noteworthy distinction, which means that with respect to a man's life noteworthiness emerges only in the second instance. It is not noteworthy that he lived, but his life exhibited one or another noteworthy trait. Among such traits may be included what he accomplished, the consequences of his life.

But the fact that God lived here on earth as an individual man is infinitely noteworthy. Even if it had no consequences whatsoever, the fact is the same, it remains just as noteworthy, infinitely noteworthy, infinitely more noteworthy than all consequences. Make the attempt of introducing here the noteworthy distinction in the second instance, and you will readily perceive the foolishness of it. How could it be noteworthy that God's life had noteworthy consequences? To talk in such a way is to twaddle.

No, the fact that God lived is the infinitely noteworthy, the in-and-for-itself noteworthy. Assume that Christ's life had no consequences—to say then that His life was not noteworthy would be blasphemy. For it is noteworthy all the same; and if anything need be said about noteworthiness in the second instance, this would be: the noteworthy fact that His life had no consequences. If on the contrary someone says that Christ's life is noteworthy because of the consequences, this again is blasphemy, for this life is in-and-for-itself noteworthy.

No emphasis falls upon the fact that a man lived, but infinite is the emphasis which falls upon the fact that God lived. God alone can attach to Himself such great weight that the fact that He lived and has lived is infinitely more important than all the consequences which are registered in history.

e

A comparison between Christ and a man who in his lifetime suffered the same opposition from his age that Christ suffered

Let us think of a man,[1] one of those glorious figures who was unjustly treated by his own age but afterwards was reinstated in his rights by history, which, by means of the consequences of his life, made it evident who he was. Incidentally be it said, however, that I am not disposed to deny that this proof from consequences is calculated rather for the *mundus qui vult decipi*. For, a non-contemporary who perceived who this glorious one was after he had reached this knowledge by aid of the consequences, only fancied that he perceived it. But this I do not intend to press; and in relation to a man it remains nevertheless true that the consequences of his life are more important than his life.

So let us think of one of those glorious ones. He lives among his contemporaries, but he is not understood, not recognized for what he is, he is misunderstood, then derided, persecuted, and finally put to death as a malefactor. But the consequences of his life make it manifest who he was; history which records these consequences does him justice, he now is acclaimed century after century as a great and noble man, his humiliation being as good as forgotten. It was due to the blindness of his age that it did not recognize him for what he was, it was due to the impiety of that generation that they scorned and derided him and finally put him to death. But let that now be forgotten; it was only after his death that he really became what he was, through the consequences of his life, which were indeed more important than his life.

Should the same be true also of Christ? It was indeed a blind-

---

[1] S. K. is thinking of course especially of Socrates. His first considerable work was characterized in the sub-title as having 'constant reference to Socrates'. This phrase might well have stood in front of the whole great literature he created, for he became constantly more and more engrossed with the figure of Socrates, learning gradually to know him better and to revere him more highly than when he wrote *The Concept of Irony*.

ness, an impiety on the part of that generation—but let that now be forgotten, history has now reinstated Him in His right, we now know from history who Jesus Christ was, we now do Him justice.

Oh, impious heedlessness, which reduces sacred history to profane history, Christ to a mere man! Can one then from history learn to know anything about Christ? (Cf. above under § *b*.) By no manner of means. Jesus Christ is the object of faith; one must either believe on Him or be offended. For to 'know' signifies exactly that the reference is not to Him. It is true enough that history furnishes knowledge in abundance, but knowledge demolishes Jesus Christ.

Again, Oh, impious heedlessness! if anyone were to have the presumption to say of Christ's humiliation, Let us now forget all that has to do with His humiliation. Yet surely Christ's humiliation was not something which merely happened to Him (even though it was the sin of that generation that they crucified Him), something which happened to Him and perhaps would not have happened to Him in a better age. Christ Himself willed to be the humiliated and lowly one. Humiliation (the fact that it pleased God to be the lowly man) is therefore something He Himself has joined together, something He wills to have knit together, a dialectical knot which no one shall presume to untie, which indeed no one can untie before He Himself has untied it by coming again in glory. With Him it is not as with a man who by the injustice of his age was not permitted to be himself or to be accounted for what he was, whereas history made this manifest; for Christ Himself willed to be the humble man, this is just what He would be accounted. Hence history must not incommode itself to do Him justice, nor must we with impious heedlessness fancy presumptuously that we know as a matter of course who He was. For no one *knows* that, and he who *believes* it must be contemporary with Him in His humiliation. When God chooses to let Himself be born in lowly station, when He who holds all possibilities in His hand clothes Himself in the form of a servant, when He goes about defenceless and lets men do with Him as they will, He surely must know well what He does and why He does it; it is He nevertheless who has men in His power, not men who have power over Him—so let not history pretend to be such a wiseacre as to explain who He was.

Finally, oh, blasphemy! if anyone presume to say that the

persecution Christ suffered expresses something accidental. Because a man is persecuted by his age, it does not follow that he has a right to say that this would have happened to him in any age. So far forth there may be something in it when posterity says, Let now all that be forgot which he suffered unjustly while he lived. Very different is the case with Jesus Christ! It is not He that, after letting Himself be born, and making his appearance in Judea, has presented Himself for an examination in history; it is He that is the Examiner, His life is the examination, and that not alone for that race and generation, but for the whole race. Woe to the generation that dared to say, Let now all the injustice He suffered be forgotten, history has now made manifest who He was and reinstated Him in His rights.

By assuming that history is capable of doing this we put Christ's humiliation in an accidental relation to Him, i.e. we make Him out to be a man, a distinguished man to whom this happened through the impiety of his age, a thing which for his part he was very far from wishing, for he would fain (that is human) have been something great in the world—whereas on the contrary Christ freely willed to be the lowly one, and though His purpose in this was to deliver man, yet he also would express what 'the truth' had to suffer in every generation and what it must always suffer. But if such is His royal will, and if only at His return will He show Himself in glory, and if He has not yet returned; and if no generation can contemplate without the compunction of repentance what that generation did to Him, with a sense of guilty participation—then woe to him who presumes to take His lowliness from Him, or to let it be forgot what injustice He suffered, decking Him fabulously in the human glory of the historical consequences, which is neither the one thing nor the other.

f

The misfortune of Christendom

But this precisely is now the misfortune of Christendom, as for many, many years it has been, that Christ is neither the one thing nor the other, neither what He was when He lived on earth, nor what (as is believed) He shall be at His return, but one about whom in an illicit way through history people have learned to know something to the effect that He was somebody or another of considerable consequence. In an unpermissible and unlawful way people have become *knowing* about Christ, for the only permissible way is to be *believing*. People have mutually confirmed one another in the notion that by the aid of the upshot of Christ's life and the 1,800 years (the consequences) they had become acquainted with the answer to the problem. By degrees, as this came to be accounted wisdom, all pith and vigour was distilled out of Christianity; the tension of the paradox was relaxed, one became a Christian without noticing it, and without in the least noticing the possibility of offence. One took possession of Christ's doctrine, turned it about and pared it down, while He of course remained surety for its truth, He whose life had such stupendous results in history. All became as simple as thrusting a foot into the stocking. And quite naturally, because in that way Christianity became paganism. In Christianity there is perpetual Sunday twaddle about Christianity's glorious and priceless truths, its sweet consolation; but it is only too evident that Christ lived 1,800 years ago. The Sign of Offence and the object of Faith has become the most romantic of all fabulous figures, a divine Uncle George.[1] One does not know what it is to be offended, still less what it is to worship. What one especially praises in Christ is precisely what one would be most embittered by if one were contemporary with it, whereas now one is quite secure in reliance upon the upshot; and in reliance upon this proof from history, that He quite certainly was the great one, one draws the conclusion: *Ergo* that was the right thing. This is to say, That is the right, the noble, the sublime, the true thing, if it was He that did it; this is the same as to say that one does not trouble oneself to learn to know in a deeper sense what it was He did, still less to try according to one's slender ability by God's help to imitate Him in doing the thing that is right and noble and sublime and true. For what that is one does not apprehend and may therefore in the situation of to-day form a judgement diametrically opposite to the truth. One is content to admire and praise, and

---

[1] The name S. K. employs is 'Godmand', alluding to Uncle Franz Godmand, a benevolent figure in a German story for children which was translated into Danish. I allude to the wise and versatile tutor in Abbott's *Rollo Books*. But though this perhaps is the nearest analogy in English (more properly American) literature, alas, I know that nowadays the reading even of our children is so various that literary allusions no longer allude.

may be (as was said of a scrupulous translator who rendered an author word for word and therefore made no meaning) 'too conscientious', perhaps also too cowardly and too feeble of heart really to wish to understand.

Christendom has done away with Christianity, without being quite aware of it. The consequence is that, if anything is to be done, one must try again to introduce Christianity into Christendom.[1]

[1] No proof could be desired more cogent than this last paragraph to demonstrate the continuity of S. K.'s thought—and, I might add, the persistence along with it of the same mental tone or feeling. Previous notes have pointed out several salient thoughts which had already emerged in the *Fragments* (1844) or in the *Postscript* (1846) and are here, not further developed, but more briefly and pointedly expressed in the style of 'direct communication'. Now it must be remarked that these same thoughts persisted to the end and constituted the spear-head of the open attack upon the Church (1855): the Christian paradox, the opposition of faith and reason, the possibility of the offence, the necessity of being contemporaneous with Christ, the vanity of the 1,800 years. Seeing that the total lapse of time here involved is only about twelve years, it might be thought that such continuity as is here remarked upon indicates no remarkable persistence. This would be true in the case of a sluggish mind; but we must remember that this includes almost the whole period (13 years) of S. K.'s restless literary activity which produced so abundantly and in such astonishing variety. Between the *Training in Christianity* (begun in 1848) and the open attack of 1855 we have a period which is relatively long, although it was characterized by a halt in production. And inasmuc as it is here especially that one may be tempted to assume a break in the continuity, an inexplicable cleft in the life of a conservative religious writer who suddenly launches a pamphleteering attack upon the Church, it is especially important to note that the thoughts which are trenchantly enough expressed in the conclusion of this section constitute the prime contention of the open attack: that 'Christendom has done away with Christianity', and that 'Christianity must be introduced again into Christendom'. These thoughts were never more strongly expressed than here, but they were later urged more relentlessly and with frequent reiteration to ensure that they would not be ignored. 'My *one* thesis', said S. K., 'is that Christianity no longer exists'; and 'my task is to reintroduce Christianity into Christendom'. His complaint against Christendom was that 'all are Christians'. S. K. was justified in saying that *Training in Christianity* (1848) would be seen to be an attack upon the Church if only the Preface and the Moral were omitted. Bishop Mynster saw that clearly enough. Others, having slight acquaintance with S. K.'s works and no understanding of his purpose, were naturally dumbfounded by the attack and were inclined to attribute it to a mental disorder. We who know the Works, and also the Journal with its revelation of persistent purpose, cannot be surprised by an attack which was so long preparing.

THE INVITER

THE Inviter, therefore, is Jesus Christ in His humiliation, and He it was who uttered these words of invitation. It was not from His glory that He uttered them. If such had been the case, Christianity is paganism and Christ is in vain—wherefore this supposition is not true. But supposing the case were such that He who sits in glory were disposed to utter this word, 'Come hither', as though it were an unambiguous invitation to rush straight into the arms of glory—what wonder then if a crowd were to come rushing up! But they who run in that fashion are on a wild-goose chase, vainly fancying that they *know* who Christ is. But that no one *knows*, and in order to believe, one must begin with the humiliation.

The Inviter who utters these words, consequently He whose words these are (whereas in the mouth of another these same words would be a falsehood), is the humiliated Jesus Christ, the lowly man, born of a despised maiden, His father a carpenter, His kindred people of the lowest class, the lowly man who at the same time (like pouring oil upon fire) declared that He was God.

It is this Jesus Christ in His humiliation who spoke these words. And you have no right to apply to yourself one word of Christ's, not one single word, you have not the least part in Him, no society with Him in the remotest way, unless you have become so contemporary with Him in His humiliation that, exactly like His immediate contemporaries, you must take heed of His warning: 'Blessed is he whosoever shall not be offended in me.' You have no right to appropriate Christ's words and mendaciously eliminate Him. You have no right to appropriate Christ's words and then transform Him fantastically into something other than He is, by means of the vain chatter of history, which while it chatters about Him really has no notion what it is chattering about.

It is Jesus Christ in His humiliation who speaks. It is historically true that *He* uttered these words. It is false that these words were uttered by *Him* the moment we alter His historical reality.

So then it is this lowly man, living in poverty, with twelve poor fellows as His disciples who were drawn from the simplest classes of society, who for a while was singled out as an object of curiosity, but later was to be found only in company with sinners, publicans, lepers, and madmen; for it might cost a man honour, life, and property, or at any rate expulsion from the synagogue (for this punishment we know was imposed), if he merely suffered himself to be helped by Him. Come now hither, all ye that labour and are heavy laden! Oh, my friend, though thou wert deaf and blind and lame and leprous, &c., though thou wert to unite (a thing never before seen or heard of) all human wretchedness in thy wretchedness, and though He stood ready to help thee by a miracle—it yet is possible that thou (for this is only human) wouldst fear more than all these sufferings the suffering imposed for letting oneself be helped by Him, the punishment of being banished from the society of other men, of being scorned and scoffed at day in and day out, of losing, perhaps, life itself. It would be human (only too human) if thou wert to say within thyself: No, I thank you; I had rather continue to be deaf, and dumb, and blind, &c., than to be helped in such a way.

'Come hither, hither, all ye that labour and are heavy laden; oh, come hither; behold how He bids you come, how He openeth His arms!' Oh, when these words are uttered by a fashionable man in a silk gown, with a pleasant and sonorous voice which resounds agreeably from the lovely, vaulted ceiling, a silken man who bestows honour and repute upon all who hear him; oh, when a king says this who is clothed in purple and velvet, with the Christmas tree in the background on which hang the splendid gifts he proposes to distribute[1]—then indeed thou wilt agree that there is some sense in what he says. But make what sense out of it thou wilt, one thing is sure, it is not Christianity, it is exactly the opposite, as contrary to Christianity as could be—for remember who the Inviter is.

And now judge for thyself—for thou hast a right to do that, whereas on the other hand thou hast no right to do what people so commonly do, to deceive thyself. That a man who makes such an appearance as that, a man who is shunned by everybody who has the least particle of common sense in his noddle and has anything in the world to lose, that He (surely that is the absurdest

---

[1] According to continental custom one of the Three Kings (Magi) appropriately distributes the Christmas gifts.

and craziest thing of all—one hardly knows whether to laugh or to weep at it), that He (surely that is the very last thing one might expect to hear from Him—for if He had said, 'Come hither and help me', or 'Let me alone', or 'Spare me', or in a proud tone, 'I despise you all', that might be understandable), but that He says, 'Come hither to me!'—what an uninviting invitation! And then further: 'All ye that labour and are heavy laden'—just as if people like that hadn't already enough troubles to bear, and then in addition would expose themselves to all the consequences of associating with Him. And finally: 'I will give you rest.' That caps the climax—He will help them! It seems to me that even the most good-natured of the scoffers who were actually His contemporaries might well say, 'That is the very last thing He should undertake—to wish to help others when He Himself is in such a plight. It is as if a beggar were to notify the police that he had been robbed. For that one who does not own anything and never has owned anything declares that he has been robbed is self-contradictory, and so also it is if one offers to help others when he himself is in need of being helped.' Humanly speaking, this is indeed the craziest contradiction, that He who literally 'has nowhere to lay his head', that a person of whom (humanly) it was appropriately said, 'Behold the man!' that He says, 'Come hither to me, all ye that suffer—I will help!'

Now examine thyself—for that thou hast a right to do. On the other hand, thou hast properly no right, without self-examination, to let thyself be deluded by 'the others', or to delude thyself into the belief that thou art a Christian—therefore examine thyself. Suppose that thou wert contemporary with Him! True enough, He said—ah, it was *He* that said it—that He was God! Many a madman has done the same—and His whole generation was of the opinion that He 'blasphemed'. That, indeed, was the reason for the punishment imposed upon those who let themselves be helped by Him. On the part of the established order and of public opinion it was god-fearing care for souls, lest anyone be led astray. They persecuted Him thus out of godly fear. Therefore before a man resolves to let himself be helped he must consider that he has not only to expect the opposition of men, but consider this too, that even if thou couldst bear all the consequences of such a step, consider this too, that human punishment is God's punishment upon the blasphemer—the Inviter!

Now come hither, all ye that labour and are heavy laden!

Here obviously there is no call for haste. There is a brief halt which might appropriately be turned to account by going round by another street. And if thou, supposing that thou wert contemporary, wilt not sneak away thus by another street, or in present-day Christendom wilt not be one of the sham Christians—then truly there is occasion for a tremendous halt, for a halt which is the condition for the very existence of faith: thou art brought to a halt by the possibility of the offence.

In order, however, to make it quite clear and vivid that the halt is due to the Inviter, that it is the Inviter who brings one to a halt by making it evident that it is not just such a simple matter, but really quite an awkward thing, to follow the invitation, because it is not permissible to accept the invitation and reject the Inviter—to make this clear I shall briefly review His life in its two periods, which, though they exhibit a certain diversity, fall *essentially* under the concept of humiliation. For it is always a humiliation for God to be man, though He were Emperor of all emperors, and *essentially* He is not more humiliated by being a poor, lowly man, mocked and (as the Scripture adds) spat upon.

A.

The First Period of His Life

And let us now speak about Him quite freely, just as His contemporaries spoke about Him, and as we speak about a contemporary, a man like the rest of us, whom one encounters occasionally in the street, knowing where he lives, on what floor of the house, what his business is, what he has to live on, who his parents are, his family connexion, what he looks like and how he dresses, with whom he associates—'and there seems to be nothing extraordinary about him, he seems just like all the others'. In short, let us speak as one speaks of a contemporary about whom one makes no great ado. For in the situation of contemporaneousness, with these thousands and thousands of *real* people, there is no occasion to take account of such a difference as that of being remembered perhaps throughout the centuries and that of being *actually* a clerk in some shop, 'just as good a man as anybody else'. —So let us speak of Him the way contemporaries speak about a contemporary. I know well what I am doing; and believe me, the affected and formal reverence we indolently conform to in speaking of Christ always with a certain sort of reverence, seeing that from history one has acquired information of a sort, and has heard so much of a sort about Him, about His having been somehow some sort of a great person—this sort of reverence, I say, is not worth a straw, it is heedlessness and mock-holiness, and as such it is blasphemy; for it is blasphemous to have a heedless reverence for Him whom one must either believe in or be offended at.

It is Jesus Christ in His humiliation, a lowly man, born of a despised virgin, his father a carpenter. But for all that, He makes His appearance under circumstances which are bound to fix very especial attention upon Him. The little nation in which He appears—God's chosen people, as it calls itself—looks forward to an Expected One who will usher in a golden age for His land and nation. It is true that the form in which He appears upon the scene was as different as possibly could be from what most people expected. On the other hand, it corresponded better to the ancient prophecy with which the nation might be supposed to be acquainted. Thus He makes His appearance. A precursor had drawn attention to Him, and He too fixes attention upon Himself by signs and wonders which are talked about in the whole land—and He is the hero of the hour, a countless multitude surrounds Him wherever He goes or stops. The sensation he awakens is prodigious, all eyes are turned toward Him, everything that can walk, yea, what can only crawl, must see this wonder—and all must have a judgement about Him, form an opinion, so that the professional purveyors of opinions and judgements are wellnigh driven to bankruptcy because the demands are so pressing and the contradictions so glaring. Yet He, the miracle-worker, continues to be the lowly man who literally has nowhere to lay His head.—And let us not forget that in the situation of contemporaneousness signs and wonders have quite a different elasticity for repelling and attracting than has this vapid affair (still more vapid when the parsons, as they are accustomed to do, serve the thing up as a warmed-over dish) of dealing with signs and wonders of . . . 1,800 years ago. Signs and wonders in the situation of contemporaneousness are an exasperatingly impertinent thing, a thing which in a highly embarrassing way pretty nearly compels one to have an opinion, and which, if one is not in the

humour to believe, may produce the utmost degree of exaspera-
tion at the misfortune of being contemporary with them, since
they make life all too strenuous, and all the more so the more
intelligent, educated, and cultured one is. It is an exceedingly
delicate matter to find oneself obliged to give assent to signs and
wonders performed by a contemporary. When one has Him at a
distance, and when the upshot of His life helps one to entertain
such a conceit, it is easy enough to fancy somehow that one believes.

So then the multitude is carried away by Him, follows Him
jubilantly, beholds signs and wonders—not only such as He
performs but such as he does not perform—exulting in the hope
that the golden age will commence when He becomes King. But
the crowd seldom can render a reason for its opinions; it thinks
one thing to-day, another to-morrow. For this cause wise and
prudent men are not in haste to adopt the opinions of the crowd.
Let us see now what the judgement of the wise and prudent is so
soon as the first impression of surprise and astonishment is past.

The wise and prudent man might say: 'Even assuming that this
person is, as He gives Himself out to be, the Extraordinary (for
all the talk of His being God I cannot but regard as an exaggeration, for which I should be quite ready to excuse and forgive Him
if I really could regard Him as the Extraordinary, for I am not
inclined to quarrel about words),[1] assuming (though about this
I have my doubts or at all events suspend my judgement) that the
things He does are actually miracles, is it not then an inexplicable
riddle that this same man can be so ignorant, so shallow, so totally
unacquainted with human nature, so weak, so good-naturedly
vain, or whatever one might prefer to call it, as to behave in such
a way, almost forcing his benefits upon people! Instead of holding
people at a distance with a proud and lordly mien, keeping them
in the deepest subjection, and receiving their worship on the rare
occasions when He permits Himself to be seen, that is to say,
being instead approachable to all, or, more properly expressed,
Himself approaching all, consorting with all, almost as if to be
the Extraordinary meant to be the servant of all, as if to be the
Extraordinary, as He Himself says He is, meant to be anxious
whether people will derive profit from Him or not, in short, as if

---

[1] In this connexion it is amusing to recall the first sentence of Renan's *Life of Jesus*.
It is as if that great man had stepped inadvertently into a trap S. K. had long before
laid to trip him up.

to be the Extraordinary were to be the most anxiously troubled of all men. On the whole, it is inexplicable to me what He wants, what His purpose is, what He is striving for, what He desires to accomplish, what the meaning of it all is. In many an individual utterance of His He discloses, as I cannot deny, so deep an insight into human nature that presumably He must know what I, with half my shrewdness, can tell Him in advance, that in such a fashion nobody can get on in the world—unless it might be that despising worldly prudence a man simple-heartedly aims at becoming a fool, or perhaps carries his simple-heartedness so far that He prefers to be put to death—but then a man is crazy, if that's what he wants. Having, as I said, a knowledge of human nature, He presumably knows that what one has to do is to deceive people and at the same time make one's deceit appear a benefaction to the whole race. In this way one stands to reap every advantage, including that which yields the most precious enjoyment of all, that of being called by one's contemporaries the benefactor of the human race—and when one is in the grave, a fig for what posterity may say. But to make such renunciation, not to take the least account of Himself, almost begging people to accept these benefactions—no, as for joining Him, such a thing could never enter my mind. And as a matter of fact He extends no invitation to me, for He invites only those who labour and are heavy laden.'

Or.—'His life is simply fantastic. Indeed this is the mildest expression one can use to describe it, for in passing that judgement one is good-humoured enough to ignore altogether this sheer madness of conceiving Himself to be God. It is fantastic. At the most one can live like that for a few years in one's youth. But He is already more than thirty years of age. And literally he is nothing. Moreover, no long time will elapse before He must lose all the popular respect and esteem He now enjoys—this being the only thing he can be said to have gained for himself hitherto. If in the long run a person would make sure of retaining popular favour (which I readily concede is quite the riskiest chance one can take), He must behave in a very different way. It will not be many months before the crowd is tired of a man who is thus at everybody's service; they will begin to regard Him as a ruined man, a sort of *mauvais sujet*, who might be thankful to end His days in some remote corner of the earth, forgetting the world and forgotten by it, provided at least that He does not obstinately hold his ground and, in conformity with the whole course of His life hitherto, want to be put to death, which is the inevitable consequence of holding His ground. What has He done to provide for His future? Nothing. Has He any definite job? No. What prospects has he? None. To speak only of a minor consideration —what will He do to pass the time when He grows older? The long winter nights, how will He occupy them? Why, He cannot even play cards. He enjoys some popular favour—verily, of all movable chattels the most movable, which in the twinkling of an eye can be transformed into popular disfavour.—To join myself to Him—no, I thank you. Praise God, I have not yet entirely lost my wits.'

Or.—'There is in fact something extraordinary about the man (though one may, on one's own behalf and on behalf of every sound human intelligence, reserve the right to refrain from any opinion with respect to His claim to be God), there is something extraordinary about Him; I have no doubt of that. In fact one might feel almost embittered at providence for entrusting to such a person what it has entrusted to Him, a person who Himself does the very opposite to that which He enjoins when He says not to cast your pearls before swine—wherefore the thing will end quite appropriately with their turning again and rending Him. This is what one can always expect of swine—but, on the other hand, one would not expect that He who Himself is aware of this truth would do exactly what He knew that other men should not do. If only one could craftily get possession of His wisdom— for as to His very peculiar personal notion that He is God, upon which He seems to set so much store, I will cheerfully leave it solely to Him as His undisputed personal possession—but if only one could craftily get possession of His wisdom ... without becoming His disciple! If one could slyly visit Him by night and get that out of Him—for I am man enough to draft and edit it, and in quite a different fashion, I assure you. To the astonishment and admiration of the whole world, something very different shall come out of it, that I warrant you. For I can perceive well enough that there is something very profound concealed in what He says, the misfortune being that He is the man He is. But, who knows, perhaps in the end it may prove possible to cajole it out of Him. Perhaps in this respect also He is idiotically good-natured enough to impart it openly. That is not improbable, for

it appears evident to me that the wisdom He is so plainly in possession of, being bestowed upon Him, has been bestowed upon a fool
—such a contradiction is the very essence. of His existence.—But
to join myself to Him, to become His disciple; no, that would be
to make a fool of myself.'

Or.—'In case (to advance an hypothesis which I leave unde-
termined) it is the Good and the True this man desires to further,
it may be said at least that He is helpful in one respect, to young
men especially, and to inexperienced youth in general, for whom
it is so profitable to understand, the sooner the better, and to
right good effect, in view of life's serious tasks, that all this high-
flown talk about living for the Good and the True has a considerable admixture of the ludicrous. He proves how exactly the poets
of our day have hit the mark when they always let the Good and
the True be impersonated by a half-wit or by a blockhead who
would serve for breaking down a door. To exert Himself as this
man does, to renounce everything except troubles and hardships,
to be at people's beck and call every hour of the day, more diligent
than a practising physician—and why? Is it because this is His
calling? No, not in the remotest sense. So far as one can judge,
it has never occurred to Him to want to have any post. Is it then
because He earns money thereby? No, not a penny. He doesn't
own a penny; and if He owned it, he would at once give it away.
Is it then to attain honour and prestige in the State? Quite the
contrary: He abhors all worldly prestige. And He who, despising
worldly prestige and practised in the art of living on nothing,
seems qualified, if any man in the world is, to pass His life in the
most agreeable *far niente* (a thing that has some sense in it after
all)—why, it is precisely He that lives more laboriously than any
government official who is rewarded with honour and prestige,
more laboriously than any business man who makes money by
the peck. Why does He exert Himself so strenuously, or (since
it is vain to put a question which can have no answer), just remark
with amazement that He exerts Himself thus to attain the good
fortune of being laughed at and derided, &c.! A queer sort of
pleasure, forsooth! That one should push through the crowd in
order to get to the spot where money is dealt out, and honour, and
glory—that one can understand. But to push oneself forward in
order to be flogged—how sublime, how Christian, how stupid!'

Or.—'So many hasty judgements are expressed by people who

understand nothing . . . and deify Him, and so many harsh
judgements by those who perhaps misunderstand Him, that for
my part I shall not give anyone occasion to charge me with a hasty
judgement; I keep perfectly cool and calm, and what is more, I
am conscious of being as indulgent and moderate as possible.
Suppose it is true (which I concede, however, only up to a certain
point) that even the understanding is not unimpressed by this
man—what judgement then must I pass upon Him? My judgement is that at the outset I can form no judgement about Him.
I do not mean with respect to the fact that He says he is God, for
about that I can never to all eternity form any judgement at all.
No, I mean an opinion about Him regarded as a man. Only the
upshot of His life can determine whether He is the Extraordinary,
or whether, deceived by His imagination, He has applied, not
only to Himself but to mankind in general, a standard far too high
for men. With the best will in the world I can do no more for
Him than this; even if He were my only friend or my own son,
I could not judge Him more indulgently or to any other effect.
But hence it follows that I cannot on sufficient grounds reach any
opinion about Him. For to have an opinion I must first see the
upshot of His life, even up to the very end. That is to say He
must be dead. Then I can (but still only perhaps) have an opinion
about Him; and this being assumed, it is still only in a non-
natural sense an opinion about Him, for then in fact He is no
more. It follows as a matter of course that I cannot possibly join
myself to Him as long as He lives. The *authority* with which He is
said to teach cannot have for me decisive significance, for it is
easy to see that it moves in a circle, appealing to the very fact He
has to prove, which in turn can only be proved by the upshot, in so
far as it does not derive from that fixed idea of His that He is
God; for if it is *therefore* He possesses authority, because He is
God, the rejoinder is . . . *if.* This much, however, I can concede
to Him, that if I could fancy myself living in a later generation,
and if then the upshot of His life, the consequences of it in history,
were to make it evident that He was the Extraordinary—then it
might not be altogether impossible that I might come very near to
being His disciple.'

A clergyman might say.——'For an impostor and seducer of the
people there is really something uncommonly honest about Him,
and for this reason He can hardly be so absolutely dangerous as

He appears to be. He appears now to be so dangerous while the storm lasts, appears so dangerous because of His immense popularity, until the storm has past over and the people—yes, precisely these people—overthrow Him. It is honesty that while desiring to make Himself out to be the Expected One, He resembles this figure so little as he does—the sort of honesty one can detect in a person who would issue false bank-notes, and makes them so badly that everyone who has any intelligence can easily detect the fraud.—True enough, we all look forward to an Expected One; but that it is God in His own person that should come is the expectation of no reasonable man, and every religious soul shudders at the blasphemy this person is guilty of. Nevertheless, we all look forward to an Expected One, in this we are all agreed. But the regiment of this world does not move forward tumultuously by leaps, the world development is (as the word itself implies) *evolutionary*, not *revolutionary*. The veritable Expected One will therefore appear totally different; He will come as the most glorious flower and the highest unfolding of the established order. Thus it is that the veritable Expected One will come; and He will act in a totally different way, He will recognize the established order as an authority, He will summon all the clergy to a council, lay before this body a report of what He has accomplished along with His credentials—and then, if by ballot He obtains a majority vote, He will be acclaimed as the extraordinary man He is, as the Expected One.

'But in this man's course of action there is an ambiguity. He is far too much the judge. It is as if He would be the judge which condemns the established order, and yet at the same time the Expected One. If it is not the former He wishes to be, to what purpose then His absolute isolation from the established order, His aloofness from everything that has to do with it! If He does not wish to be the judge, then to what purpose His fantastic flight outside reality and into the society of ignorant peasantry, to what purpose His proud contempt for all the intelligence and efficiency of the established order, and His resolution to begin entirely afresh and anew by the help of . . . fishermen and artisans! His whole mode of existence is aptly typified by the fact that He is an illegitimate child. If He wishes to be merely the Expected One, to what purpose His warning about putting a new piece of cloth upon an old garment? This is the watchword of every revolution, for it implies not merely the will to ignore the established order, but the will to do away with it—instead of joining forces with the establishment and as a reformer bettering it, or as the Expected One raising it to its highest potency. There is an ambiguity, and it is not feasible to be at once the judge and the Expected One. And this ambiguity must result in his downfall, which I have already calculated in advance. The catastrophe of the judge is rightly imagined by the dramatists as a violent death; but the thing looked forward to with hopeful expectation cannot possibly be downfall, and so He is *eo ipso* not the Expected One, that is to say, not Him whom the established order expects in order to deify Him. The people do not yet perceive this ambiguity; they regard Him as the Expected One, which the established order cannot possibly do, and the people can, the formless and fickle crowd, because they are at the farthest remove from being anything that can be called established. But as soon as the ambiguity is made manifest, it will be His downfall. Why, His precursor was a far more definitely defined figure. He was one thing only: the judge. But how confusing and bewildering to want to be both things at once, and what an extremity of confusion it is to recognize His precursor as the one who was to act as judge, which precisely means, of course, to make the established order receptive for the Expected One and to put it entirely in condition to receive Him, and then to want to be Himself the Expected One who follows close after the judge—and yet still not be willing to join hands with the established order!'

And the philosopher might say.—'Such dreadful, or, rather, insane vanity. For an individual man to want to be God is something hitherto unheard of. Never before has there been seen such an example of pure subjectivity and sheer negation carried to the utmost excess. He has no doctrine, no system, no fundamental knowledge; it is merely by detached aphoristic utterances, some bits of sententious wisdom, constantly repeated with variations, that He succeeds in dazzling the masses, for whom also He performs signs and wonders, so that they, instead of learning something and receiving instruction, come to believe in Him, who continues in the most odious manner possible to force his subjectivity upon people. There is absolutely nothing objective or positive in Him or in what He says. So far as this goes, one might say that He does not need to be brought to destruction, for philosophically considered He is already destroyed, perishableness being the very essence of subjectivity.[1] One may concede that His is a remarkable subjectivity, and that regarded as a teacher (be it as it may with His other signs and wonders) He continually repeats the miracle of the five small loaves: by the aid of a little lyric and a few aphorisms He sets the whole land in commotion. But even if one would overlook the madness revealed in the fact that *He* thinks Himself to be God, it is an incomprehensible mistake, disclosing surely a lack of philosophic culture, to suppose that God could anyhow reveal Himself in the form of a single individual. The race, the universal, the totality, is God; but surely the race is not any single individual. In general it is characteristic of subjectivity that the individual desires to be something of importance. But this you can understand. Insanity is evinced by the fact that the individual desires to be God. If this insane thing were possible, that an individual was God, then logically one must worship this individual. A greater philosophical bestiality cannot be conceived.'

The statesman might say.—'That at the moment this man is a power, cannot be denied—leaving out of account, of course, the conceit He has that He is God. One can afford to ignore once for all a private hobby like that, which need not be reckoned with practically and concerns nobody else, least of all the statesman. A statesman is interested only in what power a man possesses, and, as has already been said, at this moment He is a power to be reckoned with. But what He wants, what He is heading for, it is not easy to make out. If this is shrewdness, it must be of an entirely new and peculiar order, not unlike what commonly is called madness. He has conspicuously strong points, but He seems to annul them instead of making use of them. He expends His forces, but gets nothing in return for *Himself*. I regard Him as a phenomenon, with which—as with every phenomenon—one does best not to ally oneself, since it is always impossible to calculate on Him or on the catastrophe which confronts Him. It is possible that He may become king—that is at least possible. But it is not impossible, or rather it is equally possible, that He may end on the scaffold. What is lacking in His whole effort is seriousness.[2]

[1] Cf. Hegel's *Logic*, Part III (1st ed. of *Works*, v, p. 32 f.).
[2] S. K. found it both irksome and ridiculous that this complaint was commonly made against him.

With a vast spread of wing He hovers, merely hovers; He makes no end fast,[1] makes no businesslike reckoning—He hovers. Would He fight for national interests, or is it a communistic revolution He aims after, is it a republic He wants or a kingdom, which party will He join or which oppose, will He try to stand well with all parties, or will He struggle against them all? Get into touch with Him? No, that is the very last thing I should want to do. I do even more than avoid Him; I keep perfectly still, make as if I did not exist; for it is impossible to reckon how He might intervene to confound one, if one were to take in hand the least thing, or how things might get tangled up in His hands. The man is dangerous, in a certain sense He is tremendously dangerous; but I calculate to catch Him, just by doing nothing. For He must be overthrown—and the surest way is to let Him do it Himself, by stumbling over Himself. At this moment at least I have not the power to overthrow Him, and I know of no one who has. To undertake the least thing against Him now would be merely to get oneself crushed. No, a steady negative resistance is the thing. To do nothing! then presumably He will involve Himself in the enormous consequences He drags after Him, He will finally trip on His own train—and fall.'

Or the solid citizen might express an opinion which in his own family would be received as a verdict.—'No, let us be men.[2] Everything is good in moderation; too little and too much spoils all. And according to a French proverb which I heard from a travelling salesman, Every energy exerted to excess collapses— and as for this man, His downfall is obviously a sure thing. So I have seriously taken my son to task, warning and admonishing him that he should not drift into evil ways and join himself to that person. And why should he? Because all are running after Him. Yes, but who are these 'all'? Idle and unstable people, street loungers and vagabonds, who find it easy to run. But not very many who have their own houses and are well to do, and none

---

[1] The necessity of knotting the end of the thread in sewing was a favourite analogy of S. K.'s. He looked forward to his own martyrdom as a way of 'fastening the end'.

[2] Strangely enough, S. K. ascribes to the sententious *bourgeois* an exclamation which he himself in his youth seems to have used only too often—to judge by the parody of him which Hans Christian Andersen cruelly perpetrated in *The Lucky Galloshes*, where S. K. is the parrot which with its rasping voice has nothing to say but, 'Let us be men'.

of the wise and respected people after whom I always set my clock, not a one of them, neither Councillor Brown, nor Congressman Jones, nor the wealthy broker Robinson—nay, nay, these people know what's what. And if we look at the clergy, who surely must understand such matters best—they thank Him kindly. This is what Pastor Green said yesterday evening at the club: "That life will have a terrible ending." And he is a chap that doesn't only know how to preach. One should not hear him on Sundays in church, but on Mondays at the club—I only wish I had half of his knowledge of the world. He said quite rightly and as from his very heart, "it is only idle and unstable people that run after Him". And why do they run after Him? Because He is able to perform some miracles. But who knows whether they really are miracles, or whether He can confer the same power upon His disciples? In any case a miracle is a very uncertain thing, whereas certainty is certainty. Every serious father who has grown-up children must be truly concerned lest his sons be seduced and carried away to throw in their lot with Him and with the desperate men who follow Him, desperate men who have nothing to lose. And even these men—how does He help them? One must be mad to want to be helped in that fashion. It is true, even with regard to the poorest beggars, that He helps them out of the frying-pan into the fire, helps them into a new misery which the beggar could have avoided by remaining what he was, a mere beggar.'

And the mocker—not one who is despised by all for his malice, but one who is admired by all for his wit and liked for his good nature—the mocker might say.—'After all, that is a priceless idea, which must eventually inure to the advantage of all of us—that an individual man, just like the rest of us, says that He is God. If that is not to confer a benefit upon men, I do not know what benevolence and beneficence or beneficence and benevolence can mean. Granted that the criterion of being God is (I declare, who in all the world could hit upon such an idea! How true it is that such a thing never entered into the heart of man!), that it is just to look like all the rest of us, neither more nor less—hence we are all gods. *Quod erat demonstrandum.* Three cheers for Him, the discoverer of this invention so extraordinarily helpful to men! To-morrow I shall proclaim that I, the undersigned, am God—and the discoverer at least cannot deny it without contradicting

Himself. All cats are grey in the dark—and if to be God is to look like all the rest, then it is dark, and we are all . . . or what was I about to say? we are all and every one of us God, and no one will have ground to be invidious of another. This is the most ludicrous thing imaginable; contradiction, which always is at the bottom of the comic, is here evident in the highest degree—but the credit for it is not mine, it belongs only and solely and exclusively to the discoverer of the fact that a man just like the rest of us, only not by any means so well dressed as the average, hence a shabbily dressed person who most nearly (at least more nearly than under the rubric God) comes under the attention of the Supervisor of the poor—that He is God. It is a pity, however, for the poor Supervisor of the poor, who with this general advancement of the human race will be out of a job.'

Oh, my friend, I know well what I am doing, and my soul is eternally assured of the rightness of what I do. Imagine thyself, therefore, contemporary with Him, the Inviter. Imagine that thou wast a sufferer—but reflect to what thou dost expose thyself by becoming His disciple, by following Him. Thou dost expose thyself to the loss of almost everything accounted precious in the eyes of people who are prudent, sensible, and held in esteem. He, the Inviter, requires of thee that thou give up everything, let all go—but the common sense which is contemporary with thee in thy generation will not easily let thee go, its verdict is that to join Him is madness. And cruel mockery will taunt thee. Whereas it almost spares Him out of pity, it accounts it a madder thing than the maddest to become His disciple. 'For', says common sense, 'a fanatic is a fanatic. Bad enough. But seriously to . . . become his disciple is the greatest possible madness. There is only one possible way of being madder than a madman: it is the higher madness[1] of attaching oneself in all seriousness to a madman, regarding him as a wise man.'

Oh, say not that this whole treatment is an exaggeration. Thou knowest indeed (yet perhaps thou art not yet thoroughly sensible of it) that among all the men who were respected, enlightened, and wise, though some may have conversed with Him out of curiosity, yet there was only one, one single man, who seriously sought Him out, and he came to Him . . . by night. And thou

---

[1] In his aesthetic stage S. K. liked to boast of his proficiency in 'the higher madness'—as we learn from the letters of Judge William in *Either/Or*.

knowest well that by night one treads forbidden paths, night is chosen as the time to go to a place one would not be seen frequenting. Think what a disparaging opinion of the Inviter this implies—to visit Him was a disgrace, something no respectable person, no man of honour, could openly do—no more than to go to . . . yet, no, I would not go on with what follows this 'no more than'.

Come *now* hither *to me*, all ye that labour and are heavy laden, I will give you rest.

B.

The Second Period of His Life

It has happened to Him now as all the shrewd and prudent men, the statesmen, and citizens, and mockers, &c., foretold. And like as it was said at a moment when it would seem that even the hardest hearts might be moved to sympathy, even stones to tears, 'He helped others, let him now help himself', so has it by this time been said thousands upon thousands of times by thousands upon thousands of people, 'What did he mean when he said that his time was not yet come; might it perhaps now be come?' Whereas, alas, 'that single individual',[1] the believer, must shudder every time he thinks of it, and yet cannot withhold his eyes from gazing into that abyss of (humanly speaking) senseless lunacy—that God in human form, that this divine doctrine, that these signs and wonders, which had they been performed in Sodom and Gomorrah, must have led to repentance, that in reality they produce the very opposite effect, seeing that the Teacher is shunned, hated, despised.

It is easier at this point to perceive what He is, since men of power and repute, the opposition of the establishment as a whole and the measures put in effect against Him have attenuated the impression He produced at the first, and the people have become impatient of waiting, seeing that His career, instead of going on to ever greater and greater renown, goes more and more backward to ever greater and greater degradation. It is a truism that every man is judged by the company he keeps. And what company does he keep? Well, that can be described by saying that he is an outcast from 'human society'. The company he keeps is the lowest class of the population, including, furthermore, sinners and tax-gatherers, who are shunned by every man of any importance who values his good name and reputation; and a good name and reputation is surely the last thing one would like to lose. His

---

[1] *Hiin Enkelte.* This, S. K. desired to have inscribed on his tomb. This, he said, is 'my category', the single individual, picked out from the crowd, isolated in the presence of God, and thus enabled to be an independent force in the world. I call attention here, once for all, to this significant word, about which S. K. wrote a whole chapter, which is appended to *The Point of View for my Life as an Author.*

company consists, moreover, of lepers, who are shunned by everybody, madmen, who provoke only horror, of the sick and the needy, of poverty and wretchedness. Who then is this man that, being followed by such a train, He is still persecuted by the mighty? He is a man despised as a seducer, deceiver, blasphemer! It implies a sort of pity if any person of repute refrains from actually expressing his contempt for Him—the fact that they fear Him is another matter.—Such is now His appearance. For be on your guard not to be influenced by what you have come to learn later, to the effect that His exalted spirit, rising almost to divine majesty, never exhibited itself so evidently as just now. Oh, my friend, wert thou contemporary with a man who not only Himself was 'expelled from the synagogue', but—remember this!—a punishment was devised for everyone who let himself be helped by Him, and that punishment was 'expulsion from the synagogue'—wert thou contemporary with a man so despised, about whom everything seems correspondingly despicable (for there is nothing that cannot be interpreted in more than one way), art thou perhaps man enough to explain everything in a contrary way; or, what comes to the same thing, art thou 'that single individual', which as thou well knowest nobody wants to be, and which is regarded as a ludicrous eccentricity, perhaps as a crime?

And—to come to His principal companions, His Apostles! What madness—not to say new madness, for this is of a piece with the foregoing—His Apostles are a bunch of fishermen, who yesterday caught herring, and to-morrow (thus the logic of insanity expresses it) go out into all the world and change the face of the whole world. And it is He that says He is God, and these are His duly appointed Apostles! Is it He that is to assure respect for the Apostles, or is it perhaps the Apostles that are to ensure respect for Him? Is He, the Inviter, a crazy visionary? The procession which accompanies Him bears out this notion. No poet could invent it better. A teacher, a sage (or whatever you prefer to call Him), an ill-starred sort of genius who says of Himself that He is God—surrounded by a shouting mob, personally accompanied by a lot of publicans, criminals, and lepers, and closest to Him His chosen circle, the Apostles. And these persons, so competent to be judges of what truth is, these fishermen, tailors, and shoemakers, not only admire their teacher and master, taking every word of His for wisdom and truth, see not only what others do not see, His exalted character and holiness, no, they see God in Him and worship Him.—No poet could invent it better, indeed he might forget to mention the additional extraordinary fact that this same man is feared by the mighty, who lay their plans to destroy Him. His death is the only thing that can reassure and appease them. They have attached an ignominious penalty to the crime of joining Him, yes, even to that of letting oneself be helped by Him, and yet they cannot feel secure, they cannot feel quite certain that the whole thing is visionary madness. So much for the powerful. The people who idolized Him have more or less given Him up, only now and then for a moment does their old conception of Him flare up. There is not a single item in all the conditions of His existence that the most invidious of the envious could envy Him. And certainly the mighty did not envy Him, they require His death for the sake of their own security, that they may be at peace again when all has become as of old, only more securely settled by reason of his deterrent example.

These are the two periods of His life. It began with the people idolizing Him, whereas all who were implicated in the established order, all who had power and influence, hated Him, yet in a cowardly and underhand way spread their snare for Him. Into which He forthwith stepped? True, but He saw it clearly. Finally the people discovered that they were mistaken in Him, that the fulfilment He would consummate was at the farthest possible remove from the gold and the green gardens they were expecting. So the people fell away from Him, and the mighty drew the net closer . . . into which He forthwith stepped? True, but He saw it clearly. The mighty drew the net closer—and then the people, perceiving that they were completely deceived, turned their hate and the bitterness of their disillusionment against Him.

And (as the last straw) compassion might say, or in the society of compassion (for compassion is sociable, likes to get together, and in society with silly shallowness of feeling there is always to be found spite and envy, and even a pagan[1] has remarked that none is so inclined to compassion as the envious), in that society the discourse might run as follows. 'And yet one really can be sorry for the poor man that He comes to such an end. He was a good sort of a chap after all. I grant that it was exorbitant of Him to

[1] An unnamed philosopher in Plutarch's *De ira et odio*, cap. 7.

want to be God, yet He really was good to the poor and needy, even though it was in the queer way of making Himself entirely one with the poor and going about with beggars. But all the same, there is something touching in the case, and one can't help being sorry for the poor man that he has to be put out of the way in such a pitiable fashion. For let them say what they will, and condemn Him as severely as they will, I can't help pitying Him, I'm not hard-hearted enough for that, and I can't help showing my compassion.'

We have arrived at the last paragraph—not of sacred history, such as the Apostles and disciples who believed on Him recorded, but of the profane history which is the counterpart of it.

Come now hither, all ye that labour and are heavy laden—that is to say, if thou, of all sufferers the most miserable, still dost feel a desire to come, if thou still dost feel a desire to be helped in that fashion, that is, into still deeper misery, then come hither, He will help thee.

III

THE INVITATION AND THE INVITER

Let us now forget for a moment that in the strictest sense the offence lies in the fact that the Inviter said that He was God, and let us suppose that He represented Himself to be merely a man, and let us consider in this light the Inviter and the invitation.

The invitation is surely inviting enough; how then can one explain this incongruity in the event, this frightfully inverted proportion, that no one, or as good as none, accepted the invitation, that all, or as good as all (and, alas, it was 'all' that were expressly invited!), were at one in opposing the Inviter, in putting Him to death, yes, even in imposing a penalty for letting oneself be helped by Him. One might expect indeed that all, all sufferers especially, would come in throngs, and that all who were not sufferers but were moved by the thought of such loving-kindness and compassion would come in throngs, so that the whole race would be at one in admiring and praising the Inviter. How is the very opposite event to be explained? For that such a thing occurred is perfectly certain, and the fact that it occurred in this particular race must not be taken to signify that this race was worse than others. How could one be so thoughtless? Everyone who has any competence in such matters easily perceives that it occurred in this particular race because it was contemporary with Him. How then explain how it occurred, this frightful inversion of what it seems one might have expected?

The fact is that if the Inviter had (firstly) the aspect which the merely human conception of compassion would ascribe to His person; and if (secondly) He had had the merely human conception of what man's misery is, this surely would not have happened.

As for the first point: He should have been a thoroughly kindly and sympathetic man, who was in possession moreover of all the means for providing temporal and earthly relief, ennobling this relief with a deep and heart-felt sympathy. But he must be a man of distinction, not without a certain degree of human self-assertion, the consequence of which would be that he neither was able, in spite of his compassionate feeling, to stoop so low as to reach all sufferers, nor could clearly apprehend wherein man's misery, human misery, consists.

On the other hand, the divine compassion, its limitless *abandon* in its concern for the sufferer alone—not in the least for itself—and the absolute *abandon* with which it concerns itself for *every* sufferer—that cannot but he interpreted by men as a sort of insanity, which one hardly knows whether to laugh or to weep over. Even if there had been no other obstacle to the Inviter, this would have ensured that it would go ill with Him in the world.

Let a man merely experiment a little with divine compassion, that is to say, display some *abandon* in the practice of compassion, and then thou shalt see immediately what judgements men will form. Let one who might have a higher station in life—I do not say, let him, while maintaining the distinction of his station, give much to the poor, benevolently (i.e. as a superior) seek out the poor, and the sick, and the wretched—no, let him give up this distinction and seriously seek his society among the poor, live completely with the humble classes, with labourers, hod-carriers, mortar-mixers, and the like! Ah, in a quiet moment when one does not *see* him, most people perhaps may be touched by the thought of it; but as soon as they *see* him in this company and with this following, see him who might have been something great in the world coming along in close companionship with a brick-layer on his right and a broom-maker's apprentice on his left—what then? First of all they will have a thousand ways of explaining that it is by reason of his eccentricity and obstinacy and pride and vanity that he lives thus.[1] And even if they refrain from attributing to him such motives, they will not be able to reconcile themselves to the sight of him—in this company. Even the best men, generally speaking, will the moment they *see* it be tempted to laugh.

And though all the parsons, be they clothed in velvet, in silk, in broadcloth, or in bombasine, were to say otherwise, I would say, 'You lie, you merely deceive people with your Sunday discourses. For it will always be possible in the situation of contemporaneousness to say of such a compassionate one, who in this case therefore is a neighbour, "I believe it is vanity and hence I laugh

---

[1] In his Journals S. K. was compelled to answer frequently to the common charge that his way of life was prompted by pride and vanity or was simply to be ascribed to his eccentricity.

at him. Quite a different matter if he were the truly compassionate one, or if I had lived contemporary with that noble figure!" ' And as for these glorious ones 'who were misunderstood, &c.' (to quote the sermonizing phrase)—well, they are dead. In this way it is possible to play hide and seek. With regard to every compassionate man who ventures so far out,[1] one assumes that it is vanity—and as for the deceased, one takes it that they are deceased and that therefore they were glorious.

This, however, must be remembered with regard to differences in human life, that everybody is for his own class. This partiality constitutes a fixed point, which explains why *human* compassion never goes beyond a certain degree. The greengrocer will be of the opinion that compassion descends too far when it extends to the inmates of the poor house and expresses equality with them. The greengrocer's compassion is entoiled in one sole reference, a reference first of all to the other greengrocers, and then to the alehouse keepers. Thus this compassion is not exercised with *abandon (hensynsløs)*. And so with every class—the journalists who live off the pennies of the poor, under pretence of asserting and defending their rights, would be the first to render it ridiculous if anywhere there was manifested an example of this spirit of *abandon* in compassion.

To make oneself literally one with the most miserable (and this, this alone is *divine* compassion) is for men the 'too much', over which one weeps in the quiet hour on Sundays, and at which one bursts with laughter when one sees it in *reality*. The fact is, this is so sublime that one cannot bear to see it in daily use; to bear it one must have it at a distance. Men are not on such intimate terms with the sublime that they really can believe in it. The contradiction therefore is this: This sublimity on the one hand; and, on the other, the fact that this is daily life, quite literally daily life, in which it manifests itself. When the poet or the orator illustrates this sublimity, that is, represents it with the Poet's aloofness from reality, people then are moved—but in reality, in the actuality of daily life, to perceive this sublimity in Copenhagen, in Amager market, in the midst of the week-day business life! Oh, when the poet or the orator does it, that lasts only an hour. Just for so long a time men are capable in a way of believing in this sublimity.

---

[1] 'Venturing far out', i.e. as a swimmer in the ocean, is the figure under which S. K. thought of the bold risk he was preparing to take.

But to behold it in reality *every day*! It is indeed a monstrous contradiction that the sublime has become the everyday thing.

In view of this, it was already decided beforehand what the fate of the Inviter must be, even if nothing else had contributed to His downfall. The unconditional, everything that applies the measuring-rod of the unconditional, is *eo ipso* a sacrifice. For though it is true enough that men wish to exercise compassion and self-denial and want to have wisdom, &c., yet they wish to determine for themselves the measure, insisting that it shall be only to *a certain degree*; they are not desirous of abolishing all these glorious virtues; on the contrary they would at a good bargain and without inconvenience have the appearance of practising them. Hence the true divine compassion is unconditionally a sacrifice as soon as it manifests itself in the world. It comes in compassion for man, and it is man who treads it under foot. And while it wanders about among men, even the sufferer will hardly dare to take refuge in it for fear of men. The fact is, it is for the world a matter of great consequence to preserve the appearance of being compassionate; this, then, the divine compassion reveals as falsehood—*ergo*, Away with this divine compassion!

But the Inviter was precisely the divine compassion—and therefore He was sacrificed, and therefore even the sufferers fled from Him; they understood (and, humanly speaking, quite rightly) that, as far as most human misery is concerned, it is better to remain what one is rather than be helped by Him.

As for the second point: The Inviter had also an entirely different conception than that which is purely human of what man's wretchedness is, and to help man in this respect was what He was intent upon—on the other hand, He had not brought with Him either money or medicaments or any such thing.

Thus the Inviter is so very far from having the appearance which human compassion would bestow upon His person that he is strictly an offence. Humanly speaking, there is actually something shocking, something at which one might become so embittered that he would have an inclination to kill the man—at the thought of bidding the poor, and sick, and suffering to come to him, and then to be able to do nothing for them but only to promise them forgiveness of sins. 'Let us be men. A man is no spirit. And when a man is near to dying of hunger, then to say to him, "I promise thee the gracious forgiveness of thy sins"—that is shocking. Really, it is also ludicrous, but it is too serious a thing to laugh at.'

So then (for with these words in quotation we have merely wished to let the offence disclose the contradiction and exaggerate —we would not exaggerate) the Inviter really thought that *sin is man's ruin*. Behold now how that clears the ground!—and the Inviter did clear the ground, almost as if He had said, *procul, o procul este, profani*, or, even though He did not say this, it was as if a voice was heard which thus interpreted the Inviter's 'Come hither'. There remain not many sufferers to follow the invitation. Even if there had been one who, though he saw that there was no actual earthly help to be had from this Inviter, nevertheless followed, being touched by His compassion—now he too flees away from Him. 'It is indeed very close to being crafty of Him to pose as compassion in order to get a chance to talk about sin.'

Yes, indeed it is crafty, in case it is not clear to thee that thou art a sinner. In case it is only a toothache thou hast, or it is thy house that has burnt down, but it has escaped thy notice that thou art a sinner—then it is crafty of Him. It is crafty of the Inviter to say I have healing for all sicknesses; and then, when one comes, to tell him that there exists only one sickness, sin—for that and from that I have healing for all them that labour to labour themselves out of the power of sin, labour to resist the evil, to overcome their weakness, yet accomplish no more but to be heavy laden. From that sickness He heals 'all'; even if there were only one who on account of this sickness has recourse to Him, He heals all. On the other hand, to have recourse to Him on account of any other sickness, and on that account alone, is as if one who had broken his leg were to have recourse to a physician who employs himself only about eye diseases.

IV

CHRISTIANITY AS THE ABSOLUTE
CONTEMPORANEOUSNESS WITH CHRIST

WITH this invitation to all them 'that labour and are heavy laden' Christianity did not come into the world (as the parsons snivellingly and falsely introduce it) as an admirable example of the gentle art of consolation—but as *the absolute*. It is out of love God wills it so, but also it is *God* who wills it, and He wills what He will. He will not suffer Himself to be transformed by men and be a nice . . . human God: He will transform men, and that He wills out of love. He will have nothing to do with man's pert inquiry about why and why did Christianity come into the world: it is and shall be the absolute. Therefore everything men have hit upon relatively to explain the why and the wherefore is falsehood. Perhaps they have hit upon an explanation out of a humane compassion of a sort, which thinks that one might chaffer about the price—for God presumably does not understand men, His requirements are exorbitant, and so the parsons must be on hand to chaffer. Perhaps they hit upon an explanation in order to stand well with men and get some advantage out of preaching Christianity; for when it is toned down to the merely human, to what has 'entered into the heart of man', then naturally people will think well of it, and quite naturally also of the amiable orator who can make Christianity so gentle a thing— if the Apostles had been able to do that, people would also have thought well of the Apostles. But all this is falsehood, it is misrepresentation of Christianity, which is the absolute. But what, then, is the use of Christianity? It is, then, merely a plague to us! Ah, yes, that too can be said: relatively understood, the absolute is the greatest plague. In all moments of laxness, sluggishness, dullness, when the sensuous nature of man predominates, Christianity seems madness, since it is incommensurable with any finite wherefore. What is the use of it, then? The answer is: Hold thy peace! It is the absolute! And so it *must* be represented, viz. in such a way as to make it appear madness in the eyes of the sensuous man. And hence it is true, so true (and in another sense it is also so true) when the wise and prudent man (cf. II. A, p. 47) in the situation of contemporaneousness condemns Christ by saying, 'He is literally nothing'—most certainly true, for He is the absolute. Christianity came into the world as the absolute—not for consolation, humanly understood; on the contrary, it speaks again and again of the sufferings which a Christian must endure, or which a man must endure to become and to be a Christian, sufferings he can well avoid merely by refraining from becoming a Christian.

There is an endless yawning difference between God and man, and hence, in the situation of contemporaneousness, to become a Christian (to be transformed into likeness with God) proved to be an even greater torment and misery and pain than the greatest human torment, and hence also a crime in the eyes of one's neighbours. And so it will always prove when becoming a Christian in truth comes to mean to become contemporary with Christ. And if becoming a Christian does not come to mean this, then all the talk about becoming a Christian is nonsense and self-deception and conceit, in part even blasphemy and sin against the Second Commandment of the Law and sin against the Holy Ghost.

For in relation to the absolute there is only one tense: the present. For him who is not contemporary with the absolute—for him it has no existence. And as Christ is the absolute, it is easy to see that with respect to Him there is only one situation: that of contemporaneousness. The five, the seven, the fifteen, the eighteen hundred years are neither here nor there; they do not change Him, neither do they in any wise reveal who He was, for who He is is revealed only to faith.

Christ is (if I may express it so seriously) not a comedian, not at all a merely historical person, since as the Paradox He is an extremely unhistorical person. But this is the difference between poetry and reality: contemporaneousness. The difference between poetry and history is clearly this, that history is what really occurred, whereas poetry is the possible, the imaginary, the poetized. But what really occurred (the past) is not (except in a special sense, i.e. in contrast with poetry) the real. It lacks the determinant which is the determinant of truth (as inwardness)[1]

---

[1] S. K. here alludes to the conception of truth as subjective which he maintained in the *Postscript*, especially in Part II, 2nd section, cap. 2.

and of all religiousness, the **for thee.** The past is not reality—for me: only the contemporary is reality for me. What thou dost live contemporaneous with is reality—for thee. And thus every man can be contemporary only with the age in which he lives—and then with one thing more: with Christ's life on earth; for Christ's life on earth, sacred history, stands for itself alone outside history.

History you can read and hear about as referring to the past. Here, if you like, you can form your judgements according to the upshot. But Christ's life on earth is not a past event; in its time 1,800 years ago it did not wait, nor does it wait now, for any assistance from the upshot. An historical Christianity is galimatias and unchristian confusion; for what true Christians there are in each generation are contemporary with Christ, have nothing to do with Christians of former generations, but everything to do with the contemporary Christ. His earthly life accompanies the race, and accompanies every generation in particular, as the eternal history; His earthly life possesses the eternal contemporaneousness. And all the professional lecturing (*Doceren*) on Christianity (which lecturing has its stalking-blind and stronghold in the notion that Christianity is something past, and in the history of the 1,800 years) transforms it into the most unchristian of heresies, a fact which everyone will perceive (and therefore give up lecturing) if only he will try to imagine the generation contemporary with Christ . . . delivering lectures—but indeed every generation (of believers) is contemporary.

If thou canst not prevail upon thyself to become a Christian in the situation of contemporaneousness with Him, or if He in the situation of contemporaneousness cannot move thee and draw thee to Himself—then thou wilt never become a Christian. Thou mayest honour, praise, thank, and reward with all worldly goods him who maketh thee believe thou nevertheless art a Christian—but he deceiveth thee. Thou mightest count thyself fortunate if thou wert not contemporary with anyone who dared to say this; thou canst become exasperated to frenzy at the torture, like the sting of the 'gadfly',[1] of being contemporary with one who says it. In the first case thou art deceived; in the second, thou hast at least heard the truth.

[1] Alluding to the passage in Plato's *Apology* where Socrates says of himself that, like the gadfly on the horse, he is allotted to the Athenians to keep them alert.

If thou canst not endure contemporaneousness, canst not endure the sight in reality, if thou art unable to go out in the street and perceive that it is God in this horrible procession, and that this is thy case wert thou to fall down and worship Him—then thou art not *essentially* a Christian. What thou hast to do then is unconditionally to admit this to thyself, so that above all thou mayest preserve humility and fear and trembling with relation to what it means in truth to be a Christian. For that is the way thou must take to learn and to get training in fleeing to grace in such a wise that thou dost not take it in vain. Do not, for God's sake, repair to anyone to be 'set at ease'. For sure enough it was said, 'Blessed are the eyes which see the things that ye see', which saying the parsons make much ado about (strangely enough, it is sometimes perhaps in order to preserve a worldly smartness which precisely in the situation of contemporaneousness would be rather out of place) just as if this was not said solely and only about the contemporaries who had become believers. If the glory had been directly visible, so that everybody as a matter of course could see it, then it is false that Christ humbled Himself and took upon Him the form of a servant; it is superfluous to give warning against being offended, for how in the world could anybody be offended by glory attired in glory! And how in the world can it be explained that with Christ it fared as it did, that not everybody rushed up to see what was directly to be seen! No, there was 'nothing about Him for the eye, no glamour that we should look upon Him, no outward appearance that we should desire Him' (Isa. 53: 2 [S. K.'s version]); directly there was nothing to be seen but a lowly man, who, by signs and wonders and by affirming that He was God, continually posited the possibility of offence. A lowly man who thus expressed (1) what God understands by compassion (and the very fact of being the lowly and poor man when a man will be the compassionate one is included in this); and (2) what God understands by man's misery, which in both cases is utterly different from what man's understanding is, and which in every generation until the end of time everyone for his own part must learn from the beginning, beginning always at the same point as every other man who is contemporary with Christ, practising it in the situation of contemporaneousness. Human hot-headedness and unruliness naturally are of no help at all. In how far a man may succeed essentially in becoming a Christian, no one can tell him. But dread and fear and despair are of no avail. Candour before God is the first and last. Candidly to admit to oneself where one is, with candour before God holding the task in view—however slowly it goes, though one only creeps forward— yet one thing a man has, he is in the right position [facing forward], not misled and deceived by the trick of poetizing Christ, so that instead of being God He becomes that languishing compassion which men themselves have invented, so that Christianity instead of drawing men to heavenly places is impeded on its way and becomes the merely human.

THE MORAL

And what does all this mean? It means that everyone for himself, in quiet inwardness before God, shall humble himself before what it means in the strictest sense to be a Christian, admit candidly before God how it stands with him, so that he might yet accept the grace which is offered to everyone who is imperfect, that is, to everyone. And then no further; then for the rest let him attend to his work, be glad in it, love his wife, be glad in her, bring up his children with joyfulness, love his fellow men, rejoice in life. If anything further is required of him, God will surely let him understand, and in such case will also help him further; for the terrible language of the Law is so terrifying because it seems as if it were left to man to hold fast to Christ by his own power, whereas in the language of love it is Christ that holds him fast. So if anything further is required of him, God will surely let him understand; but this is required of everyone, that before God he shall candidly humble himself in view of the requirements of ideality. And therefore these should be heard again and again in their infinite significance. To be a Christian has become a thing of naught, mere tomfoolery, something which everyone is as a matter of course, something one slips into more easily than into the most insignificant trick of dexterity.

'But if the Christian life is something so terrible and frightful, how in the world can a person get the idea of accepting it?' Quite simply, and, if you want that too, quite in a Lutheran way: only the consciousness of sin can force one into this dreadful situation—the power on the other side being grace. And in that very instant the Christian life transforms itself and is sheer gentleness, grace, loving-kindness, and compassion. Looked at from any other point of view Christianity is and must be a sort of madness or the greatest horror. Only through the consciousness of sin is there entrance to it, and the wish to enter in by any other way is the crime of *lèse-majesté* against Christianity.

But sin, the fact that thou and I are sinners (the individual), people have abolished, or they have illicitly abated it, both with respect to life (the domestic, the civic, the ecclesiastical life) and to learning, which has invented the *doctrine* of . . . sin in general.

As a compensation they have wanted to help men into Christianity and keep them in it by means of all that about world-history, all that about the gentleness of this teaching, its exalted and profound character, &c., all of which Luther would have called bosh, and which is blasphemy, since it is impudence to wish to fraternize with God and Christ.

Only the consciousness of sin is the expression of absolute respect, and just for this reason, i.e. because Christianity requires absolute respect, it must and will display itself as madness or horror, in order that the qualitative infinite emphasis may fall upon the fact that only consciousness of sin is the way of entrance, is the vision, which, by being absolute respect, can see the gentleness, loving-kindness, and compassion of Christianity.

The simple man who humbly confesses himself to be a sinner —himself personally (the individual)—does not need at all to become aware of all the difficulties which emerge when one is neither simple nor humble. But when this is lacking, this humble consciousness of being personally a sinner (the individual)—yea, if such a one possessed all human wisdom and shrewdness along with all human talents, it would profit him little. Christianity shall in a degree corresponding to his superiority erect itself against him and transform itself into madness and terror, until he learns either to give up Christianity, or else by the help of what is very far remote from scientific propaedeutic, apologetic, &c.—that is, by the help of the torments of a contrite heart (just in proportion to *his* need of it) learns to enter by the narrow way, through the consciousness of sin, into Christianity.

TRAINING IN CHRISTIANITY

by
Anti-Climacus

Part II

'BLESSED IS HE WHOSOEVER IS NOT OFFENDED IN ME.'

A Biblical Exposition
and Christian Definition of Concepts

by
Anti-Climacus

EDITOR'S PREFACE

Refer to Preface to Part I

PRELUDE

Yea, blessed is he who is not offended in Him, blessed is he who believes that Jesus Christ lived here on earth and was the One He said He was, the lowly man and yet God, the Only Begotten of the Father—blessed is the man who knows no other to go to, but knows in every case that he may go to Him. And whatever a man's condition in life .may be, though he live in poverty and wretchedness—blessed is he who is not offended but believes that He fed five thousand men with five loaves and two small fishes; blessed is he who is not offended but believes that this occurred, is not offended because it does not now occur but believes that it occurred. And whatever a man's fate may be in the world, however the storms of life may threaten him— blessed is he who is not offended but believes fully and firmly that Peter sank for the one and only cause that he did not believe fully and firmly. And whatever a man's fault may be, though his guilt were so great that not he himself only but the human race despaired of his forgiveness—yet blessed is he who is not offended but believes that He said to the man sick of the palsy, 'Thy sins are forgiven thee', and that this was just as easy for Him to say as to say to the palsied man, 'Take up thy bed and walk'—blessed is he who is not offended but believes in the forgiveness of sinners, although they are not helped like the palsied man to believe by the certainty of healing. And whatever be the manner of a man's death when his last hour is come— blessed is he who is not offended like the contemporaries when He said, 'The damsel is not dead but sleepeth', blessed is he who is not offended but believes, who (like a child who is taught to say these words as it falls asleep) says, 'I believe' . . . and then sleeps; yea, blessed is he, he is not dead, he sleepeth. And whatever sufferings a Christian may endure here on earth on account of his faith, though he be ridiculed, persecuted, put to death—blessed is he who is not offended but believes that He, the humbled, the lowly, the despised man, He who in a sorry way learned to know what it is to be a man when it was said of Him, 'Behold the man!'[1]—blessed is he who is not offended but believes that He

[1] In view of S. K.'s frequent quotation of these words, it may be remarked once

was God, the Only Begotten of the Father, and that this experience belongs to Christ, and belongs to him who would belong to Christ. Yea, blessed is he who is not offended but believes—blessed the victory that overcometh, for faith overcometh the world by overcoming every instant the enemy within him, the possibility of offence. Fear not the world, neither poverty, nor wretchedness, nor sickness, nor need, nor opposition, nor men's injustice, their insults, their ill-treatment, have fear of nothing that can destroy the outward man; fear not him who can kill the body—but fear thyself, fear what can kill faith, and therewith can kill for thee Jesus Christ, namely the offence, which another indeed can give, but which yet is impossible if thou dost not take it. Fear and tremble; for faith is contained in a fragile earthen vessel, in the possibility of the offence. Blessed is he who is not offended in Him but believes.

'Blessed is he whosoever is not offended in Me!' Ah, if thou couldst hear Him say that Himself, hear in thine inward man that He suffers for thee also by reason of the contradiction that, in spite of love, for very love, He cannot put it beyond peradventure whether thou wilt be offended in Him or not; that He who came from far, far away, from the glory of heaven, that He who descended far, far below until He became the lowly man and now is ready to save thee also, that He the almighty who can do all things, and in love sacrifices all things, yet is . . . impotent, Himself suffering by reason of this impotence, because, though He is more concerned for thy welfare than thou art, He must leave it to thee whether thou wilt be offended or not, whether thou through His salvation wilt inherit blessedness, or make thyself unblessed and Him as sorrowful as only love can be! Oh, if thou couldst divine what is taking place in Him every time He must sorrowfully repeat the anxious word, 'Blessed is he whosoever is not offended in Me', couldst perceive that He came into the world to save all—alas, that it does not proceed so speedily, and that to each man severally He must say again and again, 'Blessed is he whosoever is not offended in Me!' Oh, if thou couldst hear Him say that and divine what is taking place in Him when He says it—to me it seems as if it must be impossible for thee to be

for all that the Danish version is, 'Look, what a man!', which all but imposes the derogatory interpretation S. K. implies.

offended in Him; if otherwise thou didst not know how important thy salvation is, if this had escaped thy notice, thou mightest learn to know it from His deep concern. So human is His divinity! With the Father He knows from all eternity that only thus can the human race be saved; He knows that no man can comprehend Him, that the moth which flies into the candle-light is not more sure of destruction than the man who attempts to will to comprehend Him or that which is in Him combined: God and man. And yet He is the Saviour, there is no salvation for any but in Him.

If for an instant I might dare to speak thus (and I do indeed dare it) I would say: Yea, if it were not for thine own cause, if it were not to thine own destruction to be offended in Him—who could be so cruel as to be offended in Him? For one can be cruel in several ways. The mighty can cruelly have a man tortured, but the weak can cruelly make it impossible for love to help him, the sole thing, alas, that love desired, and so heartily desired. Couldest thou be so cruel to Him who inwardly is as it were an endless depth of sorrow? For the greater the real superiority, the greater the sorrow. So it is always, so it is even in the relation of man to man, upon which men in general seldom reflect because they oftenest aspire to superiority and envy it, being unable to imagine themselves in its place. The superior understands, and the more truly superior he is the more deeply he understands with the concern of responsibility what is profitable to the other, desires to do everything for his profit—and beholds now with sorrow that the other understands neither his own self nor him. And now He, the God-Man—ah, what He must have suffered! not only, or rather not just from the moment when wickedness acquired power over Him to mock, scourge, and ill-treat Him; nay, all the while He went about and was the Teacher. Infinite sorrow, when He who came to save all, divinely unconcerned about attaining honour and dignity for Himself (ah, madness and mockery of God!), but every day, every hour, every moment of His life thinking only of others—infinite sorrow when he looked out upon the human multitudes and beheld everything else except faith and faith's capacity to understand, beheld curiosity which misunderstands, light-mindedness which misunderstands, instability, self-assurance, conceit, censoriousness, in short, nothing but misunderstanding with respect to Him who verily had

G

no need of them (ah, madness and mockery of God!), but of whom all had absolute need—the Truth and the Life! Infinite sorrow, that they who had gone astray did not know in the day of visitation what belonged to their peace—infinite sorrow for Him who Himself is the Visitation and would bring peace! What suffering in His sorrow when He turned His eye—upon whom?—upon the individual, upon every individual, the deluded, shallow, sinful man who would not even let himself be helped! Ah, humanly speaking this is indeed a mad relationship—between a single individual man who thus would not even let himself be helped and . . . Him! No man could bear this incongruity; that only the God-Man can bear. No man can even form a conception of this sorrow.

'Blessed is he whosoever is not offended in me!' Oh, if thou couldst form a conception of His joy over every believer—then thou wouldst be a saved man and pass over the offence. His joy over the believer is like the joy of a man at finding himself understood, entirely understood by another. He, it is true, is not like a man; He cannot be understood or comprehended, He must be believed; but in faith thou dost belong to Him entirely, and His joy is great, like that of a man who found one that understood him. How great was His joy when He declared Simon Peter blessed—'Blessed art thou, Simon'—for Peter believed. How great His joy was, you can see in this, that He thrice inquired of Peter, 'Lovest thou me?'

THE PURPORT OF THIS EXPOSITION IN BRIEF

JUST as the concept 'faith' is a highly characteristic note of
Christianity, so also is 'offence'[1] a highly characteristic note of
Christianity and stands in close relation to faith. The possibility of offence is the crossways, or it is like standing at the crossways. From the possibility of the offence a man turns either to
offence or to faith.*

Offence has essentially to do with the composite term God and
man, or with the God-Man. Speculation naturally had the notion
that it 'comprehended' God-Man—this one can easily comprehend, for speculation in speculating about the God-Man leaves
out temporal existence, contemporaneousness, and reality. It is
altogether a pitiful and dreadful thing that this (which one does

---

[1] S. K. dealt with this theme as early as 1844 in the *Philosophic Fragments*, of
which the Supplement to Chapter III bears the title: 'The Offence at the Paradox'.
He treated it more generally five years later in *The Sickness unto Death*, Second
Section, A, Cap. III, Supplement: 'The Possibility of the Offence'.

* In the works of some of the pseudonyms[2] it has been shown that in recent
philosophy confusion has been wrought by talking about doubt where one ought to
speak of despair. For this reason people are unable either to control or to master
doubt, whether in life or in philosophy. Despair, on the other hand, at once indicates
the right direction by bringing the relationship under the concept of personality (the
individual) or under the rubric of ethics. But just as people have talked confusingly
about 'doubt' instead of talking about 'despair', so also it has been customary to
employ the category 'doubt' where one ought to speak of 'offence'. The relationship
(personality's relationship) to Christ is not: either to doubt or to believe; but either
to be offended or to believe. The whole of modern philosophy (ethically and Christianly speaking) is based upon looseness of thought. Instead of holding men back
and calling them to order by talking about being in despair and being offended, it has
beckoned them on and invited them to be conceited because they doubt or have
doubted. Modern philosophy, being abstract, hovers in metaphysical indefinite-
ness. Instead then of expounding this fact about itself, and thus directing men (the
individual men) to the ethical, the religious, the existential, philosophy has made it
appear as if men could (as someone has said with blunt honesty) speculate themselves
out of their own good skin (*Skind*) and into the pure appearance (*Skin*).

---

[2] As the reference here is especially to *The Sickness unto Death*, which, like the
book we are now dealing with, was ascribed to Anti-climacus, it is obvious that S. K.
when he wrote this passage had no notion of attributing this book to the same
pseudonym. We know, in fact, that at first he purposed to acknowledge himself as
the author—not merely as 'editor'.

not characterize too strongly by saying that it is a mere prank and a way of making a fool of folks) has been fêted as profundity. No, the *situation* is inseparable from the God-Man, the situation that an individual man who stands beside you is God-Man. The God-Man is not the unity of God and mankind. Such terminology exhibits the profundity of optical illusion. The God-Man is the unity of God and an individual man. That the human race is or should be akin to God is ancient paganism; but that an individual man is God is Christianity, and this individual man is the God-Man. There is neither in heaven, nor on earth, nor in the depths, nor in the aberrations of the most fantastic thinking, the possibility of a (humanly speaking) more insane combination. As such it reveals itself in the situation of contemporaneousness; and no relationship with the God-Man is possible except by beginning with the situation of contemporaneousness.*

'The offence' in the strictest sense, offence κατ' ἐξοχήν, has to do therefore with the God-Man, and it has two forms. It either has to do with loftiness—one is offended at the fact that an individual man says of himself that he is God, or speaks in such a way as to betray[1] this thought (which is dealt with under B); or it has to do with lowliness—that He who is God is this lowly man, suffering like a lowly man (which is dealt with under C). In the first form, the offence arises in such a way that I am not in the least offended at the lowliness of the man but at the fact that he wants me to believe that he is God. And if I have believed this, the offence then arises from the other side, and consists in the fact that such a one as He should be God, this lowly, helpless man who when it comes to a test has no power to do anything. In the one case the point of departure is man, and the offence is the determining concept God; in the other case the point of departure is God and the offence is the determining concept man.

---

* As regarding this point, I may refer to the section entitled 'The Obstacle' in *Come Hither All Ye that Labour and are Heavy Laden*. [This note indicates that S. K. first thought of Part I as a separate book.]

[1] It should be noticed that although S. K. commonly speaks as if Christ were always asserting, in terms of the most 'direct communication', that He is God (in conformity with the Prologue of St. John's Gospel), yet he was emphatic in asserting that 'direct communication' was impossible for the God-Man. The word 'betray' in this passage is significant. Albert Schweitzer has used it in the same sense. Although S. K. *seems* to rely chiefly upon the Fourth Gospel, he was in fact much more devoutly attached to the Synoptic Gospels.

The God-Man is the paradox, absolutely the paradox; hence it is quite clear that the understanding must come to a standstill before it. If a man does not notice the offence which has to do with loftiness, he will on the other hand discover that which has to do with lowliness. It is not unthinkable that a man in whom imagination or feeling predominates, a man who typifies childlike or childish Christianity (since for a child the offence κατ' ἐξοχήν does not exist, and for this reason Christianity properly does not exist for the child)—it is not unthinkable that such a man might ingenuously entertain the notion that he believed this individual man to be God, and discover no offence in it. This is to be explained by the fact that such a man has no explicit conception of God, but a childlike or childish fancy about something exceedingly lofty, holy, and pure, a conception of One who somehow is greater than all kings, &c., without exactly including the quality God. This means that such a man possesses no category, and hence it was possible for him to think that he believed an individual man to be God, without stumbling at the offence. But this same man will then stumble at the offence of lowliness.

So it stands with the offence, and so too it is represented by Holy Scripture in the passages where Christ Himself warns against being offended.

But then furthermore the Scripture has something to say about an offence at Christ the possibility of which belongs to the historical past. This offence has to do in fact, not with Christ as Christ, as the God-Man (this is the essential offence, and the two forms of it last as long as temporal existence lasts, as long as faith is not done away with), but it has to do with Him as a mere man who comes into collision with the established order (which is dealt with under A).

THE EXPOSITION

A

*T*HE *possibility of offence which has not to do with Christ as Christ (the God-Man), but with Him as a mere human individual who comes into collision with the established order.*

The offence contemplated here is one which anyone might arouse in case he (the individual) does not think good to subject himself to the established order or co-ordinate himself in it. But from the fact that the individual is not willing to do this it does not follow that the individual says that he is God. One easily perceives, however, that in this case there is a quantitative reckoning in a direction towards the claim of being more than man; and this is what the established order is on the watch for. Is the individual higher than the established order? With this query, or rather with this protest, the established order would compel the individual either to back down or to declare openly that he is more than man—and with that the offence is posited.

1. Matt. 15: 1–12.—'Then there came to Jesus from Jerusalem Pharisees and scribes, saying, Why do Thy disciples transgress the ancient customs? For they wash not their hands when they eat bread. But He answered and said unto them, Why do ye also transgress the commandment of God because of your customs? For God has commanded, saying, Honour thy father and thy mother, and he that curseth father or mother shall certainly die. But ye say, Whosoever shall say to father or mother, That wherewith thou mightest have been profited by me is a gift [to the Temple], he need not honour his father or mother. Thus ye have made vain the law of God because of your customs. Ye hypocrites! Well did Isaiah prophesy of you, saying, This people keepeth close to me with their mouth and honoureth me with their lips, but their heart is far from me, But in vain do they honour me, teaching such doctrines as are the commandment of men. And he called the people to him and said to them, Hear and understand. Not that which entereth into the mouth defileth the man, but that which proceedeth out of the mouth, this defileth a man. Then

came His disciples forward and said unto him, Knowest thou that the Pharisees were *offended* when they heard this saying?'

It is a matter of course that Christ is always the God-Man; but here we have an historical situation, and the offence here spoken of has not to do with the God-Man, nor with the consideration that Jesus as an individual man gave Himself out to be God, nor with the thought that He who is God is this lowly man. Christ is here regarded in a general sense as teacher, a teacher of godly fear and inwardness, who with primitive spontaneity (without any suggestion here that he requires men to regard Him as God) insists upon inwardness in contrast with all empty externalism, a teacher who transforms externalism into inwardness. Such is the collision, a collision which recurs again and again in Christendom; briefly expressed it is the collision of pietism with the established order. The Pharisees and scribes here represent the established order, which, precisely through their sophistry and shrewd wisdom, had become empty externalism.

However, then as always, the established order plumed itself upon being objective and therefore higher than every individual, which means pure subjectivity. Now at this moment there is an individual who is unwilling to subordinate himself to the established order, or at least protests against its claim to be the truth, in fact designates it as falsehood, declaring for his own part that he is the truth, and asserting that truth consists precisely in inwardness—then the collision takes place. The established order quite naturally raises the question: What then does this individual imagine he is, does he imagine perhaps that he is God, or that he has a direct relationship with God, or does he concede that he is a mere man?

Here then is the offence, and one easily perceives that it stands in relation to a claim to be more than man. Here, however, there still remains plenty of room for relativities and quantitative reckoning with regard to the claim of being something unusual, extraordinary, &c., without precisely advancing the claim to be God. But doubtless it is the case with many men that their notion of Christ goes no farther than the thought that He was something or another quite incomparably extraordinary, pretty nearly divine. Yet doubtless they would have been offended in Him had they lived as His contemporaries. It escapes their notice, however, that the offence *sensu strictissimo* has to do with the God-Man, who is not feeling His way as it were to discover by a vague quantitative reckoning how high a price He might set upon Himself, but qualitatively defines that He is God—and requires *worship*.

This is the essential offence, which, however, is not our subject here. But it is certain that people are also offended at everyone who gives or seems to give himself the air of wanting to be more than man. People are offended in him. This, however, must not be misunderstood, as though it were always he that gave himself the air of being more than man; for this impression is often due to the fact that the opponent attributes this to him out of fanatical devotion to the established order. Every time a witness for the truth (*Sandheds Vidne*)[1] makes the truth a heart-felt matter of inwardness (and this essentially is the business of the witness for the truth), every time a genius with primitive force makes the true inwardly vivid—then also the established order will be offended in him.

One need not have much acquaintance with the human race to know that this is so, nor need one have much knowledge of the most recent philosophy to know that this will occur also in our age. Why has Hegel treated conscience, and the conscience-relationship in the individual, as 'a form of the evil'? (See *Rechtsphilosophie*.[2]) Why? Because he deified the established order. But the more he deified it, so much the more natural the conclusion, *ergo* he who disparages or opposes this divine thing, the established order, *ergo* he must come pretty near to imagining that he is God. Perhaps it is not the man himself (and in the case of the veritable witness for the truth it is certainly not he) that asserts anything blasphemous about himself. No, the blasphemy is really a projection from the ungodly veneration of the established order as divine, an acoustic illusion occasioned by the fact that the established order says to itself in a hushed voice that it

---

[1] This word represents a thought with which S. K. was deeply preoccupied. He speaks with profound reverence of the 'witness', regarding him as third in rank in the essential Christian hierarchy, coming immediately after the Apostles and the Prophets. This meant to him a heroic type, culminating in the martyr. Hence he felt so greatly outraged when Martensen proclaimed that the deceased Bishop Mynster was 'a witness for the truth, one of the long chain of witnesses which stretches from the age of the Apostles'. This afforded him the occasion for launching his newspaper and pamphleteering attack upon the Established Church.

[2] § 140. 2nd ed. of the *Werke*, viii, pp. 183 ff.

is the divine, and then owing to the presence of the witness for the truth it hears this voice, but hears it as if it were he that said he was more than man.

But that the established order has become something divine or is regarded as divine constitutes a falsehood which is made possible only by ignoring its origin. When a *bourgeois* has become a nobleman he is eager to make every effort to have his *vita ante acta* forgotten. So it is with the established order. It began with the God-relationship of the individual; but now this must be forgotten, the bridge hewn down, the established order deified.

And strangely enough it is precisely this deification of the established order which constitutes the constant rebellion, the permanent revolt against God. It desires, in fact (and, so far as this goes, no blame attaches to it), to be everything, to have the world-evolution a little bit under its thumb, or to guide the development of the race. But the deification of the established order, on the other hand, is the invention of the indolent worldly mind, which would put itself at rest and imagine that all is sheer security and peace, that now we have reached the highest attainment. And then there comes along a single individual, a Peter Malapert, who has a notion that he ought to be higher than the established order. But no, it is not necessary to say that he had this notion, it might even be possible that he was the 'gadfly' which the established order had need of to keep it from falling asleep, or, what is still worse, from falling into self-deification. Every individual ought to live in fear and trembling, and so too there is no established order which can do without fear and trembling. Fear and trembling signifies that one is in process of becoming, and every individual man, and the race as well, is or should be conscious of being in process of becoming. And fear and trembling signifies that a God exists—a fact which no man and no established order dare for an instant forget.

Thus it was that Judaism in the time of Christ had become, precisely by means of the Pharisees and scribes, a self-complacent, self-deified establishment. There had been brought about a complete commensurability as between the outward and the inward—so complete that the inward had fallen out. It is just by this one can recognize that the established order is on the point of deifying itself, just by this commensurability and congruity. Everything that might remind one of truth militant has

been done away with as something which one pretty nearly finds
ludicrous—now truth is triumphant, as once it was militant;
now it is the established order. To be in the truth cannot any
longer mean that one must suffer, and suffer more and more, the
more one is in the truth—no, here there is complete congruence:
the more one is in the truth, the more honoured and respected one
becomes. Ah! Now everything is all right! Now the established
order is deified! In case Christ were to come into the world, He
would first of all be Professor,[1] and then would be advanced more
and more just in proportion as it became clearer that He was in
the truth.

Such clearly was the opinion also of the Pharisees and the
scribes. That piety and godly fear must suffer in the world was
something quite antiquated, for now there was congruence: the
more pious and god-fearing, the more respected and esteemed.
And lest anyone might use deception, averring that he was pious
in the inner man, there was instituted (and this doubtless was
adduced as a proof of the seriousness of the established order)
a sort of examination to which piety was subjected, and everything was commensurable. People were suspicious of everything
that wanted to keep hidden in inwardness—and in this perhaps
they were not far wrong.[2] But they had also done away entirely
with the conception that the mark of true piety, when it is not

[1] 'The Professor' always suggests Martensen, who was *the* Professor of Theology
in Denmark. Bishop Mynster promptly recognized that 'half the book is written
against Martensen and half against me'. Yet it is not as though the book were evenly
divided between the two, the first half against the Professor, and the second half
against the Bishop. Mynster has already appeared in these pages as a man who deifies
the established order (i.e. the Church), although he was struck rather by several of
the 'Reflections' in Part III which 'he considered coined for him'. And of course this
book had not the petty aim of attacking individuals. It attacks the established order
which these two men typically represented. *Det Bestaende*—the existing or established order, the *status quo*—was chosen as a generic term and discussed as such, yet
now and then the reference is clearly to the Church, and as time went on, S. K., who
had at heart chiefly the religious situation, aimed more and more sharply at the
Established Church of Denmark.—By this time the reader has read enough to recognize that an open attack upon the Church was inevitable when a communication
as direct as this was ignored, and to realize that S. K. was justified in saying of this
book, at the time a second edition was published in the midst of the fiercer attack, that
by suppressing the Preface and the Moral it would be made evident that this really
was an attack and an open attack.

[2] S. K. himself had by this time begun to be suspicious of 'hidden inwardness',
which earlier he had cherished as an ideal.

kept hidden, is precisely the fact that it goes ill with it in the world. Indeed, as has been said, with the same *bravour* with which a freshly baked nobleman can forget that yesterday he was a *bourgeois*, with the same *bravour* the established order can forget its origin. And just as the individual man may aspire to become something, so does the age; and this is what it aspires to: it would build up the established order, abolish God, and through fear of men cow the individual into a mouse's hole—but this is what God will not have, and He employs the exactly opposite tactics: He employs the individual to provoke the established order out of its self-complacency.

When commensurability and congruity have set in, and the established order is deified, all fear and trembling are abolished. To live in, and more especially to attain some position in the established order is a continuation of, or rather something still safer than, hanging on to mother's apron strings—to such a degree safer that one can bank on the probability, and exempt oneself effeminately from the kind of decisions with which the 'individual' lacerates himself; for one is no 'individual', ah, far from it, one is transported by enchantment into the reliable field of probable computation, with the ravishing prospect of sure advancement straight into eternity—eternity being obliged to judge as the established order judges, since that is divine. 'Why', says the established order to the individual, 'why do you want to plague and torture yourself with the prodigious measuring-rod of the ideal? Have recourse to the established order, attach yourself to it. There is the measure. If you are a student, then you can be sure that the Professor is the measure and the truth; if you are a parson, then the Bishop is the way and the life; if you are a scrivener, the Judge is the standard. *Ne quid nimis!* The established order is the rational; and you are fortunate if you occupy the position of relativity accorded you—and for the rest let your colleagues, the Consistory, or whatever it may be, take care for . . .' 'Do you mean to say, my salvation?' 'Why, certainly. And if with regard to this matter you encounter in the end some obstacle, can you not be contented like all the others, when your last hour has come, to go well baled and crated in one of the large shipments which the established order sends straight through to heaven under its own seal and plainly addressed to "The Eternal Blessedness", with the assurance that you will be exactly as well received and just as blessed as "all the others"? In short, can you not be content with such reassuring security and guaranty as this, that the established order vouches for your blessedness in the hereafter? Very well then. Only keep this to yourself. The established order has no objection. If you keep as still as a mouse about it, you will nevertheless be just as well off as the others.'

The deification of the established order is the secularization of everything. The established order may be quite right in affirming that, so far as worldly things are concerned, one must attach oneself to the established order, be content with the relativity, &c. But in the end one secularizes also the God-relationship, insists that this shall be congruous with a certain relativity, not essentially different from one's station in life, &c.—instead of which it must be for every individual man the absolute, and it is precisely this God-relationship of the individual which must put every established order in suspense, so that God, at any instant He will, by pressure upon the individual has immediately in his God-relationship a witness, a reporter, a spy, or whatever you prefer to call it, one who in unconditional obedience, or by unconditional obedience, by persecution, suffering, and death, puts the established order in suspense.

When the individual appeals to his God-relationship in opposition to the established order, it looks indeed as if he made himself more than a man. Nevertheless, he does not by any means do that; for he concedes that every man, absolutely every man, has or should have for his part the same relationship to God. As little as one who says he is in love denies by this that others have the same experience, just so little or even less does such an individual deny that another (but always as an individual) has the same God-relationship. But the established order refuses to entertain the notion that it might consist of so loose an aggregation of millions of individuals each of which severally has his own God-relationship. The established order desires to be totalitarian, recognizing nothing over it, but having under it every individual, and judging every individual who is integrated in it. And 'that individual' (*hiin Enkelte*), who expounds the most humble, but at the same time the most humane doctrine about what it means to be a man, the established order desires to terrify by imputing to him the guilt of blasphemy.

So it was with the Pharisees who were offended in Christ because He regarded piety as absolute inwardness, not directly commensurable with the outward (rather, on the contrary, recognizable by suffering), and in any case not finding its consummation in a mere relativity. This whole construction of definitions and relativities, these marks for recognizing piety directly by honour and prestige, this objectivity, as the Pharisees and scribes doubtless would have called it, Christ ran foul of when He interpreted piety and God-fearingness as inwardness. Fully convinced that they were in the right, and presumably certain that Christ would be obliged to give in, they lay before Him the question, why His disciples transgressed the ancient custom. So it always is when the established order has come to the point of deifying itself; then in the end use and wont become articles of faith, everything becomes about equally important, or custom, use, and wont become the important things. The individual no longer feels and recognizes that he along with every individual has a God-relationship which for him must possess absolute significance. No, the God-relationship is done away with; use and wont, custom and suchlike are deified. But this sort of God-fear is just contempt for God; it does not in fact fear God, it fears man. Hence Christ replies to the Pharisees, 'Why do ye transgress God's commandment because of your customs?' So holy in fact had the Pharisees and the scribes become, and so holy do men always become when they deify the established order, that their divine worship is a way of making a fool of God. Under the pretence of serving and worshipping, they serve and worshid their own device, either in self-complacent joy at being themselves the inventors, or through fear of men.

But, as has been said, he who disparages such an established order is regarded as one who makes himself more than man, and people are offended in him, although in reality he merely makes God God and man man.

2. Matt. 17 : 24–7.—'And when they were come to Capernaum, they that collected the money for the tax came to Peter and said, Doth not your master pay the tax money? He saith, Yes. And when he was come into the house Jesus anticipated him, saying, What thinkest thou, Simon? of whom do the kings of the earth take custom or tribute? of their own children or of strangers? Peter saith unto Him, Of strangers. Jesus saith unto him, Then

are the children free. Notwithstanding, lest we should *offend*
them, go thou to the sea and cast a hook and take up the fish that
first cometh up, and when thou hast opened his mouth thou shalt
find a stater; that take unto them for thee and me.'

Here the collision again is the same, that of the individual with
the established order. That which caused them to be offended
would be that the individual would withdraw from relationship
with the established order. It must constantly be kept in mind
that in neither of these passages (the 17th and the 15th chapters)
is the possibility of the offence related to Christ *qua* God-Man.
The question here therefore is not whether He is the God-Man,
the situation does not contemplate whether He shows Himself
to be what He gives Himself out to be, the God-Man, for He is
not thus represented here. The question is about him, this
individual man, whether he will recognize the established order
by paying the tax.

Since this thing of paying a tax is an externality of no importance, Christ subjects Himself and avoids giving offence. It was
different in the case of an externality which impudently demanded
to be regarded as piety [i.e. in the passage previously dealt with].
If [in this second case] Christ had not yielded, He again would
have provoked offence, and the reason would have been, rightly,
that an individual, by withdrawing from the established order,
seems to make himself more than a man—although (to repeat
what was said above) it does not exactly follow that He qualitatively defined Himself as God.

In this story it is noteworthy, moreover, that Christ, who here
is simply the individual man in collision with the established order,
in avoiding the offence posits the essential offence. He pays the
tax, sure enough; but He gets the money by performing a
miracle, i.e. He displays Himself as the God-Man. To omit to
pay the tax is to make the offence possible with relation to Him
as the individual man, but the way by which He gets the money
posits the possibility of the essential offence with relation to Him
as the God-Man.

Now we pass on to the offence properly so called, which is
related to the God-Man. The possibility of the offence with
relation to Christ about which we have spoken is a vanishing
historical possibility which actually vanished with His death; it

existed only for His contemporaries in relation to Him as this individual man. On the other hand, the possibility of offence at Christ *qua* God-Man will last to the end of time. If you take away the possibility of this offence, it means that you also take Christ away, that you have made Him something different from what He was, the sign of offence and the object of faith.

B

*T*HE *possibility of the essential offence which has to do with exaltation, for the fact that an individual man speaks or acts as though he were God, says of himself that he is God, having to do therefore with the qualification of God by the composite term God-Man.*

1. Matt. 11 : 6 (parallel with Lk. 7 : 23). John the Baptist has sent from his prison messengers to Christ, asking if He is the one that is to come, or if they should wait for another. And Jesus answered and said unto them, 'Go and tell John the things which ye do hear and see: the blind receive their sight, and the lame walk, the lepers are cleansed, and the deaf hear, the dead are raised up, and the poor have the gospel preached unto them. And blessed is he whosoever shall not be *offended* in me.'

So Jesus does not answer *directly*. He does not say, Tell John that I am the Expected One. That is, He requires faith, and therefore to an *absent* person cannot make a direct communication.[1] To a person who was *present* He might well say it directly,

---

[1] Up to this time S. K. conceived that the truths he was most intent upon teaching could be imparted only by 'indirect communication'. He has a prodigious amount to say on this subject, and he gives this as the reason for the beginning he made with 'aesthetic' production, for his use of pseudonyms, and all the other mystifications he delighted in. In reality what deterred him from employing 'direct communication' (i.e. speaking out his own mind in the clearest terms) was the deep melancholy which oppressed him. He was in a measure relieved of this oppression by a deep religious experience in Holy Week 1848, and the significance of this new conversion is revealed by an ejaculation registered in his Journal: 'I must speak !' With that he began to suspect that there was an element of daimonia in the very principle of indirect communication upon which he had so much insisted that at one time he considered whether it might not be possible to communicate directly his doctrine of indirect communication. Now, however, he began to reflect that for a man to use indirect communication might be presumptuous and illicit. For his part he gave it up. The theme of this work, 'Come hither !', occurred to him at the very moment of his new conversion, and accordingly it is the first expression of direct, directer, and directest communication which culminated in the open attack.—But what might be a daimonia on the part of man was a necessity on God's part. Christ, at least, in His incognito could not employ direct communication. This thought is frequently reiterated here. In this perception S. K. seems to us very modern, for this is a necessary implication of 'thorough-going eschatology'.

because a person on the spot, beholding the speaker, this individual man, and because of the contradiction involved in His appearance, would not in fact receive a direct communication, inasmuch as the contradiction intervenes between what is said and what is seen, viz. what the speaker is, judging by appearances. This, however, will be duly explained in its place.

Moreover, if in truth it had been the case (as Christendom has in many periods been prone to imagine) that it was *directly* obvious to the eye that Christ was indeed what He said He was, then why such a strange reply? It would have been much simpler and more direct if Christ had comported Himself as some do in delivering a sermon, and had said to the messengers, Regard me! Then ye may behold indeed that I am God. But just try that! Nay, the simplest means of putting an end to all this sentimental paganism which in Christendom is called Christianity is quite simply to introduce it into the situation of contemporaneousness.

Further. Christ's reply comprises *in contento* all that commonly goes by the name of 'proofs[1] for the truth of Christianity', with exception only of the proof from prophecy. But John himself, being a representative of this last category, must have been able, if anybody was, to establish in the firmest possible way by the proofs from prophecy the assurance that Christ was the Expected One. Yet it is remarkable that the last of the Prophets, the Forerunner, who must have stood in the nearest possible *rapport* with prophecy, is not brought nearer by these proofs than to the point of becoming attentive—and asking the question. With exception then of the proof from prophecy, all the remaining proofs for the truth of Christianity are comprised in Christ's reply. He points to the miracles (the lame walk, the blind see, &c.) and to the doctrine itself (the gospel is preached to the poor)—and thereupon, strangely enough, He adds, 'Blessed is he whosoever is not offended in me.'—But behold how different is the custom in Christendom! There they have written these huge folios which develop the proofs of the truth of Christianity. Behind these

---

[1] S. K.'s vehement objection to 'apologetics' is everywhere evident in his works. If the professors of Christian apologetics are not to be deterred by S. K.'s arguments from continuing to *prove* the truths of Christianity, they may at least learn to be more discrete and more adroit in their employment of the proofs, and consent to leave more room for faith.

proofs and folios they feel perfectly confident and secure from every attack; for the proofs and the folios regularly conclude with the assurance, *ergo* Christ was what He said He was; by the aid of the proofs this conclusion is just as sure as that 2 and 2 make 4, and just as easy as thrusting the foot into the stocking; supported by this incontrovertible *ergo*, which makes the matter *directly* evident, the docents and the parsons strut, and the missionaries go forth to convert the heathen with the help of this *ergo*. How different it was with Christ! He does not say, *Ergo* I am the Expected One—He says (after having appealed to the proofs), 'Blessed is he whosoever is not offended in me'. That is, He makes it evident that in relation to Him there can be no question of any proofs, that a man does not come to Him by the help of proofs, that there is no *direct* transition to this thing of becoming a Christian, that at the most the proofs might serve to make a man attentive, so that once he has become attentive he may arrive at the point of deciding whether he will believe or be offended. For the proofs remain equivocal: they are the *pro et contra* of the reasoning intellect, and therefore can be used *contra et pro*. It is only by a choice that the heart is revealed (and surely it was for this cause Christ came into the world, that the thoughts of all hearts might be revealed), by the choice whether to believe or be offended. Behold the theological professor who, by availing himself of all that had previously been written on the subject, has written a new book on the proofs of the truth of Christianity. He would feel insulted if one were not to concede that now the case was proved—and, on the other hand, Christ Himself says nothing more than that the proofs might lead a man—not to faith, ah, far from that (for if such were the case it was superfluous to add, Blessed is he who is not offended), but up to the point where faith may come into existence, that they might help him to become attentive, and thereby to come into the dialectical tension out of which faith issues—the tension of, Wilt thou believe, or wilt thou be offended?

Where now does the possibility of the offence lie? Here is a miracle, and a miracle is proof, and it is by miracles they have wanted to *prove directly* the truth of Christianity! As a matter of course, the direct proof must take good care (as in fact it does) to come after, considerably after the event, thus indirectly betraying what it (like everything else that comes after) is really worth; for

in the situation of contemporaneousness the direct proof is
impossible. Let us not keep on chattering in the fog; let us not,
now that we know who Christ is (if indeed one can have *knowledge*
thereof), or else imagine that we know it—let us not, coming as we
do 1,800 years after, behold the miracles and . . . then become
convinced. What depth of nonsense! When we know who
Christ is, how can the proof be said to prove it? And besides, the·
situation here is not at all the same as with regard to certain
things, even extraordinary things, which need not interfere with
the slumber of a person who comes after. If there is to be any
sense in the assertion that miracles prove who Christ is, we must
begin with not knowing who He is, that is to say, in the situation
of contemporaneousness with an individual man, who is like
other men, in whom there is nothing *directly* to be seen, an individual man who thereupon performs a miracle and himself says
that it is a miracle he performs. What does this signify? It
signifies that this individual man makes himself out to be more
than man, makes himself out to be something pretty near to being
God. Is not this cause for offence? You see something inexplicable, miraculous (and that is all), he himself says that it is a
miracle—and with your own eyes you behold the individual man.
The miracle can prove nothing; for if you do not believe that he
is what he says he is, you deny the miracle. A miracle can make
one attentive—now thou art in a state of tension, and all depends
upon what thou dost choose, offence or faith. It is thy heart that
must be revealed.

   The contradiction in which consists the possibility of offence
is the fact of being an individual man, a lowly man—and then
acting in a way suggestive of being God. Be attentive to the
situation of contemporaneousness; and if you are not attentive
to it, you lie yourself into a deception. But the fact is that in
Christendom people have a fantastic picture of Christ, a fantastic
image of God, directly corresponding to the performance of
miracles. But this is falsehood. Christ never *looked like* this.
The Christianity of Christendom is fantastic in two directions,
both with respect to miracles, and with respect to Christ. In the
situation of contemporaneousness thou art placed between this
inexplicable thing on the one hand (which is not necessarily to be
regarded as a miracle), and on the other hand an individual man
who looks like the others—and he it is who performs this wonder.

The possibility of the offence is not to be avoided, thou must pass through it, and thou canst be saved from it in one way only —by believing. Hence Christ says, Blessed is he who is not offended in me. At that time it was not so easy as later it became —so easy as to nauseate one at the mendacity of Christendom. As soon as people heard about the blind recovering their sight and the dead coming to life they were promptly convinced who Christ was. No, at that time it required the most frightful act of decision for a man to become a Christian. Oh, dreadful contra-diction! Oh, abomination! This busy Christianity which has been able to prove and prove again the truth of Christianity; these thousands upon thousands who have believed . . . by force of proofs—and then look at Jesus Christ, the author and finisher of faith, who, pointing to the proofs, which surely must have had the strongest effect at the time when they occurred, nevertheless adds, 'Blessed is he whosoever is not offended in me', that is, He appeals to the proofs in such a way as to deny that they were the way to Him. It is as if He would say to John, as He would say likewise to us all, 'By the way of proofs no man cometh unto me; give heed to them, however, that thou mayest become attentive— and then, blessed is he whosoever is not offended in me'.

Oh, dreadful contradiction! Oh, abomination! This infatua-tion and stupidity with which people have strutted with the proofs and betrayed Christianity—and so consequently have betrayed Jesus Christ, who as a sufferer in this instance also, points indeed to the proofs, but then almost interceding for the individual, adds, Blessed is he who is not offended. Oh, mystery of suffering! That He must be the sign of offence in order to be the object of faith! With such a troubled mind He walked on earth, He who out of love came to earth. Alas, He understood, as no man under-stands or can understand, how endlessly difficult it is to become a Christian. Can it be supposed that He delights to see that in the most light-hearted way they induce thousands upon thousands to imagine that they are Christians?

2. John 6: 61. Christ says of Himself that He is the living bread, 'whosoever eateth this bread shall live'. The Jews then strove among themselves and said, 'How can this man give us his flesh to eat'. Therefore Jesus said to them, 'Verily, verily, I say unto you, except ye eat the flesh of the Son of Man and drink his blood, ye have no life in you. . . . Even many of his disciples

when they heard this said, This is a hard speech, who can bear
him [*sic*]? Then Jesus, who knew in Himself that His disciples
murmured over this, said to them, Doth this offend you?' And
from the following verse (verse 66) it appears that from that time
many of His disciples went back and walked no more with Him.

So these words offended them to such a degree that even
disciples, many disciples, fell away. In Christendom they no more
give offence. Well, naturally; the true Christians are not offended,
because they believe. But to have become believers they must
have passed through the possibility of the offence, and that is
what has been abolished in Christendom. People now put these
words in conjunction with the Lord's Supper, they have developed
a doctrine of the ubiquity of Christ's body [the Lutheran doctrine],
and with that they have in Christendom a fantastic notion of
Christ, so that all this is neither incomprehensible, nor in any
way suggestive of the possibility of offence.

But now we may once for all draw a line through the fantastic
theories of Christendom. We proceed now to consider the situation
of contemporaneousness.

Thus an individual man, to all appearance like the others, talks
in such a way about himself! What wonder, indeed, that people
are offended, that they separated themselves from him and went
each to his own affairs, deeply offended, and many of the disciples
with them.

And as in this passage we have the sorrowful word, 'Blessed
is he who is not offended in me', so there follows one like it when
Christ says to the Twelve, 'Will ye also go away?' Alas, for Christ
Himself understood, as no man can understand, how difficult it is
to become a believer. He suffers in this instance also. He desires
to save all—but to be saved they must go through the possibility
of the offence. Ah, and it is as if He, because all were offended
in Him, was about to stand alone, He, the Saviour who would
save all! The mystery of suffering, such as no man can conceive:
to be Himself a sign of offence, in order to be the object of faith!
Therefore is this word so moving, 'Will ye also go away?' Must
I then, I who came to save all, I whose love no one, no one at all
comprehends—must I be brought to the point where there
remains no one at all for whom I am salvation? Oh, to stand with
open arms and say, 'Come hither!'—and then see all flee away,
yea, not only flee away but flee away offended! What it is to be

the Saviour of the world! Hence there is an echo of this suffering in the glad words addressed to Peter, 'Blessed art thou, Simon, son of Jonas.'

But now to the passage itself, to show that the offence has to do with loftiness—recalling, however, that the historical account of how great an offence these words aroused must be taken as a sure guaranty that the same words in the same situation will arouse essentially the same offence. It is the situation of contemporaneousness with an individual man, a man like the others—and he speaks about himself in such a way! He qualifies himself in such a superhumanly spiritual way that he speaks of eating his flesh and drinking his blood, with a suggestion as fantastical as possible of the divine property of omnipresence, and yet again as paradoxically as possible when he talks of his flesh and blood. He says that only one who eats his body and drinks his blood shall he raise up at the last day—employing surely the most decisive expressions to qualify himself as God. He says that he is the bread that cometh down out of heaven—again a decisive suggestion of the divine. And when he saw that his disciples murmured and found this a hard speech, he said, 'Doth this offend you?', and follows this with the still stronger expression, 'What and if ye shall see the Son of Man ascend up where he was before?' So therefore, far from giving in and abating his claim, he directly represents himself as something entirely different from what it is to be a man, makes himself out to be divine—he, an individual man!

It is all very well for one who abandons himself to the intoxicating influence of imagination, who allows fantasy to construct a fantastic figure of Christ to which he stands related at the remote distance of imaginative vision—yes, then, perhaps, one may not notice the offence. But in reality, in truth, i.e. in the situation of contemporaneousness with that individual man, whose origin one knows all about, whom one recognizes on the street, &c.—would it occur to anybody to deny that here the possibility of the offence can be avoided only in one way, by believing? But he who believes must, in order to attain faith, have passed through the possibility of the offence.

Supplement

These two passages are the only instances where the possibility of the offence which has to do with loftiness is mentioned expressly. But it is often enough implied in the Holy Scripture, seeing that in the very nature of the situation the offence was present every instant when He (the God-Man), this individual man, spoke or acted in a way suggesting the qualification God. In this exposition, however, there is not the least need to enumerate all such passages—a superfluous exegetical labour which might also prove confusing, if it were to give the impression that the possibility of offence was present only at this or that moment, whereas in fact it is present every instant.—Thus in Matt. 9: 4 (the story of the paralytic), when Jesus says to the Pharisees, 'Wherefore think ye evil in your hearts', these evil thoughts were the offence. To forgive sinners is in the most decisive sense a qualification suggestive of God. But (to repeat it once again) when a man has only a fantastic picture of Christ, he perhaps finds nothing strange in His forgiving sins, and fails to notice the possibility of the offence. On the other hand, in reality, in truth, in the situation of contemporaneousness—an individual man like others—that he should assume to forgive sins! There is but one way to avoid the offence, viz. by believing; but he who believes has passed through the offence.—Matt. 12: 24, where the Pharisees, after Christ had healed a man possessed, who was blind and dumb, exclaim, 'This fellow doth not cast out devils but by Beelzebub, the prince of devils'—when in this connexion it is said that 'Jesus knew their thoughts', it was these thoughts again that were the offence. Matt. 26: 64, 65, where Christ says, 'Hereafter shall ye see the Son of Man sitting on the right hand of Power and coming in the clouds of heaven'—and the high priests cried out, 'He blasphemeth God, now ye have heard His blasphemy', here again it is the offence we hear. See also John 8: 48, 52 f.; the whole story about the man born blind; and John 10: 20, 30 ff.[1]

With every word suggestive of the qualification God, with

---

[1] S. K. may well refer to St. John's Gospel for illustrations of his notion of Christ as the offence and stone of stumbling, for with St. John this notion was so fundamental that it may be said that his Gospel was built up around this idea. But, on the other hand, seeing that what here provokes the offence is the exceeding directness of Jesus' communication, these passages seem to contradict S. K.'s assertion that 'direct communication' was impossible for Christ in His incognito. But S. K. has already met this criticism by remarking that even the most direct communication from the mouth of Christ could not be effectively communicated to hearers who could not receive it because they also beheld the man and perceived the contradiction.

every act that bears this suggestion, the possibility of the offence is presented. In the situation of contemporaneousness everybody will take notice of it. But in Christendom we have all become Christians without noticing the least possibility of any offence in the fact that a single individual speaks or acts in a way suggestive of being God—we have all become Christians, that goes without saying, and no one becomes a Christian except in the situation of contemporaneousness with Christ, and in the situation of contemporaneousness everyone will take notice of the offence. But in Christendom we have all become Christians without taking notice of . . . that which incidentally is the Christian weapon of defence against 'speculative comprehension' and a death-dealing weapon against it, viz. the possibility of the offence—yea, it would seem, without even noticing that it is Jesus Christ Himself that calls attention to the presence of the possibility of the offence; and surely it may be supposed that in this respect He is as well informed as the whole aggregation of speculative theological professors, without whose help and countenance indeed, as everybody knows, Christianity came into the world, whereas it is quite possible, supposing there was nothing else to hinder, that by their help and countenance it might be smuggled out of the world.

C

*T*HE *possibility of the essential offence which has to do with lowliness, for the fact that one who gives Himself out to be God shows Himself to be the poor and suffering and at last the impotent man.*

In this instance one is not offended by the claim that He is God, but by the observation that God is this man ('Behold what a man!'), whether one is now about to believe that He is God, or is merely pondering reflectively over this infinite self-contradiction that God should be such a man.

In the foregoing section the man who was about to be offended, who was brought to a halt by the possibility of offence, said, 'An individual man like us wants to be God.' Here the man who is brought to a halt by the possibility of offence says, 'Supposing for an instant that thou art God, what folly and madness it is that thou art this lowly, poor, impotent man!'

1. Matt. 13: 55 (Mk. 6: 3).—'Is not this the carpenter's son? Is not his mother called Mary, and his brethren, James, and Joses, and Simon, and Judas, and his sisters, are they not all with us? Whence hath this man all these things? And they were offended in him.'

It may be remarked that the direction of the offence is ambiguous. For if stress is laid upon, 'whence hath he all these things?' the offence is resolved into the foregoing form, they are offended that He, this lowly man, should be the extraordinary one, should be God. But the passage as a whole can be understood in the other sense: they are offended that God should be the son of a carpenter, and that this is His family. The direction of the offence is here ambiguous, and so it is also in such a passage as John 7: 27 f.

And when one has only a fantastic notion of Christ, when neither He Himself is thought of as an individual man, nor even His father, the carpenter, is so thought of as a man one knows well, nor the rest of His kindred—then it is quite possible not to be offended. But if one is not in such a sense as this contemporary with Christ, it is also impossible to become a Christian.

2. Matt. 26: 31, 33 (Mk. 14: 27, 29).—Here the possibility

of offence is quite unambiguously in the direction of lowliness. In fact, what is here said concerns the disciples, men who had believed that He was what He said He was, and it is here said that *they* will be offended in Him. But their offence cannot possibly have reference to loftiness, the doubt lest He, their teacher and master, might not be what He said He was. No, that is what they believe. It has reference to lowliness, that He, the highly exalted, the Only Begotten of the Father, should suffer in this way, should be delivered helpless into the power of his enemies.—When one talks of Peter's denial, one is inclined commonly to make the mistake of presenting it in the form of one of those climaxes which fly in the face of dialectics and so is an anticlimax, although the orator is unaware of it because he has no inkling of the secret of dialectics, but interprets it all in his declamation as a direct superlative, so that being God becomes the superlative of being man. The orator says that Peter would already have been culpable in denying Christ, if Christ had been merely a man—and then, since Christ was what he was . . .! Entirely forgetting that if Christ had been merely a man, and was regarded by Peter as merely a man, Peter surely would not have denied Him. As a matter of fact, what caused Peter to be quite beside himself, what affected him like a stroke of apoplexy, is precisely that he believed Christ to be the Only Begotten of the Father. That a man falls into the power of his enemies is human. But that He whose almighty hand had wrought signs and wonders now stands impotent and paralysed—precisely this it is that brings Peter to the point of denying Him.

Thus it is with these two passages. 'This night ye shall all be offended in Me. But Peter answered and said unto Him, Though all were to be offended in Thee, yet will I not be offended.' This is the last occasion when Jesus was alone with His disciples before His Passion, and it is about this He speaks, He foretells it. Oh, but what endless pain He foretells, pain which no man can comprehend, although it is only indirectly indicated in the sacred story. For Christ speaks laconically about what He is about to suffer, He does not tell in detail how He is to be ill-treated—and yet He foretells His Passion. His Passion, alas, His bitterest passion, for it is just this, that they all should be offended in Him, even Peter. He foretells His Passion, seemingly as if this were only an item among others in the description of its horror, as if the Passion were so horrible that all His disciples even will be offended in Him—alas, this is precisely the bitterest experience of His Passion. Ah, the man who has sense merely for the outward does not observe here at all how Christ foretells His Passion, and that this was the bitterest suffering in the night in which He was betrayed, mocked, spit upon, scourged—this, that all were offended in Him. When one sees Him nailed to the cross[1] like a criminal, one may well say that at that moment there never was a man who had accomplished so little as He and the cause He represented. One forgets the horror—for sheer horror forgets *the* horror. For the fact that His enemies and the forces of evil acquire power over Him—well, humanly speaking, one cannot for that reason say that it was in vain He had come into the world. But at the moment when all were offended in Him, even Peter—humanly speaking, was not His whole life in vain? He would save all, literally all—and all were offended in Him, literally all! And He had it in His power to remove the possibility of the offence by altering Himself a little, and, as concerning His beloved disciples, by withholding suffering from them—but then He is no longer the object of faith, then He is beguiled by human sympathy, and He beguiles them. Oh, depth of suffering, unfathomable to human understanding!—that He must be the sign of offence in order to be the object of faith!

But if there were need of any proof of the fact that the possibility of the offence belongs essentially to the experience of faith, it is exhibited here: they were all offended in Him. The disciples who had believed in His divinity, and in this respect had surmounted the offence by holding fast to their faith, are now brought to a stand by lowliness, by the possibility of offence which consists in the fact that the God-Man suffers exactly as if He were a mere man. That is to say (as was said in the first section), the possibility of offence, which is faith's protection and

[1] A reader unacquainted with S. K. might suspect that all this is nothing more than the customary Good Friday declamation. In my book on *Kierkegaard* (pp. 39 ff., 42 ff.) two stories are quoted which reveal how profoundly his sensitive soul had been affected in early childhood by the picture of the Crucifixion, and how permanent were the effects of this early experience. Thus he was extraordinarily fitted by nature and experience to be a passionate preacher of Christ's Passion; and the reader will be the more pungently affected by such passages as this when he knows that it was the thought of Christ's sufferings which impelled this writer to cherish the ambition of suffering in His likeness.

weapon of defence, is so equivocal that all human understanding must be brought to a halt by it, must stumble—so as either to be offended or to believe.

Supplement 1

Beside the passages cited above as examples of the possibility of offence at the lowliness of the God-Man, there are of course very many which imply it without using exactly this word. The whole story of the Passion is an example.

Supplement 2

The possibility of offence about which we have been speaking above has to do with the God-Man in view of His lowliness.

Christ speaks also of another possibility of offence which corresponds to this, having likewise lowliness in view, when it appears that the disciple is not above the Master but like unto Him. He is the God-Man, and one is offended that He should be so abased. But now it appears that to be a Christian, to belong truly to Christ, i.e. when one is in truth what he says he is, this it appears is the most exalted thing a man can be. And then, that to be a Christian in truth should mean in the world, in the eyes of men, to be abased, that it should mean all possible hardships, every possible sort of derision and insult, and mean at last to be punished as a criminal! Here again is the possibility of offence. Ah, and it holds good of this offence also that it may be avoided if thou, either out of hypocrisy or out of whimpering human sympathy for thyself or for others, wilt be a Christian only up to a certain point, only on the pagan principle of *ne quid nimis*; for then thou shalt be honoured and esteemed, shalt be able to avoid the possibility of offence, to accomplish a great deal in the world, and to win great multitudes who desire also to be Christians only up to a certain point. But if this is not thy desire, then thou must pass through the possibility of offence; for to be a Christian is certainly not to be Christ (what mockery of God!), but it is to be His follower—yet not the sort of fashionably rouged follower who profits by the firm's name and is content to regard Christ's sufferings as an affair of many, many centuries ago. No, to be a follower means that thy life has as great a likeness to His as it is possible for a man's life to have.

Christianity is not a doctrine. All the talk about offence in relation to Christianity as a doctrine is a misunderstanding, it is a device to mitigate the shock of offence at the scandal—as, for example, when one speaks of the offence of the *doctrine* of the God-Man and the *doctrine* of the Atonement. No, the offence is related either to Christ or to the fact of being oneself a Christian.

But as in Christendom everything has been brought to confusion, so also this; and thereby the point has been reached where Christianity has become paganism. In Christendom they preach perpetually about what happened then after Christ's death, how He triumphed, and how His disciples made a triumphal conquest of the whole world—in short, one hears only sermons which might properly end with Hurrah! rather than with Amen. No, Christ's life here upon earth is the paradigm; it is in likeness to it that I along with every Christian must strive to construct my life; and this is the essential object of the sermon, this is the end it should serve, to keep me alert when I would become slack, and to strengthen me when I would become disheartened. In such a sense He is the paradigm in the situation of contemporaneousness; in that situation there was no stuff and nonsense about what happened afterwards. But Christendom has abolished Christianity—on the other hand, it would like to inherit Him and His great name, to gain advantage from the immense consequences of his life, coming pretty close to appropriating these consequences as its own meritorious achievement and making us believe that Christendom is Christ. Every generation has to begin all over again with Christ and thus to present His life as the paradigm; but instead of this, Christendom has taken the liberty of interpreting the whole relationship simply historically, beginning by letting Him be dead—and then it triumphs! Since that time Christendom has been increasing in numbers year by year—and what wonder; for people are only too eager to take part when there is nothing whatever to do but to triumph and to join the parade.[1] And therefore to be a Christian in Christendom is as different from being a Christian in the situation of contemporaneousness as paganism is from Christianity.

In the situation of contemporaneousness, when one could

[1] This last phrase is a lame substitute for S. K.'s reference to the gala parade of heralds and guardsmen which ushered in the session of the old Parliament (*ride Herredage ind*), a ceremony which became obsolete the very year this book was published.

ascertain at any instant how far the disciple's life resembled the Master's, no world-historical hocus-pocus was possible, the disciple was construed in accordance with the paradigm—not as in established Christendom, where (assuming as one surely must that Christ is the paradigm) one cannot behold the individual Christians without being just as much astonished at the thought that they are construed in accordance with the paradigm—just as much astonished as if someone were to maintain that *domus* is declined in accordance with the paradigm *mensa*.

When one observes how people live in Christendom, one might seriously believe that in paganism men must have lived entirely without earthly sufferings and adversities and all that sort of thing—to such a degree has Christendom missed the point as to what specifically Christian suffering is, the suffering which Christ and Christianity themselves brought into the world; to such a degree has Christendom found its delight in preaching all that jargon of earthly adversity into the category of specifically Christian suffering, which is described properly by, 'because of the word', and 'for righteousness' sake', &c., while, on the other hand, they array these usual human sufferings as if they were the specifically Christian, forcing them (Oh, masterpiece of preposterousness!) into correspondence with the paradigm. Also the minor religious paradigms are customarily taken in vain. A man's wife dies. So the parson preaches about Abraham who offered up Isaac, and the widower is portrayed by the reverend orator as a sort of Abraham, a pendant to Abraham. Naturally, there is not a trace of sense in the discourse; the parson's interpretation is neither Abraham nor the widower, but the man is pleased by it and cheerfully gives ten dollars; and the congregation has no objection, for each one expects his turn to come. Might not one cheerfully give ten dollars for the honour of resembling Abraham in such an easy way?[1]

Such an instance as this, where a man's wife dies, cannot be

---

[1] Doubtless the preposterous confusion between necessary human suffering and suffering 'for righteousness' sake' is as common now as ever. One can easily imagine how S. K. must have squirmed at hearing such a sermon about Abraham; but one will not understand the passion with which he repudiates it, unless one is aware how passionately he wrote about the case of Abraham in *Fear and Trembling*, venturing to think that the sacrifice he himself made voluntarily—but so much against his will! —in giving up the woman he loved and was engaged to, found its paradigm in Abraham's sacrifice.

brought under the paradigm Abraham. It is surely not a case
where a man sacrifices his wife, or (as the parson might inadvertently say with more precision) 'was willing to put his wife to
death', for death itself has taken her off. But the point in Abraham's case, the terrible thing which infinitely intensifies the strain,
is his responsibility that Abraham wills to go forth and sacrifice
Isaac.—And so it is also with *the* paradigm, Christ Himself, and
with the derived paradigms. One has become entirely oblivious to
what is meant by Christian suffering properly so called and the
derived Christian paradigms. One has become entirely oblivious
to what is meant by Christian suffering properly so called; one
takes the common human sufferings and makes them—how it is
accomplished surpasses my understanding—but one makes them
correspond to the Christian paradigm. If in contrast to pure
Christianity one would call this applied Christianity, then one
can truly say that it is badly applied.

The decisive mark of Christian suffering is the fact that it is
voluntary, and that it is *the possibility of offence for the sufferer*. We
read of the Apostles that they forsook all to follow Christ. So it
was voluntary. Now there is a man in Christendom who is so
unfortunate as to lose all that he possessed; he has not given up
the least thing, he has lost all. So then the parson valiantly applies
himself to study out a consolatory discourse; but due to his much
study, or to whatever else it may be, everything is a confused buzz
in the brain of his Reverence; to lose all and to give up all become
synonymous, he makes losing all agree with the paradigm 'giving
up all', notwithstanding that the difference is infinite. For when
voluntarily I give up all, choosing danger and adversity, it is not
possible to ignore *the* offence (again peculiarly the category of
Christianity, though of course abolished in Christendom) which
derives from responsibility (corresponding again to the voluntary)
when they say, 'But why will you expose yourself to this and
commence such an undertaking, when you could perfectly well
leave it alone?' This is specific Christian suffering. It is a
whole musical tone deeper than common human suffering. For
when I lose all, there is no responsibility, and there is nothing
for temptation to lay hold of. But in Christendom they have
entirely abolished the voluntary, and by this the possibility of
offence as well, forasmuch as the voluntary is also a form of the
possibility of temptation. They live in an entirely heathenish way

and see no reason why they should not use their wit to deride the voluntary as a ridiculous exaggeration or a *quid nimis*. Unavoidable human sufferings one has simply to put up with once for all, just as in·paganism; but they preach them up to be Christian sufferings, preach them into relationship with Christ and the Apostles. I would venture to try the experiment of taking pagan works, without altering anything in them, except to introduce Christ's name in several places—and I shall make people believe it is a sermon or a meditation by a parson—a sermon, perhaps even a sermon 'published at the request of many', i.e. of many Christians, for surely we are all of us Christians, the Parson included.

What wonder then that, with relation to being a Christian, people are not in the least aware of *the possibility of offence*? But in the situation of contemporaneousness with Christ (that is to say, so it was once upon a time, and so it always is when there is truth in the profession of being a Christian, that being a Christian is connected with the possibility of offence) the Christian is bound to discover the possibility of offence in relation to his own life, and the question was [and is] whether he will now be offended, or whether, holding fast his faith, he will continue to be a Christian. There is no self-contradiction in the universal human afflictions; there is no self-contradiction in the fact that my wife dies, for she is mortal; no contradiction in the fact that I lose my possessions, for they are perishable, &c. Only when the self-contradiction of suffering is present is the possibility of offence also present, and that in turn, as was observed, is inseparable from being a Christian, as Christ Himself also represents it.

That this is true, that it really is self-contradiction which constitutes the possibility of offence, is to be seen moreover in the decisive passage about the possibility of offence in general, Matt. 18: 8 f. Here the possibility of offence consists in the self-contradiction that the remedy appears infinitely worse than the disease. 'Wherefore, if thy hand or thy foot offend thee, cut them off and cast them from thee: it is better for thee to enter into life halt or maimed, rather than, having two hands or two feet, to be cast into everlasting fire. And if thine eye offend thee, pluck it out and cast it from thee: it is better for thee to enter into life with one eye, rather than, having two eyes, to be cast into hell fire.' Christ is speaking [in this whole passage] about offence;

but observe that, Christianly understood, the real possibility of offence (the possibility of offence which is properly related to becoming a Christian) first emerges in the second place, i.e. in the remedy which Christ recommends as salvation from offence. The natural man has also something he calls offence, something he calls love, &c.; but just as that which the natural man calls love is, Christianly understood, only self-love, so that which the natural man calls offence is no more than a temporary disposition, and only when Christ extols the remedy against this does the possibility of offence emerge; for it is in relation to this remedy that the decision must be made, whether to be a Christian or to be offended. The natural man intends to comply with a certain standard of civic rectitude, and while he makes this effort there is something which offends him, be it his eye or his hand. It is not his intention to give in to the offence, he would gladly save his civic rectitude if this could be done by mild measures, and if the sacrifice it demanded were merely up to a certain point. But now Christianity comes along and says, If thou wouldst avoid the offence, cut off thy hand, tear thine eye out—castrate thyself, for the kingdom of heaven's sake (Matt. 19: 12). This properly is what constitutes the offence to the natural man. 'Such a remedy is mere madness, it is infinitely worse than the disease—and wherefore should I do it?' Thereto Christianity replies, 'To avoid the offence', or it says the same thing in another way, 'To enter into life'.

That is, Christ attaches infinite importance to entering into life, to eternal blessedness, regarding it as the absolute good; and hence He attaches infinite importance to avoiding the offence. What therefore really offends is the endless passion with which the eternal blessedness is conceived, corresponding to the endless fear of offence. This is precisely what offends the natural man. Such a conception of the eternal blessedness the natural man does not possess, nor does he desire to possess it; and hence he does not possess a conception of the danger of the offence.

In established Christendom this and every other possibility of offence is in effect abolished—in established Christendom one becomes a Christian in the merriest possible way, without in the least becoming aware of the possibility of offence. In established Christendom the natural man has managed to have his own way. There is no endless contrast between the Christian and the worldly.

The relation of the Christian to the worldly is conceived, at the most, as a potentialization (or more exactly under the rubric, culture), always directly; it is simply a direct comparative, the positive being civic rectitude. Such methods as Christ extols for avoiding the offence are not needed in established Christendom. One starts with the worldly. Keeping an eye upon civic rectitude (good—better—best), one makes oneself as comfortable as possible with everything one can scrape together in the way of worldly goods—the Christian element being stirred in with all this as an ingredient, a seasoner, which sometimes serves merely to refine the relish. There is no endless contrast between the Christian and the worldly, and the danger of offence has here no terrible significance—just about as much significance as blessedness. Christianity is related directly to the world, it is movement without budging from the spot—that is to say, feigned movement.

What wonder then that people are not in the least aware of the possibility of the offence in relation to being a Christian? and what wonder that established Christendom simply doesn't make sense? For when a man is convinced firmly and surely, and therefore in fear and trembling, that blessedness is to be attained only by faith in Christ, that apart from this there is only perdition, and that the offence is the danger—that he should get it into his head to venture all, does surely make some sense. But in established Christendom we pretty much all of us live with a lax conviction—certainly anything but a passionate one—that we shall somehow become blessed all of us together. From what source then might the possibility of offence in relation to becoming a Christian reach the natural man? Yet the serious Christian might well find the whole situation of established Christendom in the highest degree offensive—to use this word in another sense. But if the possibility of offence consists precisely in the fact that eternal blessedness is valued at so high a price—then the possibility of offence is removed when a person has nothing more to do about the matter but to be born in Christendom. So soon, therefore, as anyone in established Christendom is ready to express endless passion in his concern for eternal blessedness—that is, when he would express the fact that he is a Christian—established Christendom will then in a sense open its eyes and discover the possibility of offence as this showed and shows itself in the situation of contemporaneousness with Christ. For then the thing becomes serious, and hence the natural man notices the self-contradiction involved in the fact that a person in order to avoid a danger about which one might say, 'Oh, well, it would not be so great a misfortune to be offended once', should nevertheless employ such a terrible remedy as that of cutting off the hand, plucking out the eye, or castrating himself.

But now for the two passages which speak about the possibility of the offence which has to do with lowliness, the possibility of offence which, in a derived way, corresponds to the possibility of the offence which has to do with the lowliness and humiliation of the God-Man.

1. Matt. 13: 21 (Mk. 4: 17). It is the parable about the different fate of the seeds. There it is said, 'But he that receiveth the seed into stony ground, is he that heareth the word and immediately with joy receiveth it. . . . But when tribulation or persecution ariseth because of the word, immediately he is *offended*.'

The emphasis lies upon 'because of the word'. In the preacher's harangue, of course, the emphasis does not lie here, but by way of compensation strong stress is sometimes laid upon getting money for the word's sake. They preach quite Christianly about the necessity of passing through many tribulations to enter into the kingdom of heaven, saying that tribulation must be expected. Admirable! That is genuine Christianity! But listening more closely, one discovers with surprise that these many tribulations are nothing else but illness, financial difficulties, anxiety for the year to come, what one is to eat, or anxiety about 'what one ate last year—and has not paid for',[1] or the fact that one has not become what one desired to be in the world, or other such fatalities. About these things one preaches Christianly, one weeps humanly, and one crazily connects them with Gethsemane. In case it were through these many tribulations one enters into the kingdom of

---

[1] We learn from the Journal (VIII. A. 644), in date of May 17, '48, that S. K., in his comparative opulence, was much impressed by the following phrase in a letter of thanks for his *Works of Love*, which was received from a country pastor named Zeuthen, who evidently was far from opulent: commenting upon 'anxiety for the morrow', he remarks that 'there is also an anxiety for *yesterday*, with respect to what one has eaten—and not paid for. The difficulty is to keep *to-day* clear of presuppositions.' S. K. had already made use of this phrase in his Discourse about *The Lilies of the Field and the Birds of the Air*, which in 1849 'accompanied' the 2nd edition of *Either/Or*.

heaven, the heathen also must enter into the kingdom of heaven, for they also pass through the same. No, this way of preaching is in an exceedingly dangerous way the abolition of Christianity, and in part it is even blasphemous.

These tribulations and adversities stand in need of a little closer definition. This is contained in Christ's words, 'because of the word'. Christ is not speaking of softly coddled men who absolutely do not live half so efficiently as pagans, these coddled men who wish to be Christians, and then when there happens to them merely a common human suffering, no longer wish to be Christians. No, of these He does not speak—that is to say, not when the discourse is about *being offended*, though He has them in mind when in this same parable He says that covetousness and anxiety about food, &c., choke the good seed. But *offence* is a perfectly definite thought, so that one can know quite accurately whether the possibility of offence is present or not. And it is about this Christ is speaking, He is speaking about the man who is offended when tribulation and persecution arise because of the word. Because, according to His teaching, the fact that tribulation and persecution arise because of the word is the self-contradiction wherein lies the possibility of offence.

It is true that Christianity declares itself to be consolation and medicine and healing—very well then, one has recourse to it as one has recourse to a person with whom one seeks refuge, and one thanks it as one thanks a helper; for by the aid of it or by its aid one expects to be enabled to bear the suffering one sighs under. And then exactly the opposite occurs. One flees to the word in search of help—and then one has to suffer because of the word. And with respect to this suffering, the case is not the same as when one takes a medicine or subjects oneself to a cure which may be accompanied with some pain, which one supports and in which there is no self-contradiction. No, in this case tribulation overtakes a man because he has had recourse to Christ for help. When the clouds thus gather together the human understanding is darkened, so that it does not know either in or out, nor what is what. What then is Christianity? What is it for? One seeks help from it, one is willing to thank it indescribably, and then just the opposite occurs, one has to suffer for its sake—so there does not really seem to be anything to thank for. Here the understanding is brought to a halt by the possibility of offence. The help appears to be an affliction, and relief a burden; one who looks on from the outside is compelled to say, 'He is mad to expose himself to all this'—and the sufferer believed he would be helped. Let me once again make clear what is meant by, 'because of the word'. When I am ill and have recourse to a physician, he may perhaps find it necessary to prescribe a very painful cure—there is no self-contradiction in subjecting myself to it. No, but on the other hand, when I suddenly find myself in tribulation, an object of persecution, for no other reason but because I had recourse to *that* physician—yes, then there is a self-contradiction. The physician has perhaps declared that he could help me in respect to the illness I suffer from, and perhaps he can do it—but there is an *if* I had never thought of. The fact that I deal with that physician, attach myself to him, is what makes me an object of persecution. Here is the possibility of offence.

And so it is with Christianity. Now the question is, Wilt thou be offended, or wilt thou believe? If thou wilt believe, then thou must pass through the possibility of offence, accept Christianity on any terms. Then 'it is a go' [*es geht*]. So, a fig for the understanding! So you say, 'Whether it now is a help or a torment, I *will* one thing only,[1] I will belong to Christ, I will be a Christian!'

Moreover, it can easily be seen here that the possibility of offence has to do with lowliness—with the fact that this infinitely exalted thing of being a Christian should be despised, derided, spat upon, and regarded as a crime. But if this relationship is the right one, if the man so ill treated is in truth a Christian, he thus resembles the pattern as nearly as it is possible for a man to resemble it. But the contradiction is that in which the possibility of offence consists: that one should be punished for doing well.

2. John 16: 23 and Matt. 16: 23 illuminate it. Christ has spoken about what was in store for the Apostles if they should bear witness of Him on earth. 'This I have said unto you that ye should not be *offended*. They shall put you out of the synagogues; yea, the time shall come when whosoever killeth you shall think that he doeth God service.'

It is easy to perceive the contradiction in which the possibility of offence consists: that the ill treatment of God's messengers, so far from being called an injustice, will be regarded as divine

---

[1] In one the most striking of his Edifying Discourses S. K. explains that 'purity of heart is to will one thing', and that this one thing can only be the highest.

adoration. So the proper relationship is completely inverted: the Apostles are ill treated—and those responsible for this are not only highly honoured and esteemed, but more especially regarded as god-fearing and pious men. This is a relation which the human understanding cannot endure, and now it is necessary either to be offended or to believe. Such was the situation with respect to the Apostles and the first Christians. It would seem as if this were the craziest thing possible, but it is perfectly certain that in Christendom the situation has become still crazier, inasmuch as both parties are Christians. That the heathen thought to do God a service by killing an Apostle is not so crazy as that 'true Christians' are persecuted in 'Christendom', and that thus 'the Christians think that thereby they do service to God.

Thus Christ tells them beforehand so that they might not be offended, that on the contrary they might be preserved in faith, for in faith they are saved out of the possibility of offence. When a man so lives that he recognizes no higher standard for his life than that provided by the understanding, his whole life is relativity, labour for a relative end; he undertakes nothing unless the understanding, by the aid of probability, can somehow make clear to him the profit and loss and give answer to the question, why and wherefore. It is different with the absolute. At the first glance the understanding ascertains that this is madness. To relegate a whole life to suffering, to immolation, is for the understanding mere madness. If I must subject myself to suffering, says the understanding, if I must sacrifice something, or in some way sacrifice myself, then I want to know what profit or advantage I can get out of it; otherwise I am crazy if I do it. But to say to a man, 'Go now out into the world, it will befall thee thus: thou wilt be persecuted year after year, and the end of it will be that finally thou wilt come to a frightful death'—then says the understanding, 'What is there in it?' The answer is, 'Nothing'—it is an expression of the fact that the absolute exists. But this is precisely what offends the understanding.

And here one perceives also how this is connected with an objection which is often made against Christianity, and which in a sense is justly made, and at all events makes more sense than the silly defence of Christianity which is generally advanced in this connexion. The objection is that Christianity is misanthropical, as in fact it was said of the Christians in the first age

that they were [full of]¹ *odium totius generis humani*. The connexion here is this: in comparison with that which the natural
man (who loves himself selfishly or loves himself effeminately)
regards as love, friendship, and the like, Christianity seems like
hatred for the ideal of what it is to be a man, like the greatest
curse and torment to the ideal of what it is to be a man. Yes, even
a deeper man may have moments when it seems as if Christianity
were hostile to man.² For in the weaker moments one is inclined
to coddle oneself, to whimper, to get along easily in the world,
to live in quiet enjoyment. That is the womanly trait in man;
and hence it is quite certain and true that Christianity is suspicious
of marriage, and desires that along with the many married
servants it has, it might also have an unmarried person, a single
man; for Christianity knows very well that with woman and love
all this weakliness and love of coddling arises in a man, and that in
so far as the husband himself does not bethink himself of it, the
wife ordinarily pleads it with an ingenuous candour which is
exceedingly dangerous for the husband, especially for one who is
required in the strictest to serve Christianity. So it begins with
this: 'Why will you expose yourself to all the inconvenience and
exertion, all the ingratitude and opposition? Let us two enjoy
life in ease and comfort. Marriage, as the parson says, is an
honourable estate, well-pleasing to God. Indeed it is the only
estate of which this is expressly said; it is not said even of the
ecclesiastical estate. One should marry—more than this or other
than this God does not require of any man; and you have done
your part, you have married—a second time even. Give up therefore these thoughts, which are nothing but vanity and madness.
The doctrine which would thus drive a man out into the world is
misanthropy, and therefore far removed from Christianity, which,
as the parson said on Sunday, is the gentle teaching which kindly
relieves all pressure. How can you imagine for a moment that
this might be Christianity, this which was conceived by a lot of
mute and sallow hermits who have no sense for the feminine?'
   The same is true even in relation to the lesser and insignificant

---

¹ In citing these words of Tacitus S. K. says that the Christians were 'called'
odium, &c., but the context shows that he rightly understood, not that they were hated
by the human race (which was only too true), but that they were haters of men (as
Tacitus means to say here).
² Like S. K. himself—and not in his rebellious youth only.

sacrifices. And then when a whole life is in question, when it is a question of consecrating it as a sacrifice, of advancing to encounter such a future, of labouring with the utmost effort and without the least prospect of alleviation—to achieve, i.e. with the certainty of achieving in this way, the advantage of being persecuted year after year and at last put to death—Oh, even in the strongest man there are moments when it must seem to him misanthropy to require such things of a man![1]

So it was with Peter in his relation to Christ, Matt. 16: 21 f. 'Then Jesus began to show His disciples that He must go to Jerusalem, and suffer many things from the elders and the chief priests, and be killed. . . . Then Peter took Him and began to rebuke Him, saying, Lord, Lord, spare thyself. This shall not happen to Thee.'—One sees from this what extraordinary self-assurance a man must have to expose himself to the danger of having a friend. For a friend does not so much help one to venture boldly and to lay down one's life, as rather to haggle and beat down the price—and hence we can understand why so much is said in honour and praise of friendship. Therefore in case a man who wills the good, though on a more ordinary scale, is not presumptuous enough to claim an almost superhuman superiority, let him (holding fast to God in fear and trembling) above all things take the precaution to have no friend. For if Christ had not been Christ, Peter presumably would have conquered.

So Peter began to rebuke Him. Just because Peter loved Christ, because he was entirely devoted to Him, he now has the *friendly* wish that the two may have a good time together. He 'rebukes' Him; for the true friend expresses his views honestly, is not afraid of speaking sternly and rebuking his friend when he is in evil paths, that is, when he is about to decide to venture something boldly, to sacrifice himself to a cause—hence we can understand why so much is said in honour and praise of friendship; for though a man were almost weak enough to wish for himself that he might be quit of the venture, yet friendship is a glorious invention, and it is a priceless thing that it is a duty to have a friend. Peter says, 'Spare thyself';[2] for Peter is sympathetic and

[1] At this period of his life S. K. was struggling against the premonition that he personally might be required to make the utmost sacrifice.

[2] The modern Danish version, like R.V. margin, reads: God have mercy on thee.

a true friend—yet not for this reason entirely lacking in self-love, for Peter was moved for his own sake to be so severe. He says, 'This shall not *happen* unto Thee'; for it did not occur even to Peter that Christ might voluntarily expose Himself to this; and if it had occurred to him, he would have taken the liberty of speaking even more sharply.

And Christ replies, 'Get thee behind Me, Satan! Thou art an offence unto me, for thou mindest not the things of God, but the things of men.' Here one perceives very clearly wherein the possibility of offence consists, and also how it is that Christendom which minds only the things of men has abolished the possibility of offence by remodelling Christianity into the likeness of the things it 'minds'. The trait for which Peter is an offence to Christ is the exact opposite of that for which Christ is an offence to Peter. Peter is the most lovable edition of human sympathy—but of *human* sympathy, and therefore to Christ an offence.

For the relative indicates a period within the temporal for the reward of labour; the absolute seeks only the eternal. But this thing of eternity is not quite sure enough for the sensuous, the natural man, not even for the ablest, and hence the absolute is an offence to him. The believer looks upon the whole of life as the natural man does upon some few years of it. The natural man puts up with these few years—with a view to reaping the reward [in time]. The believer thus disposes of the whole of life in time.

But at the absolute the understanding stands still. The contradiction which arrests it is that a man is required to make the greatest possible sacrifice, to dedicate his whole life as a sacrifice—and wherefore? There is indeed no wherefore. 'Then it is madness', says the understanding. There is no wherefore, because there is an infinite wherefore. But whenever the understanding stands still in this wise, there is the possibility of offence. If now there is to be victorious advance, faith must be present, for faith is a new life. Without faith a man remains offended—and then perhaps he becomes something great in the world, has extraordinary good fortune, is honoured and praised by contemporaries as the greatest man of the age, &c.—this is not impossible. For let us remember that the dialectic of offence comes again into operation. If it were a fact that things must go badly in this world for the man who is offended, then the concept is abolished, then there is nothing to be offended at; the possibility of offence consists precisely in the fact that it is the believer who is regarded by the world as a criminal.

The possibility of offence, moreover, as one may easily see, as here to do with lowliness, with the fact, namely, that the endlessly exalted thing of living for the absolute finds its expression in becoming 'the refuse of the world', an object of scorn and derision, which sympathy pities while yet it also regards it in a way as a just punishment for such a person to be executed as a criminal.

CONCLUSION TO B AND C

This exposition has now displayed the two forms of offence, has gone through the passages where Christ Himself expressly gives warning against it, and in the Supplement has also alluded to many other passages where the possibility of offence in relation to the God-Man is implied in Holy Scripture. It was not its intention to go through them all, and still less to give the impression that only by going through them all would the possibility of offence be made manifest. No, the possibility of offence, in the one form or the other, accompanies the God-Man every instant, a man's shadow does not accompany a man more inseparably than the possibility of offence accompanies the God-Man, for the God-Man is the object of faith. The God-Man (and by this, as has been said, Christianity does not mean that fantastic speculation about the unity of God and man, but an individual man who is God)—the God-Man exists only for faith; but the possibility of offence is just the repellent force by which faith comes into existence—if one does not choose instead to be offended.

THOUGHTS WHICH DETERMINE THE MEANING OF 'THE OFFENCE' STRICTLY SO CALLED

In the first ages of Christendom, when even erroneous doctrines bore a stamp which testified unmistakably to the fact that people nevertheless knew what it was all about, the error with regard to the God-Man took one or another of two forms: either that of eliminating the qualification God (Ebionitism), or that of eliminating the qualification man (Gnosticism). In the modern age on the whole, which bears a stamp which unmistakably witnesses to the fact that people do not know what it is all about, the error is a different one and far more dangerous. By force of lecturing they have transformed the God-Man into that speculative unity of God and man *sub specie aeterni*, manifested, that is to say, in the nullipresent medium of pure being, whereas in truth the God-Man is the unity of God and an individual man in an actual historical situation; or else they have simply done away with Christ, cast Him out and taken possession of His teaching, almost regarding Him at last as one does an anonymous author—the doctrine is the principal thing, is the whole thing. Hence it is that they vainly conceive of Christianity simply as *direct* communication, far more direct in its simplicity than the profound dicta of the professor. They have nonsensically forgotten that here the Teacher is more important than the teaching. Wherever it is the case that the teacher is essentially involved in the teaching, there is a reduplication. Reduplication consists in the fact that the teacher is a part of it; but wherever there is reduplication, the communication is far from being the direct paragraph- or professor-communication; being reduplicated in the teacher by the fact that he 'exists' in what he teaches, it is in manifold ways a discriminating art. And now when the Teacher, who is inseparable from and more essential than the teaching, is also a paradox, all direct communication is impossible. But in our time they make everything abstract and do away with everything personal—they take Christ's teaching and do away with Christ. This means to do away with Christianity, for Christ is a person, and He is the Teacher who is more important than His teaching.—Just as Christ's life, the very fact that He lived, is infinitely more important than all the consequences of His life (as I have endeavoured to show in another work[1]), so also is Christ infinitely more important than His teaching. Only of a man can it be true that his teaching is more important than he himself is; to apply this to Christ is a blasphemy, it is to make Him a mere man.

[1] This is a reference to another part of this same work (pp. 34 ff.). The fact that S. K. speaks of it as 'another work' shows that he then proposed to publish the three parts of *Training in Christianity* as separate books. Later (but before he had written *For Self-Examination* or *Judge for Yourselves*) he thought of including *The Sickness unto Death* in one volume with the three parts of *Training in Christianity*, entitling the book *The Collected Works of the Consummation*. See IX. A. 390.

§ 1

The God-Man is a 'Sign'

What is to be understood by a 'sign?' A sign is the negation of immediacy,[1] or a second state of being, differing from the first. It is not thereby affirmed that the sign is not something immediate, but that what it is as a sign is not immediate, in other words, that as a sign it is not the immediate thing it is. A nautical mark is a sign. Immediately it is a post, a light, or some such thing, but a sign it is not immediately, that it is a sign is something different from what it immediately is.—This [viz. the failure to observe this distinction] lies at the bottom of all the mystifications by the help of 'signs'; for a sign is a sign only for one who knows that it is a sign, and in the strictest sense only for one who knows what it signifies; for everyone else the sign is only what it immediately is.—Even in case no one had erected this or that into a sign, and there was no understanding with anybody that it was to be regarded as such, yet when I see something striking and call it a sign, it is qualified as such by reflection. The striking trait is the immediate, but that I regard it as a sign (a reflective act, producing something out of myself) expresses my conception that it must signify something, but the fact that it must *signify* something means that it is something else than that which it immediately is. So I am not denying the immediacy of the thing when I regard it as a sign without knowing definitely that it is a sign or what it should signify.

A 'sign of contradiction'[2] is a sign which contains in itself a contradiction. There is no contradiction in the fact that a thing is immediately this or that and at the same time a sign; for something there must be immediately existing to serve as a sign; where there is literally nothing there is no sign. On the other hand, a sign of contradiction is a sign which contains in its very constitution a contradiction. To justify the name of 'sign' there must be something whereby it draws attention to itself or to the contradiction. But the contradictions contained in it must not be such as to

---

[1] The reader must here begin to wrestle with 'immediate' and 'immediacy'—words which are used by S. K. in a philosophical sense, as the direct apprehension of the senses, in contrast to a notion arrived at by means of reflection.

[2] This is S. K.'s version of the phrase in Lk. 2: 34, which is familiar to us as 'a sign which shall be spoken against'.

cancel the two terms and bring the sign to naught, nor must it be such that the sign becomes the opposite of a sign, an absolute secret.—A communication which is the unity of jest and earnest[1] is such a sign of contradiction. It is not by any means a direct communication, it is impossible for him who receives it to tell *directly* which is which, because the communication does not *directly* communicate either jest or earnest. The earnestness of such communication lies in another place, or in a second instance, in the intent of making the receiver independently active— which, dialectically understood, is the highest earnestness in the case of communication. Such a communication, however, must make sure of something whereby it draws attention to itself, whereby it prompts and invites one to take heed of the communication. And, on the other hand, the unity of jest and earnest must not by any means be madness, for then there would be no communication; yet a communication in which either jest or earnestness absolutely predominates is direct communication.

A sign is not what it immediately is, for no sign is immediately a sign, since 'sign' is a qualification of reflection. A sign of contradiction is one which draws attention to itself, and then, when attention is fixed upon it, shows that it contains a contradiction.

And in the Scripture the God-Man is called a sign of contradiction—but what contradiction might there be in the speculative unity of God and man in general? No, in that there is no contradiction; but the contradiction, the greatest possible, the qualitative contradiction, is that between being God and being an individual man. To be a sign is to be, beside what one immediately is, also another thing; to be a sign of contradiction is to be another thing which stands in opposition to what one immediately is. Immediately He is an individual man, just like other men, a lowly, insignificant man; but the contradiction is *that He is God*.

Yet in order that this may not result in a contradiction which exists for no one or does not exist for everyone (as when a mystification succeeds so well that its effect is null), some factor must be present to draw attention to it. The miracle serves essentially this purpose, and so does a single direct assertion about being God. Yet neither the miracle, nor the single direct assertion, is to be regarded as absolutely direct communication; for in this wise the contradiction would *eo ipso* be removed. This is

[1] A characteristic of most of S.K.'s pseudonymous works.

readily to be seen, so far as the miracle is concerned, since that is
an object of faith; and as for the other point, that the single direct
communication is not yet quite a direct communication, this will
be shown later.

The God-Man is the sign of contradiction. And why?
Because, replies the Scripture, He shall reveal the thoughts of
hearts. Has, then, this modern notion about the speculative unity
between God and man, all that about regarding Christianity
merely as a doctrine—has it the remotest resemblance to the
Christian?

No, in the modern view everything is made as direct as putting
the foot into the stocking—and the Christian is: the sign of
contradiction which reveals the thoughts of the heart. The God-
Man is an individual man, not a fantastic unity which never has
existed except *sub specie aeterni*; and He is least of all a lecturer who
teaches directly for scribbling students or dictates paragraphs to
stenographers; He does just the opposite, He reveals the thoughts
of the hearts. Oh, it is so comfortable to be a listener or a tran-
scriber when everything goes on so directly—but let these
gentlemen who listen and transcribe be on their guard . . . it is
the thoughts of *their* hearts that shall be revealed.

And this only the sign of contradiction can do: it draws attention to itself, and then it presents a contradiction. There is
something which makes it impossible for one to desist from
looking—and lo! while one looks, one sees as in a mirror, one
gets to see oneself, or He, the sign of contradiction, sees into the
depths of one's heart while one is gazing into the contradiction.
A contradiction placed directly in front of a man—if only one
can get him to look[1] upon it—is a mirror; while he is judging,
what dwells within him must be revealed. It is a riddle, but
while he is guessing, what dwells within him is revealed by how
he guesses. The contradiction puts before him a choice, and
while he is choosing, he himself is revealed.

Note. One must perceive that direct communication is an
impossibility for the God-Man, for being the sign of contradiction He cannot communicate Himself directly; even to be a sign
involves a qualification of reflection, and how much more to be a
sign of contradiction. And at the same time one must perceive

---

[1] Something of the pathos is lost here because in English the three words, 'look',
'see', and 'lo!' have to be used to translate one Danish word.

that the modern confusion has succeeded in transforming the whole of Christianity into direct communication by leaving out the Communicator, the God-Man. As soon as one does not thoughtlessly take the Communicator away, or take the communication and leave out the Communicator, as soon as one takes the Communicator into account (the Communicator who is the God-Man, a sign, and the sign of contradiction) direct communication is impossible, just as it was in the situation of contemporaneousness. It is 1,800 years since Christ lived, so He is forgotten—only His teaching remains—that is to say, Christianity has been done away with.

§ 2

The form of a servant means unrecognizableness (an incognito)

What is unrecognizableness? It means not to appear in one's proper role, as, for example, when a policeman appears in plain clothes.

And so unrecognizableness, the absolute unrecognizableness, is this: being God, to be also an individual man. To be the individual man, or an individual man (whether it be a distinguished or a lowly man is here irrelevant), is the greatest possible, the infinitely qualitative, remove from being God, and therefore the profoundest incognito.

But the modern age has done away with Christ, either by casting Him out and appropriating His teaching, or by making Him fantastic and fantastically ascribing to Him direct communication. In the situation of contemporaneousness it was different; and one must also remember that Christ willed to be incognito, just because He willed to be the sign of contradiction. But we have these eighteen centuries with all that people suppose they have learned from them; and, on the other hand, the complete ignorance and inexperience of most people about what incognito means, an ignorance and inexperience which are due to the lecturing habit which now prevails, while people have forgotten what 'existence' means—all this has confused the conception of the God-Man.

Most people now living in Christendom live, we may be sure, in the vain persuasion that, had they lived contemporary with Christ, they would at once have known and recognized Him in spite of His unrecognizableness. They are quite unconscious that they thereby betray the fact that they do not know themselves, and quite unaware that this notion of theirs, notwithstanding that it is certainly meant as praise of Christ, is really blasphemy, the blasphemy which is involved in the priest-prelate's undialectical loquacious climax: Christ was God *to such a degree* that one could at once *perceive* it directly—instead of saying as they ought: He was very God, and therefore *to such a degree* God that He was unrecognizable, so that it was not flesh and blood, but the exact opposite of flesh and blood, which prompted Peter to recognize Him.

And Christ has been completely poetized. They make of Him a man who was conscious of being the extraordinary figure, but of whom the contemporary age failed to take notice. So far this may be true. But they poetize farther, they go on to imagine that Christ would fain have been recognizable directly for the extraordinary figure He was, but that the contemporary age by reason of its blindness and iniquity would not understand Him. They betray by this that they do not understand in the least what an incognito is. It was Christ's free will and determination from all eternity to be incognito. So when people think to do Him honour by saying or thinking, 'If I had been contemporary with Him, I should have known Him directly', they really insult Him, and since it is Christ they insult, this means that they are blasphemous.

But most people do not, in a deeper sense, 'exist' at all, they have never made themselves existentially familiar with the thought of being incognito, that is, they have never sought to put such a thought into execution. Let us take simple human situations. When I wish to be incognito (whatever might be the reason for it, and whether I have a right to do it, are not questions we need here deal with), should I regard it as a compliment if one were to come up to me and say, 'I recognized you at once'? On the contrary, it is a satire upon me. But perhaps the satire was justified and my incognito a poor one. But now let us think of a man who was able to maintain his incognito: he *wills* to be incognito; he is willing, it is true, to be recognized, but not *directly*. In this case there is nothing to hinder him from being recognized directly for what he is, this disguise being in fact his free determination. But here we discover the secret: most people have no notion at all of the superiority by which a man transcends himself; and the superiority which willingly assumes an incognito of such a sort that one seems to be something much lowlier than one is they have no inkling of. Or if they have an inkling of it, they will surely think, 'What madness! What if the incognito were to be so successful that the man actually is taken for what he gives himself out to be!' Farther than this men seldom get, if they get so far. They discover here a self-contradiction, which in the service of the Good is really self-abnegation—the Good strives with might and main to maintain its incognito, and its incognito is that it is something less than it is. A man chooses then an incognito which makes him seem far lowlier than he is. He has in mind perhaps the Socratic maxim, that in order to will the Good truly, one must avoid the appearance of doing it.[1] The incognito is his free decision. He exerts himself to the utmost, employing all his inventiveness and intrepidity to maintain the incognito. This effort is either successful or unsuccessful. If it is successful, then he has, humanly speaking, done himself an injury, he has made everybody think very poorly of him. What self-abnegation! And, on the other hand, what an immense strain upon a man! For he had it in his power every instant to show himself in his real character. What self-abnegation! For what is self-abnegation without freedom? Oh, loftiest height of self-abnegation when the incognito succeeds so well that even if he now were inclined to speak directly, no one would believe him!

But that such superiority exists or could exist, no one has the least suspicion. How remote such a notion is one might learn by seeking to get from such a superior man direct communication, or might learn it in case the man of his own accord started to give it and then resumed his incognito. Let us think, for example, of a noble and sympathetic man who found it necessary to assume an incognito, either as a precaution or for any other reason what-soever. To this end he chooses, for example, to appear an egoist. Then the superior man discloses himself to another, shows his real character, and the other believes it, is impressed by it. So then they understand one another. The other perhaps supposes that he understands also the incognito—he does not observe that

[1] Plato's *Republic*, Book II, Glaucon's argument: 'There must be no seeming; for if the just man seems to be just, he will be honoured and rewarded, and then we shall not know whether he is just for the sake of justice.'

the incognito was in fact laid aside, and that he had reached that understanding by the aid of *direct* communication, that is, by the aid of him who *had been* incognito but was such no longer when he communicated to him the understanding. Let us now think that the superior man gets a notion, or for one reason or another finds it necessary, to erect again the incognito between the two who, as it was thought, understood one another. What then? Then it will be decided whether the other is just as great a dialectician as the first, or whether the other has faith in the possibility of such self-abnegation; that is to say, it will be decided whether the other possesses in himself the power to fathom the incognito, or to hold fast to his previous understanding in spite of it, or autonomously to understand it. The moment the superior man assumes the incognito he naturally does everything to maintain it, does nothing to help the other, but on the contrary excogitates the form most apt to deceive, i.e. to maintain his incognito. If now he is essentially the superior man, the device succeeds. The other makes at first a little resistance in the way of soliciting direct communication: '*This is a deceit*, you are not what you pretend.' But the incognito is maintained, no more direct communication follows, and the other returns to the opinion that the man is surely an egoist; perhaps he says, 'For a moment I believed in him, but now I too perceive that he is an egoist.' The fact is, he cannot hold fast the thought that this man would rather not be recognized as the good man he is, he can understand the incognito only so long as the unrecognizable man shows him by direct communication that it is an incognito and how it is such, in other words, so long as there is no incognito, or at least so long as the unrecognizable man is not in the role of unrecognizability and exerting all his powers to maintain it, leaving the other to make the best of it. So long as the first man helps him by direct communication about the unrecognizability, he can understand it—and he can understand the self-abnegation when in reality there is no more self-abnegation. That is, the other does not really believe in the possibility that such self-abnegation might exist.—Whether a man has a right to employ such mystification, whether he is able to do it, and if he were able to do it, whether the maieutical education of another man were not too great a responsibility, or on the other hand, whether it might not be his duty to do it, if it were done in self-abnegation and not in pride—I do not undertake to decide. Let this be regarded merely as a thought-experiment, which at least throws some light upon 'unrecognizableness'.[1]

And now in the case of the God-Man! He is God, but chooses to become the individual man. This, as we have seen, is the profoundest incognito, or the most impenetrable unrecognizableness that is possible; for the contradiction between being God and being an individual man is the greatest possible, the infinitely qualitative contradiction. But this is His will, His free determination, therefore an almightily maintained incognito. Indeed, He has in a certain sense, by suffering Himself to be born, bound Himself once for all; His incognito is so almightily maintained that in a way He is subjected to it, and the reality of His suffering consists in the fact that it is not merely apparent, but that in a sense the assumed incognito has power over Him. Only thus is there in the deepest sense real seriousness in the assertion that He became 'very man', and hence also He experiences the extremest suffering of feeling Himself forsaken of God, so that at no moment was He beyond suffering, but actually in it, and He encountered the purely human experience that reality is even more terrible than possibility, that He who had freely assumed unrecognizableness yet really suffers as though He were entrapped in unrecognizableness or had entrapped Himself. It is a strange sort of dialectic: that He who almightily . . . binds Himself, and does it so almightily that He actually feels Himself bound, suffers under the consequences of the fact that He lovingly and freely determined to become an individual man— to such a degree was it seriously true that He became a real man; but thus it must be if He were to become the sign of contradiction which reveals the thoughts of the hearts.—It is the imperfection of a man's disguise that he has the arbitrary faculty of annulling it at any instant. A disguise is the more completely serious the more one knows how to restrain this faculty and to make it less and less possible. But the unrecognizableness of the God-Man is an incognito almightily maintained, and the divine seriousness

---

[1] The reader will easily perceive that this 'thought-experiment' is designed to throw some light upon the case of Peter. But one who knows S. K. will as easily perceive the personal quality in the whole passage, the pathos which lies in the fact that S. K. had for many years maintained his incognito as the least 'serious' man in Denmark—and now began to doubt whether any *man* has a right to employ such mystification and deceit, even with the noble aim of educating people maieutically.

consists precisely in the fact that it is so almightily maintained that He Himself suffers under His unrecognizableness in a purely human way.

Note. One can easily perceive that direct communication is an impossibility, if only one will be so kind as to take the Communicator into account, and if one is not so *distrait* as to forget Christ when thinking of Christianity. In the case of unrecognizableness, or for one who is in this case, direct communication is an impossibility; for direct communication declares what one essentially is—but unrecognizableness means not being in the role which essentially belongs to one; so that here we have a contradiction which transforms direct communication into non-direct communication, that is to say, makes direct communication impossible. If there is to be a direct communication which remains direct communication, one must step out of one's incognito, for otherwise that which in the first instance is direct communication (the direct assertion) becomes in the second instance (in view of the communicator's incognito) non-direct communication.

§ 3

The impossibility of direct communication

The opposite of direct communication is indirect communication. The latter can be produced in either of two ways.

Indirect communication can be produced by the art of reduplicating the communication. This art consists in reducing oneself, the communicator, to nobody, something purely objective, and then incessantly composing qualitative opposites into unity. This is what some of the pseudonyms[1] are accustomed to call 'double reflection'. An example of such indirect communica-

---

[1] Another proof that in writing this work S. K. did not think of publishing it pseudonymously. The reference is really to *one* pseudonym, Johannes Climacus, who in the *Postscript* explains fully, but none too clearly, what is meant by 'double reflection'. I venture diffidently to express the gist of the matter in my own words. Whereas the objective thinker can perfectly well communicate directly the *result* of his own reflection, 'the subjective existing thinker' discovers an impediment to communication in the further reflection that the truth he arrives at 'interests' his existence (is part and parcel of it) and as such cannot simply be handed over to another, but to be appropriated, to become one's own, it must be acquired through the same process of reflection by which it was originally reached. Hence the communication must be indirect, *artfully* devised to prompt the other to think out the thing for himself, while the subjectivity of the communicator remains concealed.

tion is, so to compose jest and earnest that the composition is a dialectical knot—and with this to be nobody. If anyone is to profit by this sort of communication, he must himself undo the knot for himself. Another example is, to bring defence and attack together in such a unity that no one can say directly whether one is attacking or defending, so that both the most zealous partisans of the cause and its bitterest enemies can regard one as an ally— and with this to be nobody, an absentee, an objective something, not a personal man. If at a given time faith had vanished as it were from the world, had to be advertised for among 'lost articles', then it might perhaps be profitable to lure faith dialectically— whether it might really be profitable I do not, however, decide.[1] But here is an example of indirect communication, or communica- tion by double reflection: one presents faith in an eminent sense, and makes the presentation in such a way that the most orthodox sees in it a defence of faith, and the free-thinker an attack, whereas the communicator is null, a no man, an objective something— and yet perhaps he is a dexterous spy who by aid of the communi- cation succeeds in ascertaining which is which, who is the believer, who the freethinker; for this is revealed by the way they judge the production which is neither attack nor defence.

But indirect communication can be brought about also in another way, by the relationship between the communication and the communicator. Whereas in the former case the communicator was left out of account, here he is a factor, but (be it noted) with a negative reflection. Our age, however, knows in fact no other way of communication but the mediocre way of lecturing. People have quite forgotten what it is to 'exist'. All communica- tion which has regard to 'existence' requires a communicator—in other words, the communication is the reduplication of that which is communicated; to reduplicate is to 'exist' in what one understands.[2] But the mere fact that there is a communicator

[1] A strange admission when one remembers the vehemence with which Johannes Climacus of the *Postscript* affirmed the *necessity* of double reflection in every case where faith (i.e. subjective truth) had to be communicated. In fact, S. K. had begun to doubt whether such an intricate art is ever permissible or profitable—and this implied a reflection upon the futility of his pseudonymous authorship as a whole. The 'examples' he gives here aptly exemplify his methods, and the importance of reducing to nil the personality of the communicator suggests one of his reasons for writing pseudonymously.

[2] 'Reduplication' is not, like 'double reflection', an artful method, but the

who himself exists in that which he communicates does not suffice to characterize such communication as indirect communication. If, however, the communicator himself is dialectically qualified, and his own essential *being* requires reflective definition, all direct communication is impossible.

Such is the case with the God-Man. He is a sign, the sign of contradiction, and so all direct communication is impossible. For if the communication by a communicator is to be direct, it does not suffice that the communication itself is direct, but the communicator himself must be directly qualified. If not, then even the most direct communication of such a communicator becomes, by reason of the communicator, i.e. by reason of what the communicator is, non-direct communication.

When one says directly, 'I am God; the Father and I are one', that is direct communication. But when he who says it is an individual man, quite like other men, then this communication is not just perfectly direct; for it is not just perfectly clear and direct that an individual man should be God—although what he says is perfectly direct. By reason of the communicator the communication contains a contradiction, it becomes indirect communication, it puts to thee a choice, whether thou wilt believe Him or not.

One might well weep at the state Christianity has been reduced to in Christendom, considering what the parsons in their sermons again and again repeat, with the utmost assurance, as if they were saying something most striking and convincing. What they say is that Christ directly affirmed that He was God, the Only Begotten of the Father; they are horrified at any suggestion of concealment, as a thing unworthy of Christ, as vain trifling with regard to a serious matter, the most serious matter of all, the salvation of man. Ah, such parsons do not know what they are talking about, it is hidden from their eyes that they are doing away with Christianity. He who to the Jews was a stumbling-block and to the Greeks foolishness, the mystery through which

transformation of one's life or way of living in accordance with the truth one objectively knows—something therefore which goes much deeper than the intellectual act of subjective appropriation of truth. 'Existence' has here (as everywhere else in S. K.'s writings where it renders the word *Existenz*) not the meaning of mere being, but it has in view the actual character and quality of one's living. The meaning would be more promptly understood if it were translated by 'life'; but since the word has become so important by reason of the so-called Existential Philosophy in Germany, we must learn to understand the word in the sense here indicated.

everything is revealed, but in a mystery—humanly they transform Him into some sort of a public person as it were, almost as
serious as the Parson; if one will but put oneself to the trouble
of saying to Him directly with indolent good humour, 'Tell me now
seriously', then without any fear and trembling before the Deity,
without the death-struggle which is the birth-throe of faith, without the shudder which is the first experience of worship, without
the dread of the possibility of offence, one learns to know directly
that which cannot be known directly.

Yes indeed, Christ said quite directly that He was the Only
Begotten of the Father—that is, *the sign of contradiction* said this
quite directly—but what does this mean? Lo, here we are back
again at the same spot. If He is the sign of contradiction, then
He cannot give direct communication; that is to say, the utterance may be quite direct, but the fact that He is involved, that
He who says this is the sign of contradiction, turns it into indirect
communication. Yes indeed, it is true that Christ said, 'Believe
in me', and that is in fact a perfectly direct utterance. But now
when He who says it is the sign of contradiction—what then?
Why, then, this direct utterance in His mouth is the precise
expression of the fact that this thing of believing is not something
quite so direct, or that even this challenge of His to believe is
indirect communication.

And now as regards *seriousness*—these parsons have just as
much understanding of seriousness as of Christianity in general.
The seriousness consists precisely in the fact that Christ cannot
give direct communication, that the single direct utterance can
only serve, like the miracle, to make people attentive, so that once
a man is made attentive by being offended at the contradiction,
he can chose whether he will believe or not.

But they confuse the Christian conceptions in every way. They
make Christ a speculative unity of God and man; or they throw
Christ away altogether and take His teaching; or for sheer seriousness they make Christ a false god. Spirit is the negation of direct
immediacy. If Christ is very God, He must also be unrecognizable, He must assume unrecognizableness, which is the negation of all directness. Direct recognizableness is precisely the
characteristic of the pagan god. But this is what they reduce
Christ to, and that is taken for seriousness; they take a direct
utterance and fantastically construct a figure corresponding to

it (preferably sentimental: the gentle look, the kindly eye, or whatever else may occur to such a silly parson), and so it is *directly* quite certain that Christ is God.

Oh, how loathsome is this sentimental frivolity! No, at so cheap a price one does not by any means attain to become a Christian. He is the sign of contradiction, and by the direct utterance He merely rivets thine attention upon Him, that thou mayest be offended at the contradiction and the thoughts of thy heart may be revealed in the act of choosing whether thou wilt believe or not.

§ 4

The impossibility of direct communication is in Christ the mystery of His suffering

Much has been said and often, especially in earlier ages, about the sufferings of Christ, how He was derided, scourged, and crucified. But with this they seem to forget an entirely different sort of suffering, the suffering of inwardness, soul-suffering, or what one might call the mystery of His suffering, which was inseparable from a life lived in unrecognizableness, from the moment of His public appearance up to the last.

It is always painful to have to hide a heart-felt emotion and to seem to be other than one is—such is the case in a merely human relationship. Of all human suffering it is the hardest to bear, and he who suffers thus, suffers, alas, more in one day than by all bodily tortures taken together. I do not presume to decide whether such collisions actually occur, or whether a man who experiences such a collision does not also sin every instant he remains in it—I speak only of the suffering. The collision is that out of love for another one must hide a heart-felt emotion and seem to be other than one is. The pains are purely of the soul, and they are as composite as they possibly can be. But it is far from being a good thing that a pain is composite, for with every new combination it acquires an additional sting. The painfulness of this experience lies first in one's own suffering; for if it is blessed to belong to another in the perfect understanding of love or friendship, it is painful to keep to oneself this inwardness of feeling. In the next place it is suffering on account of the other; for that which in reality is the solicitude of love, of a love which is willing to do anything, even to sacrifice life for the other, finds expression here in something which has a dreadful likeness to the supremest cruelty—ah, and yet it was love! Finally the painfulness lies in the suffering of responsibility. So this is what it comes to: out of love to annihilate one's own love in its immediacy, while yet conserving it; out of love to be cruel to the beloved; out of love to assume this immense responsibility.[1]

But now in the case of the God-Man! The true God *cannot* become directly recognizable; but direct recognizableness is what the merely human, what the men to whom He came, would pray and implore of Him as the greatest alleviation. And it was out of love He became man! He is love; and yet every instant He exists he must crucify as it were all human compassion and solicitude—for He can only be the object of faith. But everything that goes by the name of human sympathy has to do with direct recognizableness. Yet in such a way He does not become the object of '*faith*', He is not very God; and if He is not very God, He does not save men. So by that step which He took for love's sake he precipitated the individual, the whole human race, once for all, into the most dreadful strife of decision. Yea, it is as though there were to be heard a lamentable cry from human compassion, 'Oh, wherefore dost Thou do this?' And yet He does it for love's sake, He does it to save men. But out there in the midst of that dreadful strife of decision He must hold men at a distance, if ever they are to belong to Him, as saved through faith —and He is love. Out of love He would do everything for men.

---

[1] Here S. K. recounts his most personal history, the poignant experience of the breach of his engagement to Regina Olsen, the beautiful girl who with all her heart responded to his affection, but whom he had to put away because a 'divine veto' prohibited his marriage—and whom he had to put away in the cruellest fashion, pretending that he was a scoundrel who had basely won her affection without reciprocating it. And all this cruelty out of love, that she might be set free from her attachment. One may wonder that a revelation so personal was included in a book which was written for publication. But S. K. knew that to the public it would reveal nothing. For he was so 'entrapped' in his incognito that he could not divest himself of it. In fact, no one had a suspicion that he was talking here about himself. The doubt he expresses, 'whether such collisions actually occur', was a thin disguise, but it was not needed. The other doubt, whether every instant of such deception might not be sin, represents his mature reflection upon the strangest and most outrageous incognito he ever assumed. When I say that 'no one' understood, I remember that Regina was the one exception. S. K. expected her to understand, and desired it; for at the moment when the book was published he was hoping for a friendly *rapprochement*.

He stakes His life for them, He suffers for them the shameful death—and for them He suffers also this life of His, the constant necessity of being so hard (humanly speaking), out of divine love and compassion, over against which all human love and compassion and mercy are to be accounted nothing. His life as a whole is the suffering of inwardness. And then when the last period of His life begins with betrayal by night, He suffers also bodily pain and ill-treatment; He suffers at being betrayed by a friend; at standing alone, derided, scourged, spat upon, wearing the crown of thorns and clad in purple, alone with His, humanly speaking, lost cause ('Behold, what a man!'); alone among His furious enemies (dreadful environment!); forsaken by all His friends (frightful lonesomeness!). Yet a man also may suffer in this way, may suffer from the desertion of his best friend—but then that is all; if this is endured, then the cup of man's suffering is drained. Here, on the contrary, it is filled up again with the bitterest drink: He suffers for the fact that this suffering of His may and does become an offence to the few believers. Truly He suffered once for all, but He is not let off like men with the endurance of suffering in its first instance, He experiences the bitterest suffering in the second instance, in His concern and solicitude over the fact that His suffering is an occasion of offence.

No man can comprehend this suffering, and the wish to comprehend it is presumptuous.

As for myself[1] personally who am endeavouring to present this subject, a little explanation may perhaps be due to the reader. Possibly I betray here and there such a knowledge of hidden inwardness, of the genuine suffering of self-denial, that possibly it might occur to some one that, though such a 'natural' man, I am yet of that ilk, one of those rare noble souls. This is very far from the truth. It is true that in a strange way—and that not precisely by reason of my virtue, but rather of my fault—I have become very thoroughly acquainted with the mysteries of 'existence', and also with its mysteriousness, which for many persons certainly have no existence. Of this I do not boast, for it was not due to my virtue. But I endeavour honestly to use this knowledge to illuminate the humanly True and the humanly Good. And

---

[1] It must have been clear to the first readers of the book that in this last paragraph S. K. is speaking in his own person, and very personally—that it is not Anti-Climacus.

I use it again to draw attention if possible to the Holy—concerning which, however, I constantly adjoin that this is something no man can comprehend, that in this relationship the beginning and the end is worship. For even if one were to comprehend, and entirely comprehend, the purely human; such understanding nevertheless is misunderstanding in relation to the God-Man. No one knows as well as I what responsibility I incur [in thus using my knowledge]. Let no one be at pains to affright me with it, for I stand in a relationship of fear and trembling to Him who can affright me on quite a different scale. But also there certainly are not many who understand as I do that in Christendom they have done away with Christianity.

§ 5

The possibility of offence lies in the refusal to employ direct communication

The possibility of offence is, as we have endeavoured to show, every instant present, and constitutes at every instant the yawning gulf between the individual and the God-Man, across which only faith can reach. So it is not (as I must again and again repeat) an accidental relation, as if some people noticed the possibility of offence and others did not. No, the possibility of offence is the stumbling-block for all, whether they chose to believe or to be offended.

So the communication begins with a thrust backward. But to begin with a thrust backward is to refuse to employ direct communication. This is readily perceived. It presents itself almost sensibly to the eye. What presents itself directly cannot be said to begin by repelling; but what presents itself thus cannot be said to present itself directly. On the other hand, it cannot be said simply that it repels; for it presents itself, but in such a way that it at first repels.

But take away the possibility of offence, as they have done in Christendom, and the whole of Christianity is direct communication; and then Christianity is done away with, for it has become an easy thing, a superficial something which neither wounds nor heals profoundly enough; it is the false invention of human sympathy which forgets the infinite qualitative difference between God and man.

§ 6

To refuse to employ direct communication is to require faith

The possibility of offence, which is the situation at the beginning, is in the deepest understanding of it an expression for the necessity of calling attention, or for the fact that there is required of man the greatest attention possible (on a scale entirely different from the merely human, for it is on the divine scale) with respect to the decision to become a believer. Direct communication also, perhaps, seeks to make the receiver of it attentive as well as it can; it begs and beseeches him, impresses upon his heart the importance of it, warns and threatens, &c.—all of which is direct communication, and hence there is not seriousness enough in it for the highest decision, nor does it sufficiently arouse attention.

No, the beginning is made by refusing direct communication—that is real seriousness. Frightful is the possibility of offence, and yet (like the Law in relation to the Gospel) it belongs essentially to seriousness. There is no direct communication, and no direct reception—there is a choice. It does not, like direct communication, employ enticement and warning and threatening—and then gradually and quite unobserved the transition is brought about little by little, to the point of accepting it, of regarding oneself as convinced by it, of being of the opinion, &c. No, an altogether distinct sort of reception is required—that of faith. And faith itself has a dialectical quality—and the receiver is the one who is revealed, whether he will believe or be offended.

But modern philosophy as a whole has done everything to delude us into the notion that faith has an immanent quality, that it is immanency; and this in turn is connected with the fact that they have done away with the possibility of offence, made Christianity a doctrine, done away with the God-Man and the situation of contemporaneousness. What the modern philosophy understands by faith is what properly is called an opinion, or what is loosely called in everyday speech believing. Christianity is made into a doctrine; this doctrine is then preached to a person, and then he believes that it is so, as this teacher says. The next stage therefore is to comprehend this doctrine—and that is what philosophy does. On the whole, this is quite right, in case Christianity were a doctrine; but since it is not that, this is a crazy proceeding. Faith in a pregnant sense has to do with the

God-Man. But the God-Man, the sign of contradiction, refuses to employ direct communication—and demands faith.

That indirect communication requires faith can be demonstrated very simply in the case of a purely human relationship, if only it be remembered that faith in the most eminent sense has to do with the God-Man. Let us carry out the demonstration, and to this end let us take the relationship between two lovers. I assume first this relationship: the lover gives the beloved assurance of his love in the most burning expressions, and his whole nature corresponds to this assurance, is almost sheer adoration—then he asks the beloved, '*Do you believe* that I love you?' Then the beloved answers, '*Yes, I believe*'. This assuredly is the way we use the word. Now let us assume, on the other hand, that the lover gets a notion to wish to put the beloved to the test, whether she believes him. What does he do then? He cuts out all direct communication, he transforms himself into a duplex being; to all appearance it is as plausible to take him for a deceiver as for the faithful lover. Thus he makes himself a riddle. But what is a riddle? A riddle is a question. And what does the question ask? It asks whether she believes him.—I do not decide whether he has a right to do this, I am merely following the indications of thought; and in any case it should be remembered that the maieutic teacher does this very thing up to a certain point; he erects the dialectical duplexity, but with the opposite intent of turning the other person away from him, of turning him in upon himself, of making him free, not of drawing the man towards him.—One will easily see what is the difference in the lover's behaviour in these two instances. In the first case he asks the question directly: 'Do you believe me?' In the second case the question is the same, but he has made himself an interrogation. He may perhaps have cause to regret bitterly that he presumed to do such a thing—I am not concerned here with such possibilities, I am merely following the indications of thought. And from a dialectical point of view it is quite certain that the latter method is a far more fundamental way of eliciting faith. The aim of the latter method is to reveal the heart of the beloved in a choice; for in this duplex possibility she is obliged to choose which character she believes to be the true one. If then she chooses the good possibility, it is revealed that she believes in him. This reveals itself, for he does nothing whatever to assist her; on the contrary, by his duplexity he has placed her in a completely solitary position, without any support whatsoever. He is a duplexity, and now the question is what judgement she will form of him; but he has another understanding of the situation, for he perceives that it is not he that is being judged, but that she is revealed by the way she judges. Whether he has a right to do this is a question I do not decide, I am merely following the indications of thought. His procedure (which perhaps occasions him indescribable suffering from inquietude and anxiety so long as he continues it) involves at one and the same time an inhuman, almost icy indifference, and yet the most intense passion.[1] But he requires faith, and dialectically he is in the right in thinking that when one gets direct communication this thing of believing is altogether too direct.

And something like this, Christianity has always understood by faith. The God-Man must require faith and must refuse direct communication. In a certain sense He can do no otherwise, and He would do no otherwise. As God-Man He is qualitatively different from every other man and therefore must refuse direct communication, He requires faith, requires that He become the *object of faith*.

In the relationship between man and man the one man must be content with the assurance of the other that he believes him. No man has a right to make himself an object of faith for another man. In case one man employs dialectical duplexity in relationship with another, he must employ it maieutically, for the sake of not becoming for the other the object of faith or anything approximating to it. The dialectical duplexity is a transitory factor, and in the next stage it becomes absolute untruthfulness

[1] Here again S. K. obviously has in mind his own experience. Although in the first instance his duplicity was not designed to draw Regina to him or to make test of her faith, but rather to thrust her from him and make her free; nevertheless, until her engagement to another man, he could not altogether dismiss the hope that on a higher plane of understanding they might again come together and experience a 'repetition'. His first great book was an either/or secretly addressed to 'her', asking whether she regarded him as a sensualist and seducer, or as a moral man with serious religious convictions. Having reason to think that she stood this test, his next two books (*Repetition* and *Fear and Trembling*) were again addressed to her, and now with a more definite hope of a 'repetition'—which even before the books were published was deluded by the news of her engagement to another. In this passage S. K. recalls his 'suffering from unrest and anxiety'. He also raises again the question of his responsibility—'whether a man has a right to do such a thing'.

if, instead of employing it merely to parry with, he presumptuously permits another man to regard him as an object of faith. Yet even with respect to maieutic teaching I do not decide how far, from a Christian point of view, it can be approved.

But only the God-Man can do no other[1] and must require that He be the object of faith. If He is not this, He is an idol—hence He must refuse direct communication because he must require faith.

§ 7

The object of faith is the God-Man precisely because the God-Man is the possibility of offence

So inseparable from faith is the possibility of offence that if the God-Man were not the possibility of offence, He could not be the object of faith. So the possibility of offence is assumed in faith, assimilated by faith, it is the negative mark of the God-Man. For if the possibility of offence were lacking, direct communication would be in place, and thus the God-Man would be an idol. Direct recognizableness is paganism.

But observe what a poor service one renders Christianity by doing away with the possibility of offence and making it an amiable, sentimental paganism.

For this is the law: he who has done away with faith has done away with the possibility of offence (as when speculation substitutes comprehension for faith); and he who does away with the possibility of offence does away with faith (as when the languishing sermon of the parson mendaciously attributes to Christ direct recognizableness). But whether one does away with faith or with the possibility of offence, one does away at the same time with something else—the God-Man. And if one does away with the God-Man, one does away with Christianity.

And verily the eighteen centuries, which have not contributed an iota to prove the truth of Christianity, have on the contrary contributed with steadily increasing power to do away with Christianity. It is by no means true, as one might consistently suppose when one acclaims the proof of the eighteen centuries, that now in the nineteenth century people are far more thoroughly convinced of the truth of Christianity than they were in the first and second generations—it is rather true (though it certainly sounds

[1] S. K. often uses Luther's expression at the Diet of Worms.

rather like a satire on the worshippers and adorers of this proof)
that just in proportion as the proof supposedly has increased in
cogency . . . fewer and fewer persons are convinced. But this is
what results when the decisive point in some question is neglected:
frightful confusions may be produced, and such as increase from
generation to generation. Now that Christianity has been *proved*,
and on a prodigious scale, there is nobody, or next to nobody,
willing to make any sacrifice for it. When people (shall I say,
'only'?) believed in the truth of it, they were ready to sacrifice life
and blood. Oh, frightful infatuation! Oh, that there were someone (like the heathen who burnt the libraries of Alexandria) able
to get these eighteen centuries out of the way—if no one can do
that, then Christianity is abolished. Oh, that there were someone
capable of making it clear to these many orators who prove the
truth of Christianity by the 1,800 years—that there were someone
who could make it clear to them (terrible as it is) that they are
betraying, denying, abolishing Christianity—if no one can do
that, then Christianity is done away with.

TRAINING IN CHRISTIANITY

by

Anti-Climacus

Part III

FROM ON HIGH
HE WILL DRAW ALL
UNTO HIMSELF

Christian Expositions

by
Anti-Climacus

EDITOR'S PREFACE

See Preface to Part II

I*

Prayer

O LORD Jesus Christ, there is so much to drag us back: empty pursuits, trivial pleasures, unworthy cares. There is so much to frighten us away: a pride too cowardly to submit to being helped, cowardly apprehensiveness which evades danger to its own destruction, anguish for sin which shuns holy cleansing as disease shuns medicine. But Thou art stronger than these, so draw Thou us now more strongly to Thee. We call Thee our Saviour and Redeemer, since Thou didst come to earth to redeem us from the servitude under which we were bound or had bound ourselves, and to save the lost. This is Thy work, which Thou didst complete, and which Thou wilt continue to complete unto the end of the world; for since Thou Thyself hast said it, therefore Thou wilt do it—lifted up from the earth Thou wilt draw all unto Thee.

John 12: 32. AND I, IF I BE LIFTED UP FROM THE EARTH, WILL DRAW ALL UNTO MYSELF.

From on high He will draw all unto Himself.

Devout hearer, if a man's life is not to be led unworthily, like that of the beast which never erects its head, if it is not to be

---

* This discourse was delivered by Magister Kierkegaard in the Church of Our Lady on Friday, Sept. 1st, 1848. Since it is this which furnished me with the title [to Part III], I have printed it here with his consent. Also, in order to round off the whole with a conclusion answerable to this beginning, I have composed No. 7 in the same tone of mildness, and with that I have deviated in a measure from my role [of austere admonition].—The above note, as the asterisk shows, is by Anti-Climacus; but I would call attention to the fact that it was four and a half months earlier, on April·18th, that this title was suggested to S. K. in the same church where this discourse was delivered, and that he then proposed to write 'seven discourses', which are evidently the 'seven reflections' comprised in Part III. In this case, therefore, as in the case of *Either/Or*, the last part of the book was written before the first, and the reader will perceive that the themes so 'mildly' presented here were later more definitely thought out and more strongly presented—with the emphasis of constant repetition which was justified as well as occasioned by men's dullness of hearing.—It needs to be observed that in Denmark the people were accustomed to communicate on Fridays, and that all of S. K.'s 'discourses on Fridays', if not actually delivered before the Holy Communion, were written in view of such an occasion—'at the foot of the altar'.

frittered away, being emptily employed with what while it lasts is vanity and when it is past is nothingness, or busily employed with what makes a noise indeed at the moment but has no echo in eternity—if a man's life is not to be dozed away in inactivity or wasted in bustling movement, there must be something higher which draws it. Now this 'something higher' may be something very various; but if it is to be truly capable of drawing, and at every instant, it must not itself be subject to 'variableness or the shadow of turning',[1] but must have passed triumphantly through every change and become transfigured like the transfigured life of a dead man.[2] And now, as there is only one name that is named among the living, the Lord Jesus Christ, so also there is only one dead man who yet lives, the Lord Jesus Christ. He from *on high* will draw all unto Himself. See, therefore, how rightly oriented is the Christian life, directed towards that which is above, towards Him who from on high will draw Christians unto Himself—in case the Christians remember Him, and he who does **not** is surely no Christian. And thou, my hearer, thou to whom this discourse is addressed, thou art come here to-day in *remembrance* of Him.

It follows as a matter of course that if He is to be able from on high to draw Christians unto Himself, there is much that has to be forgotten, much that has to be looked away from, much that has to be died from. How can this be done? Oh, in case thou, in deep distress, perhaps in distress for thy future, thy life's happiness, hast ever heartily wished to forget something: a disappointed expectation, a shattered hope, a bitter and embittering memory; or in case thou, in anxiety, alas, for thy soul's salvation, hast wished still more heartily to forget something: anguish at some sin which constantly confronts thee, a terrifying thought which will not leave thee—then thou hast surely experienced how empty is the advice the world gives when it says, 'Try to forget it!' That indeed is only a hollow mockery, if it is anything at all. No, if there is something thou art fain to forget, try to get something else to remember, and then it will succeed. Therefore if Christianity requires Christians to forget something, and in a certain sense to forget everything, to forget the multifarious, it also recommends the means: to remember something

---

[1] James 1: 17 was S. K.'s favourite text, and the text of many of his discourses.

[2] Doubtless S. K. was thinking of his father's life as it was transfigured for him.

else, to remember one thing, the Lord Jesus Christ. Therefore in case thou art aware that the world's pleasures enthral thee and thou art fain to forget, in case thou art aware that earthly anxieties distress thee so that thou art fain to forget, in case thou art aware that the bustle of life carries thee away as the current carries the swimmer, and thou art fain to forget, in case the dread of temptation overpowers thee and thou art heartily fain to forget—then remember Him, the Lord Jesus Christ, and it will succeed. If indeed it might be possible for thee—as now to-day thou eatest bread and drinkest wine in remembrance of Him—if it might be possible for thee to have Him in remembrance every day as thy constant thought in everything thou undertakest to do—with this thou wouldst also have forgotten everything that ought to be forgotten, thou wouldst be as forgetful as a feeble old man with regard to everything that ought to be forgotten, as oblivious to it all as one who in a foreign land has forgotten his mother tongue and babbles without meaning, as oblivious as the absent-minded —thou wouldst be completely drawn to the heights with Him who from on high will draw all unto Himself.[1]

From on high He will draw all unto Himself.

From on high—for here upon earth He went about in lowliness, in the lowly form of a servant, in poverty and wretchedness, in suffering. This indeed was Christianity, not that a rich man makes the poor rich, but that the poorest of all makes all men rich, both the rich and the poor. And this indeed was Christianity, not that it is the happy man who comforts the afflicted, but that it is He who of all men is the most afflicted.—He will draw all to Himself—*draw* them to Himself, for He would *entice* no one. To draw to Himself truly, means in *one* sense to repel men. In thy nature and in mine and in that of every man there is something He would do away with; with respect to all this He repels men. Lowliness and humiliation are the stone of stumbling, the possibility of offence, and thou art situated between His humiliation which lies behind, and the exaltation—this is the reason why it is said that He draws to Himself. To entice is an untrue way of drawing to Himself; but He would entice no one; humiliation

---

[1] It is remarkable that at this very same time Horace Bushnell, who was nine years older than S. K., was preaching in America the same doctrine of 'the expulsive power of a new affection', affection for the Lord Jesus Christ.

belongs to Him just as essentially as exaltation. In case there was one who could love Him only in His exaltation—such a man's vision is confused, he knows not Christ, neither loves Him at all, but takes Him in vain. Christ was the truth [in His humiliation] and is the truth. If then one can love Him only in His exaltation, what does that signify? It signifies that he can love the truth . . . only when it has conquered, when it is in possession of and surrounded by power and honour and glory. But while it was in conflict it was foolishness, to the Jews a stumbling-block, to the Greeks a foolish thing. So long as it was scorned, ridiculed, and (as the Scripture says) spat upon, he desired to hold himself aloof from it. Thus he desired to keep the truth from him, but this in fact means precisely to be in untruth. It is as essential for 'the truth' to suffer in this world as to triumph in another world, the world of truth—and Christ Jesus is the same in His humiliation as in His exaltation. But, on the other hand, in case one could feel himself drawn to Christ and able to love Him only in His humiliation, in case such a man would refuse to hear anything about this exaltation when power and honour and glory are His— in case (oh, pitiable perversity!), with the impatience of an unstable mind, tired (as he would express it) of Christendom's triumphant boast of 'seeing good days', he longs only for the spectacle of horror, to be with Him when He was scorned and persecuted— such a man's vision also is confused, he knows not Christ, neither loves Him at all. For melancholy is no closer to Christianity than light mindedness,[1] both are equally worldly, equally remote from Christianity, both equally in need of conversion.

My hearer, thou to whom my discourse is addressed,[2] thou who to-day art come in His remembrance, our Lord Jesus Christ's, art come hither as drawn by Him who from on high will draw all unto Himself. But it is precisely on this day thou art reminded of His humiliation, His suffering and death, so that it is He that draws thee to Him. Though He is raised up on high, He has not forgotten thee—and thou art not forgetful of His humiliation,

---

[1] *Tungsind/Letsind*—literally, heavy-minded/light-minded. Here S. K. evidently condemns his own melancholy, which in its darkest periods disposed him to a gloomy and 'perverse' view of Christianity.

[2] It is characteristic of S. K. that even in public addresses he singled out 'that individual'—'my hearer', not hearers. For this reason I feel bound to use the second person singular, notwithstanding that it is strange to our ears, except as we read the Bible.

dost love Him in His humiliation, but at the same time dost love His glorious revelation.

From on high He will draw all unto Himself.

It is now eighteen centuries since He left the earth and ascended up on high. Since that time the form of the world has undergone more than one change, thrones have been erected and overthrown, great names have cropped up and been forgotten; and on a smaller scale, in thy daily life, changes regularly occur, the sun rises and sets, the wind shifts in its courses, now something new is sought out and soon is forgotten again, and again something new—and from Him, in a certain sense, we hear nothing. And yet He has said that from on high He will draw all unto Himself. So also on high He is not resting, but He works hitherto, employed and concerned with drawing all unto Himself. Amazing! Thus thou beholdest in nature all about thee the many forces stirring; but the power which supports all thou dost not behold, thou seest not God's almightiness—and yet it is fully certain that He also works, that a single instant without Him, and the world is nothing. So likewise He is invisible on high, yet everywhere present, employed in drawing all unto Himself—while in this world, alas, there is worldly talk about everything else but Him, as though He did not exist. He employs the most various things as the way and the means of drawing unto Himself—but this we cannot dwell upon here, least of all to-day, when a period unusually short is prescribed for the address, because the sacred action predominates and the Communion is our divine service. But though the means He employs are so many, all ways come together at one point, the consciousness of sin—through that passes 'the way' by which He draws a man, the repentant sinner, to Himself.

My hearer, thou to whom my discourse is addressed, thou who to-day art come hither in remembrance of Him to partake of a holy feast, the Lord's Supper—to-day thou didst go first to confession before coming to the altar. From on high He hath drawn thee to Himself, but it was through the consciousness of sin. For He will not entice all to Himself, He will draw all to Himself.

From on high He will draw all unto Himself.

My hearer, thou to whom my discourse is addressed! To-day He is indeed with thee, as though He were come nearer, as though

He were touching the earth. He is present at the altar where thou seekest Him; He is present—but only in order to draw thee from on high unto Himself. For because thou dost feel thyself drawn to Him, and therefore art come hither to-day, it does not necessarily follow that thou mayest venture to conceive that He has already drawn thee entirely to Himself. 'Lord, increase my faith.' He who made that prayer was not an unbeliever but a believer; and so it is also with this prayer, 'Lord, draw me entirely to Thee'; for he who rightly makes this prayer must already feel himself drawn. Ah, and is it not true that precisely to-day, and precisely because thou dost feel thyself drawn, thou wilt to-day be ready to admit how much is still lacking, how far thou art from being drawn entirely to Him—drawn up on high, far from all the base and the earthly which hold thee back? Ah, it is not I, my hearer, nor any other man, that says this to thee, or might presume to say it. No, every man has enough to do with saying this to himself. I do not know, my hearer, who thou art, how far He has perhaps already drawn thee to Himself, how far perhaps thou art advanced beyond me and many another in the way of being a Christian— but God grant that this day, whoever thou art, and whereunto-soever thou hast attained, thou who art come hither to-day to partake of the holy feast of the Lord's Supper—that this day may be to thee truly blessed; God grant that at this sacred moment thou mayest thyself be entirely drawn to Him and be sensible of His presence. He is there—He from whom in a sense thou dost separate when thou departest from the altar, but who nevertheless will not forget thee if thou dost not forget Him; yea, will not forget thee even when, alas, thou dost sometimes forget Him, who from on high continues to draw thee unto Himself, until the last blessed end when thou shalt be by Him, and with Him on high.

II

O LORD Jesus Christ, weak is our foolish heart, and only too ready to let itself be drawn—and there is so much that would draw it to itself. There is pleasure with its seducing power, the manifold with its confusing distractions, the moment with its deceptive importance, and bustle with its vain toil, and frivolity's careless squandering of time, and melancholy's gloomy brooding—all of these would draw us away from our own self and to them, in order to deceive us. But Thou who art the truth, only Thou our Saviour and Redeemer, canst truly draw a man to Thee, which indeed Thou hast promised to do, to draw all unto Thyself. So God grant that we by entering into our selves may come to our selves, so that Thou, according to Thy word, canst draw us to Thee—from on high, but through lowliness and humiliation.

JOHN 12: 32. AND I, IF I BE LIFTED UP FROM THE EARTH, WILL DRAW ALL UNTO MYSELF

Devout hearer, let us first, by way of introduction, get clearly in mind what precisely is contained in the thought of *drawing unto oneself*, so that we may understand the better and the more inwardly what is meant by the sacred text which has just been read: that *Christ*, lifted up from the earth (i.e. *from on high*), will *draw* all *unto Himself*.

What does it mean to draw to oneself? Is it not fundamentally false to use the expression, 'draw to itself', for that which only deceitfully draws to itself, or draws to itself in order to receive, or deceives by drawing to itself?[1] For in such a case it would be more correct and more truthful to say simply, 'it deceives'—not one word more. If in such a case a man says, 'It draws', it is as if for an instant he would suppress the decisive point, as if for an instant he would linger upon the first and not come out at once with the decisive word—though truth is always prompt of speech and hastily flees

[1] The sentence sounds flat because it is impossible to render in English the play on words: *bedragende bedrage* (deceivingly draws); and in the following paragraphs, as the reader must keep in mind, the same words recur again and again.

from the lie. In case a man were to say of that which seduces that it 'leads'[1]—refraining from adding anything more, or only after a long interval adding . . . 'to seduction'—would not that be an expression of the fact that the man was essentially in the power of seduction? Verily, it is dangerous and highly suspicious when a man spells his words out thus and is so slow to put them together. It is a dangerous dallying with the forbidden thing—or rather than dallying, it is as though one had pleasure in going along a piece of the way, in being led a little distance in the path of seduction. It would also be improper for a man to say to another who already was in the power of seduction, 'Take care! That leads to seduction'. Ah, one who is deeply concerned for his own or for another man's salvation speaks more promptly and more impatiently. Even when he (humanly speaking) is yet far remote from seduction, he does not give it a single finger, lest it take the whole hand, he does not jest with it, does not coquet.

Say not that this stress upon words is hair-splitting pedantry, at the remotest remove from edification; and believe me it is highly important that a man's speech be accurate and true, for so then will his thought be. And furthermore, although to understand and to speak rightly is not everything, inasmuch as one is also required to act rightly, yet in relation to action the right understanding is like the spring-board from which the jumper makes his leap. The clearer, the more exact, the more passionate (in a good sense) one's understanding of a matter is, by just so much does it lighten[2] one's weight for action, or just so much easier is it for one who has to act to render himself light[2] for action, just as it is easier[2] for the bird to take off[2] from the swaying branch, which by reason of its pliability is most nearly related to flight and affords the easiest[2] transition to it.

Therefore that which can be said truly to draw to *itself*, must first of all be something in itself, or be a something which is in its self. For that which cannot be said to be in its self, cannot

---

[1] In this paragraph we are embarrassed by an additional play on words: *fører*—*forfører* = lead—seduce.

At this point we begin to find cause to remark how suddenly S. K.'s style changes. We perceive now that the first 'reflection' was not only 'milder' but simpler—like the style of Thomas à Kempis contrasted with Thomas Aquinas.

[2] Perhaps this is not an intentional play upon words; but unfortunately for us *lettere* may be either an adjective or a verb, and may have more than the four meanings attached to it here: 'easier', 'lighter', 'to make light', and 'to take off'.

possibly draw to its *self*. But such is the case with the sensuous, the worldly, the momentary, the manifold, with all that which in itself is nothing, is empty. Hence in the last analysis it cannot draw (*drage*) to itself, it can only deceive (*bedrage*). This, that it deceives, is the last consequence; but this last is what ought first to be said, and said at once: 'It deceives'.

That which can be said truly to draw to itself must be the higher, the nobler, which draws up the lower to itself—that is to say: truly to draw unto oneself is to draw upward, not to draw downward. When a lower draws a higher to itself, it does not draw, it pulls downward, it deceives. This, the deceit, is doubtless what comes last to evidence; yet this last is what ought first to be said, and said at once: 'It deceives'.

Furthermore, with a deeper understanding of the matter, what is meant by drawing to itself depends upon the nature of that which is to be drawn. If it is in itself a self, then the phrase 'to draw truly to oneself', cannot mean merely to draw it away from being its own self, to draw it in such a way that it loses its own existence by being drawn into that which draws it unto itself. No, in the case of that which is truly a self, to be drawn in such a way is again to be deceived. This, the deceit, will doubtless be the last thing to come to evidence; yet this last is what ought first to be said, and said at once: 'It deceives'. No, when that which is to be drawn is in itself a self, the real meaning of truly drawing to oneself is, first to help it to become truly its own self, so as then to draw it to oneself, or it means to help it to become its own self with and by the drawing of it to oneself.—So here the meaning of truly drawing to oneself is duplex: first to make that which is to be drawn its own self, and then to draw it to oneself.[1]

What is it, then, to be a self? It is a duplication. Hence in this case the phrase, 'truly draw to oneself', has a duplex meaning. The magnet draws iron to itself, but iron is not a self: hence in this case 'draw to itself' indicates a single and simple act. But a self is a duplication, it is freedom: hence in this case 'drawing truly to oneself' means to present a choice. In the case of iron which is drawn, there is not and cannot be any question of a choice. But

---

[1] This complicated thought does not emerge here for the first time in S. K.'s works. It results from his constant reflection upon what he called 'my category', viz. 'that single individual' (*hiin Enkelte*); and in *The Sickness unto Death*, which was published a year earlier than this book, he considers profoundly what 'the self' is.

a self can be truly drawn to another only through a choice, so that 'truly drawing to oneself' is a composite act.

Then again: that which can be said to draw truly to itself must be something in itself, or something which is in its self. So it is when the truth draws to itself; for the truth is in itself, is in-and-by-itself—and Christ is the truth. It must be the higher which draws the lower to itself—as when Christ, the infinitely highest, very God and very man, from on high draws all unto Himself. But man, of whom we are here discoursing, is in his own self a self. Hence Christ would first and foremost help every man to become himself, would require of him first and foremost that by entering into himself he should become himself, so as then to draw him unto Himself. He would draw man unto Himself, and in order to draw him truly to Himself, He would draw him only as a free being, and so through a choice. Therefore will He who humbled Himself, He the humiliated one, from on high draw man to Himself. Yet whether in lowliness or in exaltation, He is one and the same; and this choice would not be the right one if anyone were to mean by it that he should choose between Christ in His lowliness and Christ in His exaltation, for Christ is not divided, He is one and the same. The choice is not between lowliness and exaltation; no, the choice is Christ; but Christ is composite, though one and the same, He is the humbled one and the exalted, so that by means of the two He prevents the choosing of one or the other, or the fact that the two sides are there makes it impossible to be drawn to Him except through a choice. For if He were able to draw to Himself without any choice, He must be a single thing, either the exalted or the humiliated, but He is both. There is nothing, no power of nature, nothing in all the world that can thus draw to itself through a doubleness; only spirit can do that, and can thus in turn draw spirit unto itself.

From on high He will draw all unto Himself.

And surely this has indeed come to pass, with these thousands and thousands and millions He has drawn and continues to draw unto Himself—whereas in His humiliation He drew only twelve, and of these twelve, one betrayed Him and the others denied Him. But all these thousands and millions whom He draws unto Himself from on high hold fast to Him. Maybe! But suppose He were again to assume lowliness—and come to those who are in the strictest sense 'His own' . . . what would the consequence be?

Is not this, however, His own word, that from on high He will draw all unto Himself? So what could be more natural than that it comes to pass as He foretold it would come to pass? And how reasonable it is then that these many thousands and millions feel themselves drawn unto Him from on high. But what does it mean 'to draw unto Himself'? It means to draw unto Himself through a contradiction, through a choice, hence not immediately but mediately, so that the choice (as has been said) does not consist in choosing one or the other of the contraries, but in choosing a unity of two contraries, a thing that cannot be done immediately. In view of this He cannot be said to *draw* only from on high, as though He were simply the highly exalted One and never had been anything else.

But who is the speaker? Is it the exalted One that speaks? By no means, for in that case the saying must have been expressed differently, it would have to be, 'I who am lifted up will draw all unto me'. On the contrary it reads, 'But I—if I be lifted up'. So the 'I' that speaks is not the exalted One: 'I' (that means I, the humiliated One), 'if I be lifted up, will draw all unto me'. It is the exalted One who shall do this, but it is the humbled One who has said that He will do it. In case the humbled One had not lived, we should have known nothing about the exalted One; and in case the humbled One had not uttered this word, we should have known nothing about the promise that He from on high will draw all unto Himself.

How then should these words be understood? For the under-standing of any speech, especially of a speech made in the first person with emphasis upon the 'I', it does not suffice to understand the words that are spoken, but we must also observe attentively who the speaker is. And the speaker is the humbled One—and in addition to this it must be remarked that, historically considered, the words He spoke were not uttered last year nor the year before last, but 1,800 years ago, when the humbled One was not exalted. But when a person undergoes such a change and alteration as that of humiliation–exaltation, it is of the utmost importance for the simple and direct understanding of his utterance to ascertain at what period of his life he made it. With respect to the life of Jesus Christ this is easily ascer-tained, because His exaltation began with His ascension into heaven—and since that time not a single word has been heard

M

from Him, so that every word He has uttered was uttered in His humiliation.

But let us now construct a perfectly simple case, in order to show, in the instance of an utterance made by a man who has gone through significant changes in his life, how important it is to ascertain in what period of his life he made it. Let us think of a pious poor man. Naturally he lives lonely and forsaken, everyone is glad to see him go by his door, and when one sees him coming, one is glad to observe it in time to lock the door or leave word that one is 'not at home'. It is related of him that he once said, 'When I have become the richest of the rich, all will seek after me'. Now let us think that this thing came to pass which, without grumbling at his poverty, but rather happy in it, he had piously hoped: he became the richest of the rich—and now all seek after him. Let us think that many, many years elapsed between the first and the second period of his life—if then one understood this utterance in such a way as to forget that it was the poor man that said this . . . did he then understand it? No, he misunderstood it.

The remarkable thing was precisely the fact that it was the poor man, while he was poor, who uttered this saying, which without doubt seemed madness to most people when he said it. The remarkable thing was that in the days of his poverty he had this faith and trust in God, that God would make him the richest of the rich. Is not this remarkable? Or is there anything remarkable in the fact that all seek after the rich man? Is there anything remarkable in foretelling that this will occur? It is a thing everyone, the fool as well as the wise man, can foretell. So the noteworthiness consists in the relationship between the utterance and the man's situation when he uttered it. Hence when the poor man uttered these words, 'When I become the richest of the rich, then, . . .' people likely replied derisively, 'Oh, yes, . . . when!' That is to say, though they did wrong to deride, yet they rightly understood that what was really remarkable in this speech was the speaker, or the fact that it was a poor man that spoke these words.

And so it is also with regard to the sacred text we have read about Him, the exalted One: the remarkable thing is that He who said it was the humbled One, that one who was despised, mocked, derided, spat upon, said 'I, when[1] I am lifted up, will

[1] In Danish *naar* means when as well as if.

draw all unto me'. For that the exalted, the mighty, the victorious
Christ will draw all to Him is not so remarkable; a fool could
foretell it almost as well as a wise man. If such prognostication
were prophecy, we all of us, great and small, would be equally
great prophets. But the remarkable thing was that the humbled
One said it. And hence no doubt the contemporaries said, 'Oh,
yes, . ·. when!' That is to say, they rightly discovered wherein
lies the emphasis which made this saying so remarkable. It is
exactly as in the case of the poor man's utterance. Yet there is this
infinite difference, that he, at the time he uttered this word 'when'
with a childlike faith and trust in God, was able at the utmost to
hope the possibility, to hope that such a thing might be possible.
Moreover, it was literally true that he, the poor man, when he was
poor, was really poor. But He, the humbled One, *knew* that He
would be exalted, He knew it with eternal certitude, indeed in
one sense He was the exalted One even when He was humbled.
And this you see is the remarkable thing: one so humbled—and
such a word from one so humbled! But, as has been said, if this
word is really to be understood, it must above all be remembered
that it is the humbled One who speaks.

If a man then is vividly conscious of this, so that it is as though
he knew nothing about the exaltation, but only hears the humbled
One speaking—then there is also another way of getting to
understand the saying better. For to understand the utterance
of a man, it is not only necessary to understand what was said,
but also, as we have seen, to learn to know who the speaker is,
and (in case his life has been tried by decisive changes) to what
period of his life this saying belongs—and then one thing more is
necessary: to know in what mood he uttered these words.

Let us again think of that poor man. He is now the rich man,
sought after by all. But these 'all' will wish to consign to oblivion
the fact that he was once poor, and especially that it was as a poor
man he said this—for otherwise these words would remind them
that when he was poor no one sought after him. That is to say,
these words really acquire their sting only now, when he is rich
and all . . . seek after him. The sting must be got rid of, for
otherwise one cannot have all the profit from the rich man one
might have. What does one do then? One says, 'Ah, let that be
forgotten, it is a sad and gloomy memory.' One casts aside the
first part of the saying, 'when I become', and lets it appear as

though he said merely, 'I shall be sought after by all'. How profound the saying now becomes—almost as profound as when one says on a sunny day, 'It is a fair day to-day'. And this is what people regard as truth, they think that it was capitally expressed by him. Thus it is, thus it will be, it is always in order, that all seek after the rich man especially, who is so witty, so clever, who with the exuberant feeling of *joie de vivre*, with a smiling mien, says with such hearty satisfaction, 'I am sought after by all.'

But, but it was the poor man that said the words, 'When I have become the richest of the rich, then all will seek after me'. Let us above all remember the situation in which he uttered these words, and then we shall be on the trace of his mood—indeed there may even have been bitterness in the poor man's soul when he said this. 'Oh, wretched world', he may have thought. 'While I was poor all fled from me.' And supposing there was depth in this man's soul, he must first and foremost upon becoming rich have repented humbly before God of the bitterness which was in his heart when he said these words—but verily he was disgusted with existence when he saw all fleeing from the poor; and, oh, he was far more disgusted with it when he saw all seeking after the rich. For if there was depth in his soul, he did not wish to be held in derision. And in a deeper sense he was not held in derision when all fled from him, the poor man; but he could easily become an object of derision when all sought after him, the rich man; he could easily become that—for, in a deeper sense, to become an object of derision does not depend upon what others do to one, but upon what one is—supposing he fatuously went his way and forgot what as a poor man he had learnt.

And now with regard to Him, the humbled One! Verily, in his soul there was no bitterness, not even when He said, 'How long shall I suffer this generation?' For He was love; in His case bitterness came from without, but it never availed to embitter Him. On the other hand, it availed to make His life bitter, the life He lived at the mercy of every lie and calumny and ill-treatment and persecution and the witness his pain bore to the universal weakness and cowardice and selfishness—shunned as He was by all. Then it was He said, 'But I, if I be lifted up, will draw all unto myself.' But can we suppose that He who said, 'How long shall I suffer this generation?' meant to speak only of that generation, and that the generations which were eager to leap over the lowliness in order to share in His highness—can we suppose that they were essentially better and more easily 'suffered'? Can we suppose that He really might be deluded by the fact that when He is exalted all are eager to join themselves to Him? Are we to suppose that this might delude Him and alter in the slightest degree His judgement of the truth, who Himself is the truth? But if this is an impossibility, more impossible than the greatest impossibility in the order of nature—then He has not forgotten in the slightest degree what His life was when He was the humbled One.

Then at bottom there is a sting, the sting of truth, in these words, 'But I, if I be lifted up, will draw all unto myself'. At the time this was said by Him, the humbled One, this sting of truth lay in the fact that He, the humbled One, knew Himself to be the highly exalted. As we have seen, He was not bitter, yet He said, 'How long shall I suffer this generation?'. And then when He became the exalted One, and it came to pass that He from on high drew all unto Himself—the sting (the sting of truth) is that it was the humbled One who said these words. And neither shalt thou nor all the millions of men, or . . . all the millions of Christians, succeed in deluding Him or in making Him forget anything—as the merry house-guests who toasted the one-time poor man, now the rich man, were so eager to make him forget that it was in his poverty he uttered these words, make him forget what as a poor man he had learnt to know about the world, make him imagine that it is a splendid world—for are not all flocking to him?

No, a man may very well become a bit forgetful in the course of years, and forget in the good days of wealth the experience and truth learnt in the days of poverty; but for Him, the exalted One, everything is eternally present—the 1,800 years are as one day. His exaltation cannot alter Him; He is Himself so vividly present that even to-day He is the same in the words which He uttered, so lively a memory He has that He was the humbled One. He is the humbled One who says to men now living, 'From on high I will draw all unto myself'.

But then it is true, is it not, that He said that from on high He will draw all unto Himself? Yes, verily—He the humbled One said it. He does not allow Himself to be deluded—thou canst not get rid of the humiliation; for if the saying reminds us of the exaltation, the speaker reminds us of the humiliation. Thou canst not choose one or the other without being guilty of an untruth, wherewith thou deludest only thyself and not Him, and deludest thyself of the truth which He is.

III

O LORD Jesus Christ, many and various are the things to which a man may feel himself drawn, but one thing there is to which no man ever felt himself drawn in any way, that is, to suffering and humiliation. This we men think we ought to shun as far as possible, and in any case that we must be compelled to it. But Thou, our Saviour and Redeemer, Thou who wast humbled yet without compulsion, and least of all compelled to that humiliation in the imitation of which man discovers his highest honour; ah, that the picture of Thee in thy humiliation might be so vivid to us that we may feel ourselves drawn unto Thee in lowliness, unto Thee who from on high wilt draw all unto Thyself.

John 12: 32. AND I, IF I BE LIFTED UP FROM THE EARTH, WILL DRAW ALL UNTO MYSELF.

Who, then, is this that is 'lifted up?' It is God's only begotten Son, our Lord, who from eternity was with God and was God, who came to earth, then was raised up to heaven, where He sits at the right hand of the Father, glorified with the glory which He had before the world was. He it is to whom all power is given in heaven and on earth, He in whose name every knee shall bow, of things in heaven, and things on earth, and things under the earth; He to whose praise and honour eternity resounds and ever shall resound; He who shall come again upon the clouds, surrounded by His holy angels, to judge the world and to save those who have believed and are expecting His glorious appearing.

But is nothing else known of Him? Yes, indeed; and what is known of Him is for the most part something entirely different from this, namely, that He was the humbled One. He was born as an illegitimate child, and if the father, good-natured man that he was, had followed his own counsel, he would not indeed have put away openly, but he would have quietly deserted the despised virgin who was the mother. However, the intention of the step-father was changed; so far as concerns tender care and sacrifice for the child, he became a real father; but, on the other hand, the whole race in which this child grew to manhood as a member became a cruel stepfather—to this illegitimate child which the race refused to recognize. Yes, just as one sees occasionally a poor bird which all the other birds of the same species continually persecute, maltreat, and peck at, because it is not altogether like the others, until finally they succeed in their desire to take its life so as to put an end to this kinship—so the race would not have any kinship with this child or this man; it was of the utmost consequence to it, yea, it had a vital importance, to take this man's life, so as to put an end to this kinship.—This story, the story of constant maltreatment which finally ended in death, or shall I say the story of this suffering, is the story of His [whole] life. It can be told in several ways. It can be told briefly in two words, nay even in one: it was the story of the Passion. It can be told also more diffusely, but even thus it cannot be quite truly told, for then it would be so diffuse that no one could recite it. Otherwise than in these two ways it cannot be told. It is by reason of a human misunderstanding[1] that people have abbreviated it in such a way that the last part [only] is called 'the story of the Passion'. This is through a misunderstanding. True enough, there was a time, a period in His life which almost looked like glory. But did not the race also at that time peck at Him with the torture of the misunderstanding they inflicted upon Him? And regarding even that moment of His life which, humanly, seemed glorious, one readily observes that this glory was more volcanic than secure, a thing not to be relied upon; one has a presentiment that this glory must signify something else, must be related to and is obscurely in correspondence with its exact opposite, the terror of

[1] This 'misunderstanding' was in fact the understanding of the few important lives of Jesus which were published before S. K.'s death (by Schleiermacher in 1832, by David Strauss in 1835, by Neander in 1837), and the same understanding or misunderstanding was repeated in all the many subsequent *Lives*, which were the principal contribution of the nineteenth century to the understanding (or misunderstanding) of Christianity—until in the first year of the twentieth century Albert Schweitzer rudely stigmatized it again as a misunderstanding (*Skizze des Lebens Jesu*, 1901. My translation, made in 1913, *The Mystery of the Kingdom of God*, is published by A. & C. Black.) From that time on, no man of light and leading can, with a good conscience, or with a good face, continue to propagate this misunderstanding. Nevertheless, almost all the 'biographers' of Jesus have continued to do this; and so far as the people are concerned nothing else is offered to them but this 'misunderstanding' (a Jesus who, as Schweitzer trenchantly says, 'never existed'), and it may be that the people are not yet ready to accept such an understanding as was offered by Kierkegaard so long ago.

destruction (like the height from which one falls), that it is ambiguous, like the moment when the woman anointed Him with
precious ointment. Yet on this occasion one hardly has the
impression of festive security at the supper, and He Himself says,
'She hath kept this (i.e. the ointment) against the day of My
burial'.—as indeed every day of His life was a day of burial for
Him who was appointed to be a sacrifice.—And so too all this, the
glory of a brief instant, was only with a view to destruction, signifying destruction or preparation for destruction. They would
acclaim Him king. But does He look at all like a candidate for
election to kingship, like one who himself aspires to it and hence
does everything to make it sure? No, in relation to the suggestion
that He should be king He prefers to play the part of an alien
because He knew that this episode had no serious importance
except in relation to that which He conceived He should be—the
sacrifice. The thought of acclaiming Him king! It is as strange
and mad a thing as to present all the world's treasures to one who
under a sacred vow was living in poverty. What could such a one
do with it—and what could He do with kingly power who was
the most indifferent of all men with respect to everything worldly?
The small nation to which He belonged was under foreign domi-
nation, and naturally all were intent upon the thought of shaking
off the hated yoke. Hence they would acclaim Him king. But,
lo, when they show Him a coin and would constrain Him against
His will to take sides with one party or the other—what then?
Oh, worldly passion of partisanship, even when thou callest
thyself holy and national—nay, so far thou canst not stretch as to
ensnare His indifference! He asks, 'Whose image is this that is
stamped upon the coin?' They answer, 'The Emperor's'.—'Then
give to the Emperor what belongs to the Emperor, and to God
what is God's.' Infinite indifference! Whether the Emperor be
called Herod or Shalmanezer, whether he be Roman or Japanese,
is to Him the most indifferent of all things. But, on the other
hand—the infinite yawning difference which He posits between
God and the Emperor:[1] 'Give unto God what is God's!' For they

---

[1] And yet to-day almost all the 'authorities' who comment upon the Gospels like
to see in this an example of Jesus's perfect balance of mind ... as between the claims
of the world and of God; they like to see in it more particularly a solution of the
conflict between the Church and secular society—a beautiful example of equanimity.
S. K. had pondered profoundly the difficulties of adjusting the claims of all the

with worldly wisdom would make it a question of religion, of duty to God, whether it was lawful to pay tribute to the Emperor. Worldliness is so eager to embellish itself as godliness, and in this case God and the Emperor are blended together in the question, as if these two had obviously and directly something to do with each other, as if perhaps they were rivals one of the other, and as if God were a sort of emperor—that is to say, the question takes God in vain and secularizes Him. But Christ draws the distinction, the infinite distinction, and He does this by treating the question about paying tribute to the Emperor as the most indifferent thing in the world, regarding it as something which one should do without wasting a word or an instant in talking about it—so as to get so much more time for giving unto God what is God's. And it is Him they would proclaim king! Oh, but what suffering to be so misunderstood!—And thus He was misunderstood in every way. No day passed, not an hour of any day, but that misunderstanding, as well it can (and perhaps with greater tortures than bodily suffering) crucified Him. His teaching they misunderstood and took it in vain, His miracles they misunderstood and took them in vain, Himself they misunderstood and took Him in vain, His association with sinners and publicans they misunderstood and became offended, His renunciation of all they misunderstood and became offended, His prediction of suffering and death they misunderstood and became offended. Yes, with exception of the Apostles, that woman was likely one of the few who understood Him, and yet she misunderstood Him, for she did not understand that what she did in anointing Him was in view of His death. Oh, shuddering horror! that there is such a mysterious interpretation of that which seems to be the very opposite, that this instant at the supper when He is anointed with precious ointment signifies His burial! Picture the humbled One whom the race would not recognize, while all in different ways unite in crying, 'Behold, what a man!' His life was heterogeneous from first to last. 'Behold, what a man!' cried the race when they would have made Him king; and,

---

relative and finite ends which inevitably 'draw' us—and the absolute claim of God. Everyone who knows his works at all is familiar with the concise formula in which he expressed the result of so much reflection. His maxim is: 'To comport oneself relatively with respect to the relative ends, and absolutely with respect to the absolute *telos.*'

'Behold, what a man!' they cried when they crucified Him. 'Behold, what a man!' That is as it were the story of His life's suffering summed up in one single word.[1]

And He, the humbled One, was love; He desired but one thing, to save men; He desired this at any price, relinquishing for it the glory of heaven; He desired this at any price, sacrificing for it His own life. Thus—one cannot indeed say that thus He started out in the world, but thus, with this resolution, He descended to earth, and then started out in the world. One might suppose that He would have moved all, but He moved none—and yet in a way He did move, and moved all, that is, He roused them all against Him. What suffering! What suffering of love!

Cannot this sight move thee? But surely thou wilt be honest with thyself, and though one or another of the eloquent preachers who does ill, or knows not what he does, would deceive thee by his eloquence, by talking beguilingly about the sufferings of Christ, or let us say by stationing himself beguilingly beside the cross of Christ—as an onlooker, so that from that point of view he can contemplate the world, universal history, and mankind—surely thou wilt not suffer thyself to be deceived by him. Thou wilt bear in mind that if there is to be any seriousness in stationing oneself or standing beside the cross, it must be in the situation of contemporaneousness, where it will mean *actually* to incur suffering with Him, not to propose subjects for reflection at the foot of the cross, but perhaps to be nailed oneself to a cross alongside of Him—there to propose subjects for reflection. Therefore (for the sake of seriousness, or in order that the thing may become serious) do not think upon Him reflectively, but think first of all upon thyself with the aim of becoming in thy thought contemporary with Him. Cannot now this sight move thee?—I do not say to tears, which here are out of place and superfluous, if it is not over thine own self thou weepest—but in all seriousness, with a view to action, with a view perhaps to suffering somehow in His likeness.[2] Thou art not compelled against thy will; but blessed art

[1] S. K. was in a position to perceive this, because also the story of his life's suffering could be summed up in the one word, 'heterogeneous'. For this reason he was 'pecked at' by the other birds, and a comic paper egged on his own people to cry after him on the street, 'Behold, what a man!'

[2] This especially, no doubt, was the passage in the 'Reflections' which Bishop Mynster recognized as 'coined expressly for him'. He had a faculty for moving his

thou if thy will compels thee to say, 'I can do no other; for this sight compels me'. Thou art not compelled against thy will. Ah, do not misunderstand me; it is a point of honour which is raised here. If thou wilt not do it, if it seems too hard for thee, thou canst readily be free—in this case it is only a point of honour from which thou dost liberate thyself . . . does this perhaps seem to thee easier? But say for thyself, oh, say to thyself, what opinion wilt thou have of a lady-love who would consent to belong to her lover only after he had withstood all difficulties and triumphed over all dangers, who loved him only when he was on high? Is this love? Yes, in a way, for it is self-love—but is this love? Think of two lovers, and suppose that the man had passed through many and indescribable experiences in life, had been compelled to stand alone in the world, impoverished, misunderstood by all, despised and derided—but the situation changed, his cause triumphed, and now he is admired by all, courted by all. Then for the first time he makes the acquaintance of a maiden who becomes his beloved. So she is entirely without fault for the fact that she has not shared his sufferings with him, she did not even know him in the days of his sufferings; but in case she is a true lover, would she not then (here is an exaggeration, I admit, but an exaggeration of true love)—would she not then almost reproach herself as for a sort of unfaithfulness, or feel at least that her love was imperfect, because she did not know him in the days of his sufferings, would she not feel ashamed that she should share with him only his glory?

But in the case of Christ, no one can say of himself that he first learned to know Him when He had entered into glory; for everyone who has learnt to know Him learns to know Him in lowliness, and if he truly learns to know Him he learns first to know Him in lowliness. Moreover, no one can say truly that it is impossible to share His lowliness with Him because this is past and long passed. No, in case thou dost become contemporary with Him in His humiliation, and in case this sight moves thee to desire to suffer with Him, then there shall be given thee—that He warrants thee—opportunity enough to suffer in His likeness; and even if the opportunity were not to be given, it is really not so much a question of opportunity as of willingness to suffer in

hearers to tears, and S. K. once proposed to gather up all the tears he had shed in the pulpit.

His likeness. To suffer in His likeness—and surely thou wilt not deceive thyself, thou wilt be honest with thyself; for the fact is that thou art a lover, and hence cannot remotely wish to seek evasions or deceitful shifts, as they do who in various ways speculate upon the exaltation in order to avoid the suffering. No, he who loves Christ can very well understand, quite simply and without the aid of eloquence, what is meant by suffering in His likeness. Although thou, or some person, let us say, has adversities in life, and although it may perhaps go very ill with him—that is not properly called suffering in likeness with Jesus Christ. Such sufferings are the universal human experience, in which the heathen are (or were) just as severely tried as the Christians. The Christian may be recognized in the fact that he bears these sufferings patiently; but however patiently he bears them, it never occurs to him that this might be to suffer in likeness with Christ— this very notion would mean un-Christian impatience. To suffer in likeness with Christ does not mean to encounter the unavoidable with patience, but it means to suffer ill at the hands of men because as a Christian or by being a Christian one desires and strives after the Good, so that one could avoid the suffering by ceasing to will the Good. As, for example, when a man endeavours like a Christian to bear his burden patiently—and then is ridiculed and derided by people because he would be patient. For so it was that Christ suffered. He suffered because He was the truth and would not be anything other than He was, namely, the truth.

Look once again upon Him, the humbled One! For surely it is this, the humiliation, that ought to be preached—no guidance is needed for sharing His glory with Him or for instruction how to behave in that instance. The humiliation is what must be preached, the fact that if thou wilt not share with Him His humiliation, neither will He share with thee His glory, and hence that thou must share His humiliation with Him. Look upon Him, the humbled One! And if this sight affects thee deeply, so that thou art ready for any suffering along with Him—then, yes, then I say, 'Thou *shalt* suffer with Him'. And to speak thus is blessed. It is disagreeable to have to say to one who is unwilling, 'Thou shalt'. But when someone desires nothing but this one thing, to have to suffer with Him, and desires this as his only desire,[1]

---

[1] Lest the reader imagine that this is mere 'eloquence', he should remember that such in fact was S. K.'s 'melancholy desire'.

it is blessed to say to him, 'Good cheer, my friend, thou shalt'. It is blessed to say that; and then too the word 'shall', in the best sense, is in the right place. The word 'shall' in this case does not so much express a commandment (for what is the use of a commandment to one who enthusiastically desires what the commandment commands?) as the need for sanctification, purification, that in this zeal there might be no precipitancy, no conceited exaggeration, no defiling thought of anything meritorious.[1]

So look again upon Him, the humbled One! What effect does this sight produce? Might it not move thee in some way to wish to suffer in His likeness, and so to wish to witness for the truth, with the danger of having to suffer on this account? Forget, if for an instant thou canst, all thou knowest about Him, divest thyself of what may be a customary and indolent way of knowing about Him, let it be as if for the first time thou didst hear the narrative of His humiliation. Or, if this seems to thee impossible, then let us seek assistance from a child, a child unspoiled by learning as a task in school a jargon that has to be memorized about Christ's suffering and death, a child who now for the first time hears it told. Let us see then what effect this will produce, if we tell it only tolerably well.[2]

Think then of a child, and give this child delight by showing it some of those pictures one buys on the stalls, which are so trivial artistically, but so dear to children. This one here on the snorting steed, with a tossing feather in his hat, with a lordly mien, riding at the head of the thousands upon thousands which you do not

---

[1] Although Karl Barth has rudely shaken himself free from dependence upon S. K., recognizing that he is not in agreement with him upon a point which he regards as the fundamental distinction between Catholic and Protestant, it is not to be supposed that he would minimize the magnitude of a debt which is still so obvious. Lately Alfred de Quervain, writing in *Theologische Existenz heute*, No. 34, an article on 'Das Gesetz Gottes', reflects and substantiates the thought which S. K. develops in this paragraph. The 'Thou shalt not' of the Ten Commandments he regards as a future rather than as an imperative. It is God's expectation that His people will be ready to do His will, and He gives expression to this expectation in the 'Ten Words': 'Thou wilt have none other gods before Me; thou wilt not take the name of the Lord thy God in vain; thou wilt not steal', &c. May not a father expect this of his sons? 'Thou wilt love the Lord thy God with all thy heart, and thou wilt love thy neighbour as thyself.'

[2] It is commonly recognized that in what follows up to the end of this 'Reflection' is the narrative of S. K.'s own experience as a child.

see, with hand outstretched to command, 'Forward!' forward
over the summits of the mountains which you see in front of you,
forward to victory—this is the Emperor, the one and only,
Napoleon. And so now you tell the child a little about Napoleon.
—This one here is dressed as a huntsman; he stands leaning upon
his bow and gazes straight before him with glance so piercing, so
self-confident, and yet so anxious. That is William Tell. You
now relate to the child something about him, and about that
extraordinary glance of his, explaining that with this same glance
he has at once an eye for the beloved child, that he may not harm
him, and for the apple, that he may not miss it. And thus you
show the child many pictures, to the child's unspeakable delight.
Then you come to one which intentionally was laid among the
others. It represents a man crucified. The child will not at once
nor quite directly understand this picture, and will ask what it
means, why he hangs like that on a tree. So you explain to the
child that this is a cross, and that to hang on it means to be crucified, and that in that land crucifixion was not only the most
painful death penalty but was also an ignominious mode of
execution employed only for the grossest malefactors. What
impression will that make upon the child? The child
will be in a strange state of mind, it will surely wonder that
it could occur to you to put such an ugly picture among all
the other lovely ones, the picture of a gross malefactor among all
these heroes and glorious figures. For just as a reproach to the
Jews there was written above His cross, 'The King of the Jews',
so this picture, which regularly is published every year as a reproach to the human race, is a remembrance which the race
never can and never should be rid of, it never should be represented differently; and it will seem as if it were *this* generation
which crucified Him, as often as *this* generation for the first time
shows this picture to the child of the new generation, explaining
for the first time how things go in this world; and the child, the
first time it hears this, will become anxious and sorrowful, for his
parents, for the world, and for himself; and the other pictures—
surely (as the ballad relates)[1] they must turn their faces away, this
picture being so different. However—and we have not yet reached

---

[1] A well-known ballad about Agnes and the Merman, which recounts that when
Agnes entered the church with the secret of her clandestine love, the saints pictured
on the walls turned their faces away from her.

the decisive point, the child has not learned who this gross male-factor was—with the curiosity children always have, the child will no doubt ask, 'Who is it, what did he do? Tell me.' Then tell the child that this crucified man is the Saviour of the world. Yet to this he will not be able to attach any clear conceptions; so tell him merely that this crucified man was the most loving person that ever lived. Oh, in common intercourse, where everyone knows that story by rote as familiar patter, in common intercourse, where a half-word thrown out as a hint is enough to apprise everyone what is meant—there it goes so glibly; but verily it must be a wonderful man, or rather an inhuman one, who does not instinctively cast down his eyes and stand almost like a poor sinner the moment he must tell this to a child for the first time, to a child who has never heard a word about it before, and conse-quently has never surmised such a thing. But then at that moment the parent stands as an accuser, who accuses himself and the whole race!—What impression now do you think it will make upon the child, who naturally will ask, 'But why were people so bad to him then?'

Now the moment has arrived. If already you have not made too strong an impression upon the child, then tell him now about the exalted One who from on high will draw all unto Himself. Tell him that this exalted One is the crucified man. Tell the child that He was love, that He came to the world out of love, took upon Him the form of a humble servant, lived only for one end, to love men and to help them, especially all those who were sick and sorrowful and suffering and unhappy.. Then tell the child what befell Him in life, how one of the few that were close to Him betrayed Him, that the other few denied Him, and all the rest scoffed at and derided Him, until at last they nailed Him to the cross—as the picture shows—requiring that His blood might be upon them and upon their children, whereas He prayed for them that this might not come to pass, that the heavenly Father would forgive them their fault. Tell this to the child in as vivid a way as if you had never heard it before or never told it to anyone; tell it as if you yourself had poetically imagined the whole story; but forget no single incident that has been handed down, only as you tell it you must forget that it has been handed down. Tell the child that contemporary with this loving One there lived a notori-ous robber who was condemned to death—for him the people demanded release, they cried, '*Viva*! Long live Barabbas!' But as for the loving One, they cried, 'Crucify, crucify!' So that the loving One not only was crucified as a malefactor, but as such a monster of a malefactor that this notorious robber became a kind of honest man in comparison with the loving One.

What effect do you think this narrative will make upon the child? In order to throw light upon this question, make a test; continue the story of the crucified One, relating that thereafter He rose from the dead on the third day, then was carried up into heaven, to enter into glory with the Father of heaven—make the test, and you will see that at first the child will almost ignore this; the account of His sufferings will have made so deep an impression upon the child that he is not in a mood to hear about the glory which succeeded. For one must be pretty thoroughly spoiled and pampered by learning in the course of many years to know the whole story of His humiliation, suffering, and death flippantly and by rote before one reaches the point where, without feeling any check, one can at once grasp at the exaltation.

So then, what effect do you think this account will produce upon the child? First and foremost surely this, that he has entirely forgotten the other pictures you have showed him; for now he had got something entirely different to think about. And now the child will be in the deepest amazement at the fact that God did nothing to prevent this being done; or that this was done without God raining down fire from heaven (if not earlier, at least at the last minute) to prevent His death; that this happened without the earth opening to swallow up the ungodly. And so, too, the elders would be obliged to understand the matter, if they did not understand that it was voluntary suffering, hence all the harder to bear, and that the humbled One had it in His power every instant to pray, and then the Father would have sent Him legions of angels to ward off this terrible end.—That surely was the first impression. But by degrees, the more the child reflected upon the story, the more his passion would be aroused, he would be able to think of nothing but weapons and war—for the child would have decided that when he grew up he would slay all these ungodly men who had dealt thus with the loving One; that was his resolve, forgetting that it was 1,800 years ago they lived.

Then when the child became a youth he would not have forgotten the impression of childhood, but he would now understand it differently, he would know that it was not possible to carry out what the child—overlooking the 1,800 years—had resolved to do; but nevertheless he would think with the same passion of combating the world in which they spat upon the holy One, the world in which they crucify love and beg acquittal for the robber.

Then when he became older and mature he would not have forgotten the impression of childhood, but he would understand it differently. He would no longer wish to smite; for, said he, 'I should attain to no likeness with Him the humbled One, who did not smite even when He Himself was smitten'. No, he wished now only one thing, to suffer in some measure as He suffered in this world, which the philosophers always have called the best of worlds, but which nevertheless crucified love and cried *Viva*! to Barabbas—showing that after all a thing may be true in philosophy which is not true in theology. Indeed, the world has showed again and again on a smaller scale that not only is he who (humanly) loves the Good obliged suffer, but that (for the sake of the contrast for which the world has such a fondness, just to show how contrasted the world is to the Good) there commonly lives at the same time a worthless, despicable, and base man to whom, by way of contrast, the world cries *Viva*!

So *can* the sight of this humiliation move. Cannot it also move thee thus? So it moved the Apostles, who knew nothing and were resolved to know nothing save Christ and Him crucified— can it not also move thee thus? From this it does not follow that thou dost become an Apostle. Presumptuous thought! No, it follows merely that thou dost become a Christian. So this sight moved those glorious ones whom the Church remembers as its Fathers and Teachers, who like the Apostles knew nothing and were resolved to know nothing save Christ and Him crucified— cannot it also move thee thus? From which it does not follow that thou dost become such as they. Vain thought! It follows merely that thou dost become a Christian. For why did this sight move them thus? Because they loved Him. Therefore they discovered His sufferings; for only he who loves Him understands that He was love, and hence only he can become observant to discover how He suffered: how hard it was, how torturing, and how He suffered; how gentle He was, how loving, how He suffered; how just His cause was, how He suffered; and what injustice! If this sight does not move thee thus, it must be because thou dost not love Him. Yet do not therefore let it go, for it may be that the sight of this humbled One in His sufferings may yet move thee to love Him. If such be the case, thou wilt get to see this sight a second time [with other eyes], and then it will move thee also to wish to suffer in His likeness—who from on high will draw all unto Himself.

IV

O LORD Jesus Christ, Thou who indeed didst not come to judge, but wilt come again to judge the world, Thy life on earth is in reality the judgement by which we shall be judged. Wherefore everyone who calls himself a Christian must test his life by this judgement, to discern whether he loves Thee in Thy humiliation, or loves Thee only in Thine exaltation, or simply whether he loves Thee, for if it is only in one of these two ways he loves Thee, he loves Thee not. But if he loves Thee, he surely shall experience humiliation (for he loves Thee in thy humiliation), but not as when the worldly mind succumbs to humiliation—for it was not thus Thou didst walk here on earth in humiliation. No, such a lover, though humiliated, is raised above humiliation, his mind, his eye, being directed to the high places wherein Thou hast entered, and where he looks forward to being with Thee who from on high wilt draw all unto Thyself.

John 12: 32. AND I, IF I BE LIFTED UP, WILL DRAW ALL UNTO MYSELF

'Many are called, but few are chosen'—from on high He will draw *all* unto Himself. But because many are called, it does not follow that many are chosen; on the contrary, it is said expressly that few are chosen. And so, from the statement that He will draw all unto Himself, it does not follow that all will permit themselves to be drawn. Only it is not in Him the fault is to be sought, if this does not come to pass, for He will draw all unto Himself.

'From on high'—for when He walked upon earth in lowliness He wished indeed to draw to Himself all them that labour and are heavy laden, He went unto them that were sick and sorrowful, but at the same time He had another purpose to carry out, He must in His own life give expression to the truth, and as very man He had this other purpose as His task—a task He must Himself bring to perfection. He himself had something to perfect, He Himself learned by what He suffered—He learned obedience. He was developed to become and to be the Truth— if we may speak quite humanly, and surely we may rightly do so of Him who was very man. In and with the act of perfecting this task He sought to draw all unto Himself. Then when He had perfected this task which was set before Him, becoming obedient unto death, yea, the death of the cross, He ascended up on high! He had now finished the race, His work was perfected, the work of obedience which was laid upon Him, or which He freely had assumed. Then from on high He begins a second time; He has no longer need of being developed, there is nothing more for Him to learn, He is now occupied solely with drawing all unto Himself—from on high He will draw all unto Himself.

So from on high He begins a second time, and there He begins with that which from henceforth is His sole work—to draw all unto Himself. But where should we begin? Because He now is in the high places, can we therefore also begin with the high places, and so, because He inherited such elevation, can we therefore anticipate such elevation?

Let us regard Him and His life, let us speak about this quite humanly, for He was indeed very man. He began His life in lowliness and carried it on in lowliness and humiliation until the last, and then He ascended up on high. What does that mean? It means that for Him the temporal in its whole extent was suffering, and victory, exaltation, came only in eternity. So it is not as sometimes one sees in the life of a man who perhaps for several years experiences lowliness and humiliation, suffers misunderstanding and persecution, but then, still within the bounds of time, he triumphs and attains high place. No, He ended as He began; born in poverty, as if He were hardly a man (for only in a stable was place found for the tiny babe), He ended as if He were hardly a man, with a shameful death, crucified like a malefactor—and then only did He ascend on high.

Regarding our earthly existence as a test, we must say of Him (if for an instant we may ignore the infinite significance of His death as an atonement and consider Him merely as a man) that He has now completed His test, has passed it successfully, is now perfected, and is raised up on high. But it is true that this earthly existence of ours is a test, it is the period of trial; such is the teaching of Christianity, and hence Christian orthodoxy always has so regarded it. To be a man, to live here in this world, is to be put on trial. To use a foreign word (partly because it so exactly characterizes the situation, and partly because it so promptly and definitely reminds everyone of what one should remember), it is an examination. And the greatest examination a man has to take, an examination which involves one's whole life, is that of becoming and being a Christian. Whatsoever he undertakes, whether his influence is the greatest possible, or whether it is very limited, the whole thing signifies for him merely that he is being examined. I know very well that people generally speak differently, that they are busy about trying to accomplish something in the world, and busy talking about what others have accomplished; I know that they would teach us that 'history is the judgement'[1] but I know also that this is an invention of human shrewdness which does away with the God-relationship, would make itself important and play the part of providence, and for this reason is concerned only about the consequences of a life, instead of reflecting that every instant a man is examined only by God. As for 'accomplishing' anything, a man has nothing to do with it, it is God's affair, God's bestowal upon the individual; but as for the individual himself, his whole life and every act of it must never have any other significance than that of a test to which he is subjected, God being the Examiner. Even Christ's life, regarding Him merely as a man (though it would be superfluous to speak of what He accomplished), was for Him simply an examination, an examination in obedience. But He passed it at every instant up to the death on the cross, wherefore also God hath highly exalted Him—and now He, the perfected One, is on high. Let us speak of this quite humanly: He passed His test, He developed the pattern, He is now on high. It is just as in any other case when one has passed his test, and then, being perfected, is engaged in leading others. From on high He will draw all unto Himself. Here it is of the first importance not to get through an illusion the picture of His life, the life of the pattern, drawn, if I may so speak, wrong end foremost. If thou hadst lived contemporary with Him, thou wouldst naturally have begun like Him with lowliness and humiliation. But since He is now on high and would draw all unto Himself, and it comes thy turn to begin, it may so easily seem to dazzled eyes as if thou wert to *begin* with the high place, as He certainly did not do, for He, being perfected, ended with the high place. Thou wilt easily perceive, and surely also easily understand, what I mean when I say that the picture

[1] Quoted from Schiller's *Resignation*, penultimate strophe.

of His life, which is the pattern, may be drawn in either of two ways: In the one case lowliness and humiliation compose the picture essentially, and in the remote distance, barely indicated as the object of faith, is lofty dignity; the other is a picture of lofty dignity, and far, far in the background, as an almost forgotten memory, lie lowliness and humiliation. But since it is from on high He draws thee, the possibility of deception is all too near.

When thou dost look upon Him, His life's probation seems so easy, when once He, the perfected One, has passed it. Viewing it in this way, there is no reason to wonder that He draws all unto Himself. But it was precisely in view of this that I called attention earlier to a saying which here provides an apt interpretation: 'Many are called, but few are chosen.' The invited guest is also commonly said to be called. Having regard only to the word 'called', the thing seems so easy. Then comes the more precise meaning—and only a few are the chosen.

But is not this like a deceit on His part, that from on high He draws me in this wise unto Himself? Has He not suppressed something? To be the truth, is it enough for Him to draw, is He not quite as much required to warn him who lets himself be drawn, reminding him constantly of the difference between them, that He the perfected One is in the environment of perfection, whereas the other is in the environment of actuality, of worldliness, of the temporal, where this loftiness must exhibit itself inversely as lowliness and humiliation, so that He draws from on high, and the man who feels himself drawn and follows finds himself, just in proportion as he follows heartily, in exactly the opposite case, of being in and sinking deeper into humiliation and lowliness? It is not difficult to give an answer to this query of impatience and misunderstanding. First of all, it could not be otherwise; He has endured His probation and is perfected, and this must have enduring significance, unless indeed He must begin all over again with every generation, be born in every generation, and suffer and die as He did the first time—but this would be to render vain the significance of His suffering and death.——No one can properly say that He has suppressed anything, for His life as he led it in humiliation and lowliness is surely well known. So it is not He who suppresses something, but perhaps it may be the individual who forgets something, who by looking only and with false passion upon the loftiness actually takes Him in vain, and therewith falls into forgetfulness of lowliness and humiliation, until it ends with his wandering too far off and finding himself where he least expected to be, where he lays the blame upon Him who from on high draws all unto Himself.—That instead of drawing unto Himself He should warn away, is in fact a self-contradiction; for when a man's mind is Christianly transformed he understands that there is no relationship between humiliation and glory. But in any case, His own life is there as a warning, if one so will, i.e. as a warning against the frivolity which will only take His loftiness in vain.

Thus it is He draws unto Himself from on high, and so it is also that the man who at a later time than those who were contemporary with His humiliation is to become a Christian begins in a sense with the easiest; for loftiness is naturally an easy thing, and to feel oneself drawn to it is easy enough. But Christ who from on high draws men unto Himself does not take them out of the world where they live, and therefore to everyone who is drawn unto Him in the heights lowliness and humiliation come as a matter of course.

This Christ knows very well; and He knows also that the permission to begin with the easiest, or with what seems the easiest, is a necessary deceit in the process of education, and that the fact of its becoming then harder and harder is in order that life may become in truth a probation and examination. Even to the Apostles, though they were contemporary with Him, He did not at once foretell all that they would suffer; indeed, when He was parted from them He had still much to say unto them, but did not say it because they were not yet able to bear it. Man is a frail creature, not like the God-Man capable of knowing everything beforehand, his sufferings and the certainty and necessity of his destruction, and yet able to live day after day tranquilly, with devotion to God, as if He understood it all as good. A man has to be handled carefully, and hence it is only little by little his task is made clear to him, little by little he is screwed tighter and tighter by the greater and greater and greater effort of probation and examination. So little by little it becomes for the individual a serious truth that to live is to be examined, and the highest examination is this: whether one will be in truth a Christian or not.

Let us make perfectly clear to ourselves how it goes generally with man's upbringing in the school of life, or with the necessity of passing life's examination; the same thing will then hold good with regard to the highest upbringing in life's school, that of becoming and being a Christian.

Every man possesses in a greater or less degree a talent which is called imagination, the power which is the first condition determining what a man will turn out to be; for the second condition is the will, which in the final resort is decisive. Memory is strongest in youth and decreases with years. We will now think of a youth. With his imagination he constructs one or another picture (ideal) of perfection, whether it be one handed down by history, that is, belonging to a time past, so that it has been actual, has possessed the reality of being, or whether it be formed by the imagination alone, so that it has no relation to time or place and receives no definition by them, but has only the reality of thought. To this picture (which—since for the youth it has existence only in imagination, that is, in imagination's endless remoteness from reality—is the picture of completed perfection, not of striving and suffering perfection), to this picture the youth is now drawn by his imagination, or his imagination draws this picture to him; he falls in love with this picture, or the picture becomes the object of his love, of his enthusiasm, becomes his more perfect (ideal) self; he does not let this picture go, not even in his sleep, it renders him sleepless, as was the case with that well-known youth,[1] until he himself became as great a conqueror as the man whose renown had made him sleepless. So the imagination deals with this picture of perfection, and so even if it were with the picture of *that* perfected One whose perfection consisted precisely in the fact of having endured, not only frightful sufferings, but also what is most opposed to perfection (ideality), namely, daily indignity and maltreatment and vexation throughout a long life—as imagination presents this picture it looks so easy, one beholds only the perfection, even the striving perfection is seen only as it is completed. For the imagination is itself more perfect than the sufferings of reality, it is timelessly qualified, soaring above the sufferings of reality, it is capable of presenting perfection admirably, it possesses all the splendid colours for portraying it; but suffering, on the other hand, is something the

[1] Themistocles, who was rendered sleepless by the thought of the exploits of Miltiades.

imagination cannot represent, except in a rendering which represents it as already perfected (idealized), that is, softened, toned-down, foreshortened. For the imaginary picture, that is, the picture which the imagination presents and fixes, is after all, in certain sense, unreality, it lacks the reality of time and duration and of the earthly life with its difficulties and sufferings. The true perfection consists in the fact that this perfection—I do not say *was*, as of a definite time (for that concerns the perfect one, not me), but *is* continuously tried day after day by the actual sufferings of reality. But this is what the imagination cannot render—in fact it cannot be rendered, it can only *be*, and hence it is that the picture of perfection as imagination presents it always looks so easy, so persuasive.

A youth commonly has but little conception of reality and its sufferings or of what it means when they become real; and even if he had such a conception, or (since this simply cannot be the case) even if an older man were to come to his aid with his whole experience, and even if such efforts were made as never were made by any poet, and even if such success were attained as no poet hitherto has attained in expressing the picture of perfection with inclusion of the sufferings as well, it nevertheless remains a thing which essentially cannot be done; for (as has been said) imagination has to do with the expression of perfection, but suffering, however accurately it is reported, is already made to seem easy by the mere fact that it is within the sphere of imagination—for it comes into existence by means of imagination. An actor clad in rags (even if in defiance of stage convention they were actual rags) is, as the mere deceit of an hour, a totally different thing from being clad in rags in the everyday life of reality. No, however great the effort of imagination to make this imaginary picture of reality, it cannot be accomplished. If it could, if by the aid of his imagination a man might experience exactly the same thing as in reality, live through it in exactly the same way as if he were to live through it in reality, learn to know himself just as accurately and fundamentally as in the experience of reality—then there would be no meaning in life, then the providential governance of life would be entirely preposterous; for of what use then is reality if by imagination one were able with complete actuality to conceive it in advance, of what use the seventy years if in his twenty-second year a man could experience everything! But it is not thus by any means; and hence again the picture which imagination presents is not the picture of true perfection, there is something it lacks, namely, the suffering of reality or the reality of suffering. The true perfection is this very perfection, only that the suffering is real. It is this very perfection which day after day and year after year is present in the suffering of reality. It is this frightful contradiction—not that perfection does not exist in the more perfect man, but that it exists in the endlessly more imperfect. And here precisely lies the imperfection of the imaginary picture, in the fact namely that the imperfection is not expressed; and this, alas, is the pitiful thing, that in the sphere of reality, which is the only place where true perfection can find true expression, it is so rare because it is so hard—yes, so hard that for this very cause to be perfect in the sphere of reality is the only true perfection.[1]

Now let us turn back to the young man. He is in love with this picture of perfection; one can see this by looking at him: his eye beholds nothing of that which lies closest to him on all sides, it seeks only this picture; he walks like a dreamer, and yet he is wide awake, as one may perceive by the fire in his eye; he walks like a stranger, and yet he is at home, for in imagination he constantly is at home with this picture which he desires to resemble. And as it comes to pass so beautifully with lovers that they get to resemble one another, so likewise is this youth transformed into likeness with this picture which stamps or expresses itself upon all his thinking and upon his every utterance, while with his eyes directed to this picture, as has been said, he has not watched his step, has paid no attention to where he is. He desires to resemble this picture, he already begins to resemble it—and then suddenly he discovers an environment of reality in which he is placed and the relation of this environment to him.

In case the power which directs man's life were an evil power of

[1] The translator ventures diffidently to express his feeling that these last six paragraphs are dull reading. Certainly they are hard to translate, for here S. K. has not expressed his thought with the usual clearness and precision. And yet this can be forgiven, for it now becomes evident that he is endeavouring to say what hitherto never had been said, to formulate a paragraph of existential philosophy before appropriate terms were invented to express it. Something like this Robert Browning was feeling after when in 'Easter-Day' he sought to show why 'it is so very hard to be a Christian'. And now, when we 'turn back to the young man', it becomes evident that S. K. was intent upon his own difficulty in becoming a Christian.

seduction, it would at this moment say of the youth, 'Look now, he is caught'—just as the environing world says of him, 'Look, here is a youth who has allowed himself to be enticed by his imagination to go too far out, so that he has become eccentric and ridiculous, does not fit into reality.' But the power which directs man's life is love, and if it might be said that it has partiality, then it would be a partiality for this youth, as we read indeed that Christ was well pleased with that rich young man, not because he became worldlywise and turned away, but because he had gone so far out that Christ had begun to hope for him. Loving providence therefore does not judge the youth unlovingly as the world judges, but it says, 'Hail to thee! Now life's seriousness begins for thee, now thou hast come so far out that thou canst take seriously the notion that to live is to take an examination.' For life's seriousness does not consist in all this busyness about business and temporal things, about livelihood and employment and place-finding and the procreation of children, but life's seriousness consists in the *will* to be and to express perfection (ideality) in everyday reality, *willing* this in such a way that it may not turn out to one's own perdition, when once for all one busily cancels the whole thing, or presumptuously takes it in vain, regarding it as a dream—what lack of seriousness in both cases!—but humbly *wills* in reality.

In a certain sense the youth's imagination has deceived him, but verily, if he himself will, it has not deceived him to his hurt, it has deceived him into the truth, as though by a deceit it played God into his hands; if the youth will—God in heaven waits for him, willing to help, in such ways as help can be given in an examination which yet must have the seriousness of the highest examination. Imagination has deceived the youth; by the aid of this picture of perfection it has made him forget that he is in the real world: and now he stands there—in exactly the right posture. True enough, he may experience a momentary shudder as he now contemplates the situation; but to escape from the picture— no, that he cannot persuade himself to do. On the other hand, he cannot in any wise escape suffering as long as he cannot persuade himself to escape from the picture; for since the picture he would resemble is the picture of perfection, and since the reality in which he finds himself and in which he would express this resemblance is anything but perfect, suffering is assured and

unavoidable. So he finds himself—God be praised! (for away
with cowardly talk! and accursed be paltry jesting! where only
congratulation is in place)—he finds himself—God be praised!—
in a serious strait. It depends upon divine governance (but let us
never forget that this is love) how many holes (if I may speak
thus) it will bore in him, how hot (if I may speak thus) it will heat
the oven in which like gold he is to be tried. Perhaps he is yet
far from having a complete survey of the true situation, for
governance is love, and though his probation is taken seriously,
there is nothing cruel about this seriousness, which deals gently
with a man and never tempts him beyond his capacity to bear.
He has seen what he is going to suffer, he has seen what this love
will cost him, 'But maybe,' says he, 'better times may come, help
will yet come, and all may yet be well.' So he does not let go the
picture, but advances tranquilly into the suffering whereto he is
led. For governance is love; in its indulgence towards this ardent
youth it has not the heart to let him understand at once that here
there awaits him a disappointment, that he is reckoning without
his host. But this he could not yet endure to understand, and
therefore (oh, infinite solicitude of love!) he is not able to understand it. He holds out, and by thus holding out he is strengthened,
as one is strengthened by suffering—now he loves doubly that
picture of perfection, for what one suffers for, one loves more
dearly. Splendid! But, on the other hand, something is lacking
to him: no help came in the way he had hoped; only in an entirely
different sense has he been helped, for he has become stronger.

Thus governance deals with him many times, and each time it
helps him farther and farther out into suffering, because he will
not let go that picture which he desires to resemble. Then there
comes a moment when everything becomes clear to him; he
understands that this hope of help and of better times was a
youthful hope, he understands now that there is no chance of
escaping suffering, and that it will increase with each forward
step he takes. Now existence has racked him as hard as it can
rack a man; to live under or hold out under this pressure is what
may be called emphatically to exist as a man. If existence had
done this at once, it would have crushed him. Now he is able to
endure it—indeed he must be able to, since it is governance that
does this to him, governance which is love. And yet he shudders
at it. The Tempter whispers to him that he should let that picture

go. But he cannot persuade himself to let it go, and now he exclaims, 'I can do no other. God help me!'[1] Let us now suppose that he holds out until his death—then he has passed his examination. He himself became that picture of perfection which he loved, and verily imagination has not deceived him, nor has governance. To enter into the kingdom of heaven one must become again a little child, but in order that one's life may express the fact that one has entered into the kingdom of heaven, one must become for a second time a youth.[2] To *be* a child or to *be* a youth when one simply is such is an easy thing; but the *second time*—the second time is decisive. To become again a child, to become as nothing, without any selfishness, to become again a youth, notwithstanding one has become shrewd, shrewd by experience, shrewd in worldly wisdom, and then to despise the thought of behaving shrewdly, to *will* to be a youth, to *will* to retain youth's enthusiasm with its spontaneity unabated, to *will* to reacquire it by valiant effort, more apprehensive and shame-faced at the thought of chaffering and bargaining to win earthly advantage than a modest maiden is made by an indecent action—yes, that is the task.

Let us now think of Him who from on high will draw all unto Himself, understanding therefore that life's examination is this: to become and to be a Christian.

Here again the beginning is made with the easiest thing, with exaltation. Just as imagination led that youth on, so also does this picture, the picture of Him, the perfected One, who is on high, draw a man on. Let us think of a youth. He gazes upon this picture to which he feels himself altogether drawn, and he gazes so long that this picture becomes his sole thought. This youth, we can well assume, has heard the narrative of the life which this exalted One lived upon earth in humiliation and lowliness. We assume that this youth is not what might be called frivolous, and that therefore he makes every possible effort by the aid of imagination to represent to himself this suffering. But imagination, which is the faculty of representing perfection (idealization), has to do essentially with exaltation, perfection, and only imperfectly deals with imperfection. Even when this youth represents to

---

[1] Luther's exclamation at the Diet of Worms.

[2] Elsewhere, reflecting upon his own experience, S. K. calls this 'the second immediacy'—but the first youth, the first immediacy, he himself had never known.

himself most vividly the suffering of humiliation, imagination is
prompt to lay emphasis upon the lovingness, the gentleness, the
infinite loftiness of the humiliated One, in *such a way* (for up to
this point there is nothing false in imagination's rendering of the
picture, it is only here the falsehood begins) that the opposition
of the world, all the thousands and thousands of fools, and all
the world's mockery, become in comparison so insignificant—so
insignificant that the thing looks easy. The difficulty which
imagination always has in representing suffering is here increased by a new difficulty: the greater the loftiness and purity
are, so much the more insignificant must the opposition of
the world appear by contrast, whereas in reality the suffering is all the greater and more intense in proportion to the
loftiness.

So the youth goes out into the world with this picture before
his eyes; he does not need, as piety once prompted, to make the
long pilgrimage to the Holy Land in order to put himself back
in time, for the picture is so vividly present to him that in another
sense he can nevertheless be said to have journeyed forth, although
he has remained in the usual place, in the old environment—but
is engaged solely with the desire to resemble this picture. And
this exercises its power over him, the power of love, which indeed
is all-powerful, especially to bring about likeness. His whole
inward man is reconstructed little by little, and it is as if he were
beginning, however imperfectly, to resemble this picture for the
sake of which he has now forgotten everything else—even the
world in which he is, which now seems to him strange and
astonishing.

Now he is caught, now it must come to seriousness. To give
up the picture he cannot persuade himself; but if he does not
give it up, the very fact that he does not, and the picture itself,
will lead him to resemble the very opposite of exaltation and glory.
For that truth is exalted in the world of truth, where He the
humiliated One is now exalted, that indeed is quite natural; but to
will to resemble the truth, though weakly and imperfectly, in the
world of untruth, that must bring one to lowliness and humiliation,
this also is entirely natural. Yet even this the youth has perhaps
understood and apprehended by the aid of imagination, but he
has not experienced it—now for the first time it begins to be
seriousness. Yet he cannot persuade himself to give the picture

up, or (what comes to the same thing) to give up becoming or being a Christian.

And then it will be as with that former youth: he holds fast to the picture and suffers what follows naturally upon holding it fast, but like that youth he will comfort himself in this situation with the human hope that things may get better. Conscious as he is of willing the Good and the True, might he not then succeed in winning men? might not God help him, help him to conquer? God will indeed help him to conquer; but in this world truth conquers only by suffering, by defeat. This, however, the youth does not fully understand. For governance is loving—how could it then have the heart to let a youth at once understand it fully?

Governance now helps him farther and farther out in suffering and danger, for he cannot persuade himself to let go the picture, and as this comes about little by little, he is really hardly observant of the fact that exactly the opposite is occurring from that which he was promised by that hope. But then there will come an instant when, tried as already he is by the sufferings of reality, he will get a survey of the whole situation, and then eternity itself says, 'From now on it is seriousness.' So he himself is already acquainted with sufferings, and now he is to get an understanding of the picture, which at this instant seems shudderingly close. 'There lies before me,' he says, 'a whole life, long or short, but suffering up to the end. This I learn from the picture.' To bring to a stop an object which is rolling down a steep slope is as easy as to bring suffering to a stop before the moment of death, which, in so far as that is part of suffering, will not be tranquil and peaceful for one. And not only is there no let up of suffering, but the painfulness of it increases with its continuance. To be cast out of human society, an abhorrence to all, which then has an effect upon the few who are closest to one and upon whom one has counted, so that they find the price of friendship too dear—to be betrayed, sold by a confidant, to hear from the mouth of the only friend upon whom one had relied up to the last, 'I know him not!' Frightful! Unless a man loses his senses so that he no longer knows himself, speaks of himself in the third person, answering to the scorn which names his name, 'I know not the man!' Ah, when one is oneself living in luxury or at least well provided for, one can read of such things, perhaps talk of them, perhaps also in the course of his talk let fall a few tears—and yet perhaps he is inwardly tranquil, personally unmoved by that about which he is speaking. But when one has already been initiated into suffering, one can doubtless better understand the situation, but then too one has the thing one understands as dreadfully near as possible. However, he is not yet done for. 'Let this picture go?' he says. 'No, that I cannot do. In God's name! let there come upon me what will, I can do no other; let all these sufferings come, I have my hope in God, not as my earliest days, but in another and more inward way, so I will not let this picture go'—but at this same instant he looks again at the Pattern and sees that suffering does not stop even here, there is still an intensification of it, the very last: at the bitterest moment to be deserted by the last support . . . by God. He had thought that in reliance upon God he should bear all these sufferings, all the tortures and pangs which men can invent, but it had never occurred to him that he might be deserted by God, that God who is generally so loving, and everywhere is so quick to help, that yet He should one time leave a man in the lurch and retire—and this just at the moment (how dreadful!), the one moment in all the history of the world, the moment when His help was needed as never before it had been or could be needed.

Let us now suppose that this youth of whom we have been speaking has already, though not many years have passed, become like an old man;[1] let us suppose that with the comfort of the thought that, even though God should desert him, it would be but for an instant—he chooses not to let the picture go. And why? Indeed, the only answer he can give is, 'I can do no other.' Let us then suppose that he holds out unto the last. Thus he stood his test, became and continued to be a Christian, drawn by Him who from on high will draw all unto Himself. Perhaps there lay before him a long life, perhaps only a short one. Perhaps at a given moment he said with blissful confidence, 'Yet a little while' (that is, in a little while I shall be perfected), and yet had at the same time a conception that it might be many years, but eternity was so close to him that he could say, 'Yet a little while.' Perhaps at another moment he sighed, 'Eventually' (meaning, eventually I shall attain blessedness), and yet perhaps he had not in mind a longer period than before, but felt himself weaker and eternity farther away. For these words, 'yet a little while' and 'eventually',

[1] S. K. was 'like an old man' when at the age of forty-two years he died.

mean the same thing in a different way; if it were only a half-hour, one might say, 'yet a little while', but also, 'eventually'; and, conversely, one might say of the longest time, 'eventually', but also, 'yet a little while'. However, to return to our assumption, to this youth, or to this old man, as he had now become—he held out unto the last; then when the 'little while' was passed he entered (after standing the test of becoming and remaining a Christian) eventually into blessedness, with Him who from on high will draw all unto Himself.

This is the test: to become and to remain a Christian, through sufferings with which no other human sufferings can compare in painfulness and anguish. Yet it is not Christianity that is cruel, nor is it Christ. No, Christ in Himself is gentleness and love, He is gentleness and love itself; the cruelty consists in the fact that the Christian has to live in this world and express in the environment of this world what it is to be a Christian—for Christ is not so gentle, i.e. so weak, that He would take the Christian out of the world. In a passionate mood prompted by the possibility of offence it will seem to one as if Christianity were cruel; but this is not so, it is the world which is cruel, Christianity is gentleness and love. Yet, as has been said, the suffering is the most agonizing, and for the individual Christian there is reserved a suffering by which the God-Man could not be tried. It is a frightful thing to discover that the truth is persecuted, but the suffering assumes a different character, depending upon who it is makes this discovery. A foolish, conceited man who is extraordinarily satisfied with himself does not suffer greatly at the discovery that truth is persecuted—if indeed it were possible for such a man to make this discovery. On the other hand, the God-Man knows within Himself and with eternal certainty that He is the truth, and He surely suffers for the fact that as the truth or in spite of being the truth he is persecuted; but He does not suffer inwardly at another spot concerning how thoroughly He Himself at every instant is in the truth. But such is the case with the individual Christian. It naturally could never occur to him to desire blasphemously to be the truth, he is before God a lowly, sinful man who only very imperfectly relates himself to the truth. But the more the Christian is thus inwardly in fear and trembling before God, so much the more is he in dread of every false step, so much the more is he inclined only to accuse himself. In this situation it might sometimes be a comfort to him if others thought well of him. But exactly the opposite is the case, he is accused of every evil, and every instant is forced back again into concern about himself, whether after all the fault might not lie in him—and he shudders. Yet the more he labours in fear and trembling, struggling all the more to be entirely unselfish, devoted and loving, all the more do men accuse him of self-love. And if he lives in Christendom, this is accompanied by a humming and buzzing of fantastic figures belonging to that section of the clergy which may be called so-called priests, who with a view to their livings asseverate that the loving man is loved by God and men, and that this is what Christianity is—not that the loving person is sacrificed, but that the loving person is the one to whom sacrifice is offered—without observing that this is indeed to mock Christ, for if this is true, then Christ (who was sacrificed) was not the loving One. But so in fact does a Christian in Christendom suffer the sufferings here described, augmented by the fact that men say of him that he is not a Christian, that his life is an unchristian exaggeration, because he will not like the other Christians treat Christianity as a thing which must presumably be hidden in the inward man—perhaps so well concealed that it is not there at all. So it is agonizing for the individual Christian, already disturbed by deep self-concern, to make at the same time the discovery—not that the truth must suffer (for that is a discovery which no Christian can truly be said to make, but only the God-Man who was the truth), but that even love for the truth must suffer. In case this—shall we now say this *suffering* Christian? no, that is superfluous, for every Christian suffers—in case this Christian had not the Pattern to look upon, he could not hold out, he could not dare to believe in love within himself when men thus bear witness against him. But the Pattern, who eternally knew within Himself that He was love, whom therefore no world, not even all the world, could shake in this conviction, has precisely expressed the fact that love is hated, truth persecuted. With this picture before his eyes the Christian therefore holds out in humiliation, drawn unto Him who from on high will draw all unto Himself.

Such is the relationship between exaltation and lowliness. The humiliation of the true Christian is not plain humiliation, it is merely the reflected image of exaltation, but the reflection of it in this world, where exaltation must appear conversely as lowliness and humiliation. In reality the star is situated high in the heavens, and it is no less high for the fact that seen in the ocean it seems to be below the earth. Likewise, to be a true Christian is the highest exaltation, although as reflected in this world it must appear the deepest humiliation. Humiliation is therefore in a certain sense exaltation. As soon as you eliminate the world, the turbid element which confuses the reflection, that is, as soon as the Christian dies, he is exalted on high, where he already was before, though it could not be perceived here on earth, any more than a man who was unable to lift up his head, and so could only see the star deep below at the bottom of the sea, could get the notion that in reality it is on high. And so it is with the true Christian; in his humiliation he is not supported by the recognition of others that this humiliation is really exaltation or is the converse reflection of exaltation due to the character of the reflecting medium. If such were the case, if he had such support, the humiliation could not be taken seriously. The situation is not like that of a prince who is known and yet unknown; but it is as when a prince has so disguised himself that he is ensured against anybody recognizing him, or when he lives in a foreign land where nobody knows him, and there he is regarded as a man who pretends to be a prince, one to whom they will therefore say, 'No, enough of that, you do not deceive us; for you to make out that you are royalty or something great is a sheer lie and vanity and delusion. You are either mad or you are a deceiver.'

And how does this situation come about? It comes about in this way: He who from on high will draw all unto Himself draws a man unto Himself in such wise that he becomes and remains a Christian; but this Christian is here upon earth, and therefore it is the exaltation of Him who draws which is reflected in this Christian's humiliation.

V

O LORD Jesus Christ, doubtless it is from on high Thou dost draw a man to Thyself, and it is to victory Thou dost call him, but this is to say that Thou dost call upon him to strive and dost promise him victory in the strife whereunto Thou dost call him, O Thou mighty Victor. So then preserve us, we pray Thee, as from all other errors, so also from this, that we might imagine we are members of a Church already triumphant here in the world. Thy kingdom indeed was not of this world and is not; this world is not the abode of Thy Church, there is only room for it if it will strive and by striving make room for itself to exist in. But if it will strive, it shall never be driven out of the world, that Thou dost vouch for. On the other hand, if it imagines that it is to triumph[1] here in the world, then, alas, it is itself to blame for that Thou didst withdraw Thy support, then it has perished, then it has confounded itself with the world. Be then with Thy militant Church, that it never may come to pass (in the only way in which it could come to pass) that it should be blotted out from the earth by becoming a triumphant Church.

John 12: 32. AND I, IF I BE LIFTED UP FROM THE EARTH, WILL DRAW ALL UNTO MYSELF

'Yes, this is easy to understand: He has triumphed, and we have merely to join ourselves to Him in order to share the triumph with Him—only no quirks and captiousness, and the thing is quite simple.' Hardly will anyone express himself exactly in these words, yet perhaps there has been one and another who has thought thus within himself. And what then have we to say for our part?

One might call attention to the fact that (if there were no other obstacle) this is not so easy a thing to do, inasmuch as Christ's life in a sense is outside of the direct relationship which exists between every individual in the human race, for the fact that as God-Man, although truly man, He is yet so heterogeneous, so unlike the individual man, that it is not just simply a matter of

---

[1] *Stridende* (striving, combating) and *triumpherede* allude to the distinction between the Church militant and the Church triumphant.

course that with a kind of impudent forwardness one should want in a way to take sides with Him. One might call attention to the fact that the heterogeneity of Christ (the God-Man), His difference from all individual men, is expressed also by the doctrine of the second coming. For it is not with Him as with some other man who lived once upon a time, who perhaps won some great victory or another, the consequences of which we as a matter of course appropriate, whereas nothing more is heard of him, least of all that he might come again to make a reckoning with us, to sit in judgement upon us by requiring of us his own again or his own self. With Christ it is different. He lived here on earth, this life of His is the pattern. Thereupon He ascends up on high, and He says to the race directly, 'Now you begin'. And what is it they should begin with? By living in conformity with the Pattern—'But', He adds, 'one day at the end of time I shall come again.' This form of existence (if I may so express myself) makes the whole existence of the Church here on earth a parenthesis, a parenthesis in Christ's life; the content of this parenthesis begins with Christ's Ascension, and with His second coming it ends. So here the case is not similar to every other historical relationship between an individual and others who profit as a matter of course by his victory; for neither is such an individual the pattern, nor is such an individual he that shall come again. It is only Christ that can make His life a test for all men. When He ascends up to heaven the examination period begins; it has now lasted 1,800 years, it will perhaps last 18,000. But (and this contributes expressly to define the intervening period as an examination) He is coming again. And if this is so, then all direct adherence to Him, with the aim of profiting by His triumph as a matter of course, is more impossible than in the case of any other man.

Upon this, however, we will not dwell any longer, we prefer to insist upon another consideration. Is 'truth' the sort of thing one might conceivably appropriate without more ado by means of another man? Without more ado—that is, without being willing to be developed and tried, to fight and to suffer, just as he did who acquired the truth for himself? Is not that as impossible as to sleep or dream oneself into the truth? Is it not just as impossible to appropriate it thus without more ado however wide awake one may be? Or is one really wide awake, is not this a vain

conceit, when one does not understand or will not understand
that with respect to the truth there is no short cut which dispenses
with the necessity of acquiring it, and that with respect to acquiring it from generation to generation there is no essential
short cut, so that every generation and every individual in the
generation must essentially begin again from the start?

For what is truth? and in what sense was Christ the truth?
The first of these questions was asked by Pilate, as every one
knows, and it is another question whether he really was interested
in getting an answer to it. In any case, his question was in one
sense as perfectly in place as it possibly could be, and in another
sense as entirely out of place as possible. Pilate put to Christ
the question, 'What is truth?' But in fact Christ was the truth,
and so the question was perfectly in place. Yes—and yet, in
another sense, no. The fact that at that instant it could occur to
Pilate to put such a question to Christ is precise proof that he had
absolutely no eye for the truth. For Christ's life was the truth,
and therefore He Himself says (as a more precise explanation of
the words, 'My kingdom is not of this world: if My kingdom
were of this world, then would My servants fight, that I should
not be delivered to the Jews'): 'To this end was I born, and for
this cause came I into the world, that I should bear witness unto
the truth.' Christ's life upon earth, every instant of this life, was
the truth. Wherein then lies the fundamental confusion in Pilate's
question? It lies in the fact that it could occur to him to ask such
a question of *Christ*; for in asking such a question he denounces
himself, he reveals that Christ's life has not made clear to him
what truth is—but how then could Christ explain this to Pilate
in words, when that which is the truth, Christ's own life, has not
opened Pilate's eyes to what truth is? It seems as if Pilate were
avid of knowledge, eager to learn, but verily his question is as
foolish a one as could be—not the fact that he asks what truth is,
but that he puts this question to Christ, whose life precisely is the
truth, and who therefore by His life is at every instant a more
potent demonstration of what truth is than are the prolix lectures
of all the cleverest thinkers. Every other man, a thinker, a
teacher of science, &c., indeed any other man you please, a
serving-man, a letter-carrier—to ask of him what truth is, that
makes sense in a way; but to ask it of Christ who stands bodily
before one, to ask this of Christ is the most complete confusion

possible. If Christ were to reply to such a question, He must momentarily admit with tacit untruth the implication that He is not the truth. No man, with the exception of Christ, is the truth; in the case of every other man the truth is something endlessly higher than he is, and therefore it naturally occurs to him to ask, 'What is truth?' and to make answer to this question. Pilate's notion with regard to Christ evidently was, that Christ was a man pretty much like the rest of them, and then only with his question seemed to single Him out (untruly) as some sort of a thinker or who knows what; and he put the question to Him rather in the role of the highly superior person who in reality looks down upon thinking as something which has no practical bearing, but takes pleasure in talking to the man for a moment in a tone of lofty condescension not unmixed with roguish jest—so it is that Pilate asks of Christ, 'What is truth?' And Christ *is* the truth! Poor Pilate! There has been handed down that commiserating word of thine, 'Look, what a man!'[1] but in view of thy question there is good reason to say of thee, 'Look, what a fool! For this question of thine, though thou wert not able to understand it thus, is absolutely the most foolish and the most confused question that ever was asked.' The question is just as foolish, precisely as foolish, as if one were to inquire of a man with whom one was talking, 'Dost thou exist?' For Christ *is* the truth. And what could that man say in reply? He must say, 'If one who stands here talking to me cannot feel sure that I exist, my asseveration can be of no avail, for that is something much less than my existence.' And so it is also with Christ in relation to Pilate. Christ is the truth. 'If my life', He might say, 'does not open thine eyes to what truth is, then it is of all things the most impossible for Me to tell thee what it is. Herein lies the difference between Me and all other men: doubtless what some other man says in answer to the question, "What is truth?" is not always quite true, but I am the only man that cannot reply to this question at all, for I am the truth.'

Christ is the truth in such a sense that to *be* the truth is the only true explanation of what truth is. Hence one may ask an Apostle, one may ask a Christian, what truth is, and then the Apostle or the Christian will point to Christ and say, 'Behold Him, learn of Him, He was the truth.' That is to say, the truth, in the sense in

[1] So reads the Danish version—not without plausibility.

which Christ was the truth, is not a sum of sentences, not a definition of concepts, &c., but a life. Truth in its very being is not the duplication of being in terms of thought, which yields only the thought of being, merely ensures that the act of thinking shall not be a cobweb of the brain without relation to reality, guaranteeing the validity of thought, that the thing thought actually is, i.e. has validity. No, truth in its very being is the reduplication in me, in thee, in him, so that my, that thy, that his life, approximately, in the striving to attain it, expresses the truth, so that my, that thy, that his life, approximately, in the striving to attain it, is the very being of truth, is a *life*, as the truth was in Christ, for He was the truth.

And hence, Christianly understood, the truth consists not in knowing the truth but in being the truth. In spite of the newest philosophy, there is an infinite difference between these two, which can best be seen in Christ's relation to Pilate; for Christ could not, or could only untruly, reply to the question about what truth is, for the reason precisely that He was not one who knew what truth is, but He was the truth. Not as though He did not know what truth is; but when one is the truth, and when the requirement is to be the truth, this thing of knowing the truth is untruth. For knowing the truth is something which follows as a matter of course from being the truth, and not conversely; and precisely for this reason it becomes untruth when knowing the truth is separated from being the truth, or when knowing the truth is treated as one and the same thing as being the truth, since the true relation is the converse of this: to be the truth is one and the same thing as knowing the truth, and Christ would never have known the truth in case He had not been the truth; no man knows more of the truth than what he is of the truth. Indeed, properly speaking, one cannot know the truth; for if one knows the truth, he must know that to be the truth is the truth, and so in his knowledge of the truth he knows that this thing of knowing the truth is an untruth. If a man were to say that by knowing the truth one is the truth, then he himself says that truth is, to be the truth, when he says that to know the truth is to be the truth; for in the other case he must say, the truth is, to know the truth, otherwise the question about truth merely returns again, so that the question receives no answer, the decisive answer is merely adjourned until one can know whether he is the truth or not. That is to say, knowledge has a relation to truth, but with that I am (untruly) outside of myself; within me (that is, when I am truly within myself, not untruly outside of myself) truth is, if it is at all, a being, a *life*. Therefore it is said, 'This is life eternal, to know the only true God and Him whom He hath sent', the Truth. That is to say, only then do I truly know the truth when it becomes a life in me. Therefore Christ compares truth with food, and the appropriation of it with eating; for just as food, corporally, by being appropriated (assimilated) becomes the sustenance of life, so also is truth, spiritually, both the giver of life and its sustenance; it is life. And hence one sees what a monstrous error it is, very nearly the greatest possible error, to impart Christianity by lecturing; and how Christianity has been changed by this perpetual lecturing may be seen in the fact that all expressions have been constructed in view of the notion that truth is understanding, knowledge (one constantly talks of comprehending, speculating, reflecting, &c.), whereas in primitive Christianity all expressions were constructed with a view to truth as a form of being.

There is a difference between truth and truths, and this difference is made especially evident by the definition of truth as being, or it is evident from the fact that a distinction is drawn between the '*way*' and the final decision, what is attained at the end, the '*result*'. With respect to that sort of truth which permits a distinction between the way and the point ultimately reached by travelling along that way, the successor may find himself in a different position in comparison with the foregoer, he may be in a position to begin at a different point and slip into the truth more easily; in fine, the difference consists in the fact that the way is shortened, in certain cases indeed it is shortened to such a degree that it drops out, as it were, entirely. But when the truth is the way, when it is being the truth, when it is a life (and so it is Christ says of Himself, 'I am the way, the truth and the life'), then no essential change is conceivable as between the foregoer and the successor. The change reflected upon above consisted in the fact that the way was shortened, and that was possible because the way had not essentially the same significance as the truth. But when the truth itself is the way, the way cannot be shortened or drop out, without the truth being corrupted or dropping out.

This is not so difficult to understand if only one will give oneself a little time to understand it. It may, however, become

clearer when it is illuminated by several examples; and it is
important that it be made clear, this difference between truth and
truths, for what always has produced confusion in Christianity,
and what in great part is responsible for the vain conceit of a
triumphant Church, is this, that people have regarded Christianity
as truth in the sense of a result, whereas instead it is truth in the
sense of 'the way'.—Here are a few examples. A man discovers
something, gun-powder, for example. He, the discoverer, has
perhaps spent many, many years of his life pondering and rumi-
nating; perhaps many men before him have in vain spent a long
time in a similar way—now he succeeds, now powder is discovered. At that same instant the way as good as drops out, to
such a degree is it shortened. What it took him twenty years to do,
another man, by the help of his advance, can do, if he goes about
it rightly, in the space of half an hour. The twenty years stand
in an entirely fortuitous relation to the invention; one cannot
properly say that he employed twenty years in the discovery of
gun-powder; no, he too actually discovered gun-powder in half
an hour; one might say more justly that in twenty years he did not
discover gun-powder, in a certain sense these years have no value,
since they did not contribute to the discovery but represent a vain
attempt to discover gun-powder, or were spent in not discovering
powder. Suppose it could be proved conclusively that he laboured
full twenty years to discover gun-powder, and did not discover
it—in this case 'the way' has absolutely no significance in itself.
Suppose that the discoverer made his discovery as he was coming
home drunk from a party and stumbled over the kerbstone—
the way is a thing absolutely indifferent, in this case the discoverer
would merely be on a par with the dog which discovered purple,[1]
yet his discovery would have been just as valuable to the human
race, which might perhaps have called him, if the discovery had
been of a different sort, the benefactor of the race—but not its
teacher, for to be a teacher, especially a teacher of the race, 'the
teacher of mankind', answers to the conception of truth as 'the
way'.—A man works laboriously to get an understanding of an
obscure period of history upon which hitherto no investigation
has been able to throw any light—finally, after spending twenty
years on this work, he succeeds in bringing the historic truth to

[1] Refering to the story that purple dye was discovered when a dog thrust its
muzzle into the shell of the mussel which secretes this colour.

light and rendering it incontestable. This outcome inures to the advantage of the successor; the way is very considerably shortened, the successor requires perhaps barely three months to familiarize himself completely with the true situation in that obscure period.—A man cultivates a language which no one hitherto has known. He makes prodigious efforts a whole life long, but also leaves behind him as the outcome of his life and effort substantial aids to study, by the help of which the successor perhaps in the course of two years gets just as far as he did in twenty years. Here the way is considerably shortened for the successor. The disciple (in spite of the fact that he is perhaps a mere bungler in comparison with the master) is constantly ahead of the master; by reason of the master's preliminary work he is in a position to begin at another point and to reach farther than he did. And such more or less is the situation wherever truth is knowledge.

But it is different when truth is being, when it is 'the way'. Here it is not possible for any essential difference to exist as between the foregoer and the successor, or as between one generation and another, even if the world were to last for 1,800 years, for truth is not different from the way but is the way itself. Christ was the truth, He was the way, or He was the way in the sense that the truth is the way. The fact that He has travelled the way to the end does not alter anything in the situation of the successor, who, if he is of the truth and desires to be of the truth, can be so only by following 'the way'; the fact that at a given time there have lived thirty generations which have followed the way alters nothing in the situation of the next generation or of every individual in it who must always begin over again at the same point at the beginning of the way in order to follow it. So there is no occasion or opportunity for triumphing; for only he who has followed the way to the end could triumph, but he is no longer in this world, he has gone up on high, as Christ also was the way when He ascended up to heaven. If, however, a late comer would take occasion to triumph because someone before him had followed the way, this would be just as foolish as if a student were to triumph because another student had passed his examination.

If a man will hold fast to this which is indeed Christ's own saying, that the truth is the way, he will perceive ever more clearly that a Church triumphant in this world is a vain conceit, that in this world there can be question only of a Church militant. But the Church militant is related to and feels itself drawn to Christ in lowliness; the Church triumphant has taken the Church of Christ in vain. To make this clear is the purpose of this argument, and it should be remembered that in speaking here of a triumphant Church we mean a Church which would triumph in this world, for it is entirely appropriate to speak of a Church triumphant in eternity, corresponding to Christ's reception into glory.

How could one ever get the notion of a triumphant Church? and what is to be understood by a triumphant Church?

It has been remarked above that what especially has contributed to the error concerning a triumphant Church is the fact that people have conceived of Christianity as that sort of truth which can be distinguished from the way, or have conceived of the truth of Christianity as a result, as what might be called a surplus, a dividend, for in the case of truth as the way the emphasis falls precisely upon the fact that there is no surplus, no dividend, which accrues to the successor from the predecessor, that there is no result. If Christianity were the truth in the sense people so commonly suppose, then the notion of triumphing would be entirely appropriate. The human race has a triumphant relation to the discovery of gun-powder, of printing, &c., to the many conquests made in the realm of science and art, &c., for here truth is a result, here the emphasis does not fall upon 'the way,' and upon 'every single individual', who, responsible before God, has to decide for himself whether he will walk in the way or not, regardless, completely regardless, as to whether no one else or all men are following the same way, completely regardless as to whether no one or countless millions have followed the same way —no, here the emphasis falls upon truth as knowledge, upon the 'dividend', and upon the race, human society, the partnership, the *corporation*, which as a matter of course assumes possession of the truth, and it is an accident that an individual invented it, discovered it, verified it, &c. If, for example, Christ had been a teacher of the truth, a thinker, who had made a discovery or verified something which had cost him perhaps indescribable cudgelling of the brain, but which also might become a result (because the way stood in an accidental relationship to the truth) —then it would be quite appropriate for the generation following to behave triumphantly with regard to it. The successor, exempted from the necessity of such prodigious cudgelling of the brain, of these many, many years of effort, might at the most feel obliged to remember gratefully the man who had endured all this, but for the rest there would be nothing to do but to triumph. That this is an error has already been shown, and here it need only be added that for this reason Christ's teaching is infinitely exalted above all the discoveries of time or of the ages, that it is an eternity older and an eternity higher than all systems, even than the very newest one,[1] even than that which ten thousand years hence will be the newest; for His teaching is the truth, but in the sense that the truth is the way; as the God-Man He Himself is and remains the way, which no man without blasphemy dare assert of himself, however zealous he is in professing that the truth is the way.

But besides this error which has missed the point of Christianity as confusedly as possible by conceiving of truth as a result, there is at the same time another error which has contributed to bring about the conceit of a triumphant Church. This error is the specious notion which has arisen in the course of the ages, that in a way we are all Christians. For if this is posited, the Church militant seems an impossibility. Wherever there seems to be, or people assume that there is, an established Christendom, there is an attempt to construct a triumphant Church, even if this word is not used; for the Church militant is in process of becoming, *established* Christendom simply *is*, does not become.

Finally, this conceit of a triumphant Church is connected with the human impatience which would lay hold in advance of what belongs later; and as it is almost universally observable that children and youth desire to experience by anticipation the whole of life, leaving nothing for manhood and old age, so has the race, the human race, or Christendom, with like impatience desired to anticipate eternity, and (instead of what is God's invention and His notion with regard to existence as a whole, that the temporal, this life of ours here, is the period of probation, eternity the period of triumph)—instead of this they would introduce triumph within the temporal, which means to abolish Christianity. What Christ said about His kingdom not being of this world was not said with special reference to those times when He uttered this saying; it is an eternally valid utterance about the relation of Christ's kingdom to this world, and so it is valid for every age.

[1] Hegelianism, of course.

As soon as Christ's kingdom comes to terms with the world, Christianity is abolished. If, on the other hand, Christ is the truth, His is truly enough a kingdom in this world, but not of this world, that is to say, it is militant.

What then is to be understood by a triumphant Church? By this we are to understand that the time for contending is past, that the Church, although it is still in this world, has nothing to contend for or to contend about. But then the Church and this world have become synonymous; and such in fact is precisely the case, not only with all that has called itself the triumphant Church, but with all that is called an established Christendom. For in this world Christ's Church can truly survive only by contending, that is, by fighting for its survival every instant. If it is the established Church, this implies that it has triumphed. The militant Church survives only by contending, and the Church which is called established must surely be one which survives after it has triumphed.

And this triumphant Church, or established Christendom, does not resemble the Church militant any more than a quadrangle resembles a circle. Imagine a Christian of those ages when the Church was truly militant—it would be perfectly impossible for him to recognize the Church in its present perversion. He would hear Christianity preached, and would hear that what was said was quite true, but to his great amazement he would see that the actual conditions for being a Christian were exactly the opposite to what they were in his time, so that to be a Christian now is no more like being a Christian in his time than walking on one's legs is like walking on one's head.

To be a Christian in this militant Church means to express what it is to be a Christian within an environment which is the opposite to Christian. To be a Christian in a triumphant, an established Christendom means to express what it is to be a Christian within an environment which is synonymous, homogeneous with Christianity. If in the former case I am a true Christian, then as a matter of course (seeing that the stage-setting is the opposite) this will be recognizable *conversely* by the opposition I suffer; and just in proportion as there is more truth in my claim to be a Christian, will this be recognizable by the fact that the opposition is greater. In the second case (seeing that the stage-setting is congruous) the fact of being a Christian will as a matter of course be recognizable *directly* by the favour, honour, and esteem I win in Christendom. Just in proportion as there is more truth in my claim to be a Christian, this too will be recognizable by the extraordinary esteem I enjoy in Christendom. This is an inevitable consequence when the assumption is a triumphant Church. At the precise place where suffering would have come if I had been living in a militant Church, now comes reward; there, where scorn and derision would overtake me if I had been living in a militant Church, now honour and esteem beckon to me; there, where death would be unavoidable, I now celebrate the highest triumph. For since (according to the assumption) all among whom I live are Christians, they must promptly recognize my genuine Christian character, and so, instead of opposing me, they hasten towards me with honours and distinctions. Indeed, if we can imagine a member of the Christian Church from the age when it was militant becoming a witness of this situation, he surely must for an instant be moved almost to laughter at beholding that what in his age was frightful earnest had become a charming game. There stands Christianity with its requirement of self-denial: 'Deny thyself—and suffer therefore, because thou dost deny thyself.' This was Christianity. Now how different. I imagine a youth who with lovable simplicity determined to direct his life in accordance with the Holy Scriptures—how astonished he would be, how could be ever stop laughing at himself? For precisely at the instant when, in accordance with Christ's directions, he had prepared himself to suffer—what comes to pass? He receives honour and esteem. He girds himself to withstand opposition, he dares to take the step—and he is greeted with acclamation. He prepares himself at least for icy coldness and ridicule, and he is received with the warm embrace of almost feminine admiration. The youth had forgotten (what is not to be found at all in the Bible) that it was in Christendom he was living, in Christendom where all are Christians, in the triumphant Church where there is no longer any combat, but where for being a true Christian one is rewarded with distinction.

Such is the situation in the *triumphant* Church, where it pays exceedingly well to be a Christian, and where the only thing that doesn't pay is not to be a Christian. On the other hand, if so-called established Christendom maybe does not expressly call itself the Church triumphant, perhaps disdaining this name as an externality, it nevertheless produces the same confusion by means of *'hidden inwardness'*;[1] for, again, established Christendom, where all are Christians, but only in hidden inwardness, resembles the militant Church just as little as the stillness of death resembles vociferous passion.

Nothing but the vain conceit of a triumphant Church could succeed in making the notion prevail that in a stricter sense only one particular order in the Church was really Christian. The exclusive task or business of this order was that of being Christian, and here the rule applied with direct force, that the more truly a Christian one was, the higher he rose in honour and general esteem. The rest of the world actually constituted only an audience, the chorus, and with this provided no opposition to the thing of being a Christian, but rather an admiring circle about that order which represented what it was to be a Christian. Then, however, when the distinction of this order vanished, there vanished also the triumphant Church. The direct recognition of Christian character (the degree of the attainment of true Christianity corresponding directly to the honour and esteem enjoyed) stumbled at a peculiar difficulty which rendered it impossible— the difficulty that everybody desired to take part in the game.[2] Essentially, the clergy have nothing else to do but to express what it is to be a Christian; and as long as the multitude of Christians were content to behold themselves in the representative order, this notion of the triumphant Church was viable. But it was different when the distinction of this order no longer contented the multitude of Christians. The multitude of Christians had at the same time—indeed as viewed from the outside they had principally—something else to attend to in the world besides expressing (in the sense of the triumphant Church) what it is to be a Christian. How then could the direct recognizability of this thing of being a Christian be expressed in a medium which is heterogeneous to this thing of being a Christian, yet not hostile, only indifferent? That, in fact, was an impossibility. In the militant Church direct recognition is impossible because the fact

---

[1] Bishop Mynster dwelt unctuously upon the virtue of 'hidden inwardness', and S. K. too was inclined to exalt it so long as he was an anonymous Christian. Only after 1848 did he begin to recognize it as a sham.

[2] S. K. has in mind the polemical emphasis of Protestantism upon the 'priesthood of all believers'.

of being a Christian finds expression within an environment which is contrary to it. Now, however, direct recognition has become impossible because the fact of being a Christian has to be expressed within an environment which is indifferent. Understand me aright. A simple citizen, for example, is a Christian. Let us suppose that he is a shoemaker. That is his livelihood, the greater part of the day he naturally is employed in the exercise of his handicraft. If now the direct recognition of the fact that he is a Christian were possible, he among shoemakers who was the truest Christian, or the fact that he was the truest Christian, must be recognizable in the observation that he had the most to do, had the most apprentices, and perhaps the King and Queen together with the whole royal family had their shoes made by him—or at least the clergy had. That this principle could not be applied became naturally in the course of time more and more evident. The direct recognition of Christian character encountered a different sort of opposition to that which the militant Church knew. The opposition was not the contrary to the thing of being a Christian, but the indifferent. This 'opposition of indifference' does not convert the situation to converse recognizableness as in the militant Church, but it nevertheless makes direct recognition impossible.

So in Christendom there came about a complete change in the stage-setting with respect to what it is to be a Christian. People gave up the conceit of a triumphant Church; they let the whole external arrangement continue to exist, and along with this they accepted the law of indifference with respect to being a Christian, the law that the best shoemaker is the one who makes the best shoes, the best poet the one who writes the best poetry, &c. With this they gave up the external marks of being a Christian and transformed the whole thing into inwardness. There is posited and assumed a general clearing of accounts for us all, we all receive an acquittance, we are all of us Christians, exactly in the same sense in which we are all of us men, the assumption with which the game of life or of reality first begins, so that it would be stupidity, indeed madness, for anyone to advance a special claim for himself that he is a man, that being an assumption which is assumed once for all and of all and lies at the bottom of all.

Here we have the concept of established Christendom. In established Christendom we are all true Christians, but it is in

hidden inwardness. The external world has nothing whatever to
do with the fact that I am a Christian; my being a Christian is
therefore not measurable. If I am an innkeeper, I do not require
in the least that my character as a Christian should be recognized
in the fact that I have the best patronage. No, if as an innkeeper
I am to have the best patronage, it depends upon how well I know
how to satisfy 'a highly esteemed cultured public', and the true
Christian I am is a thing for itself, a thing for myself, something
I am in hidden inwardness—quite like all the others, not merely
like all the other innkeepers, but quite literally like every other
man in Christendom; to such a degree is it true that I am a Christian that in my case it is just exactly as true as in the case of all the
others. If I am a parson, I do not require in the least that my true
Christian character be recognized by the fact that I have the most
hearers and am the most acclaimed preacher. No, if as a parson
I am to have the most patronage, it depends artistically upon what
gifts of eloquence I possess, it depends upon whether I have a
voice, how the preaching gown becomes me, how well I have
studied the newest philosophy so that I can satisfy 'the requirements of the age'; the true Christian I am is a thing for itself, a
thing for myself, something I am in hidden inwardness—quite
like all the others; but that I am a true Christian is sure enough,
it is just as sure as that all the others are.

And why, then, this hiddenness? why this hiddenness which I
so carefully watch over and preserve? Well, naturally, because
I am fearful lest, in case it came to be known to what a degree
I am a true Christian, I should be rewarded for it with extraordinary honour and esteem; and I am too true a Christian to wish
to be honoured and esteemed *because* I am a true Christian. This
you see, is the reason why I keep it laid away in hidden inwardness;
for if people came to know it, it would be inevitable that I should
be exceedingly honoured and esteemed for it, since I live in
established Christendom where we are all of us true Christians.

If a Christian of the age when the Church was militant were to
be transported into established Christendom, he would fall into
the profoundest amazement. In the militant Church the fact of
being a Christian could be recognized by the opposition one
suffered. In the triumphant Church it could be recognized by
the honour and esteem one enjoyed. But established Christendom has discovered something new: one keeps hidden the fact that

one is a Christian—for fear it might (unchristianly) be rewarded by honour and esteem. In the militant Church it sometimes no doubt was the case that one or another kept hidden the fact that he was a Christian for fear of the opposition which was linked to being a Christian; but in 'established Christendom' it is for fear of enjoying honour and esteem. And yet, for all this, established Christendom is something infinitely higher than the militant Church, which hardly had an inkling of so lofty a piety! In the militant Church it was piety to confess Christianity; in established Christendom piety consists precisely in being silent about it. Oh, infinite depth of piety! since the whole thing might so easily, with such infinite ease, be merely illusion! Oh, countless hosts of the pious, when the collective millions of every land are pious men of such a sort—and that surely we all of us are! Put off thy shoes from off thy feet, for the place whereon thou standest is holy ground, when thou standest in Christendom, where there are nothing but true Christians! Let God keep eternity for Himself, where taken all in all He hardly gets as many true Christians as there are at any one instant in established Christendom where all are true Christians.

If one were to imagine a youth who had grown up in established Christendom, but unacquainted as yet with the realities which he was about to face, living in almost monastic remoteness from life, brought up upon the Holy Scriptures—his experience will be strange in the highest degree, and in a sense ludicrous. He is well instructed in Christianity—assuming that this is possible by means of the Holy Scriptures, and for the sake of the poor young man one may be inclined to admit this assumption. He was told that the requirement is to confess Christ before the world. He is well instructed—so far, that is to say, as one can be well instructed by means of the Holy Scriptures, and for the young man's sake one may be inclined to admit this assumption. He is instructed about what the consequence will be—having pondered all this well, the youth is resolved to direct his life in accordance with the precepts. But what happens? He chances to live in established Christendom. While he makes as if he would venture to take the decisive step, there comes up to him a kindly man, a sort of pastor of souls, and 'delivers a sort of a speech':[1] 'My

---

[1] Quoted from Holberg: *Ulysses von Ithaca*, Act II, sc. 3. Holophernes delivers a sort of a speech.

young friend, thou art in error, thou art not aware what place thou art in, it is established Christendom, and that verily is not the place to confess Christ. For between us be it said (but this remains between us, and for me to have said so much is already a weakness, an inadvertence), we are all Christians, and the true Christian is precisely he who keeps it most hidden.' In case a youth who in his childhood had been brought up on fairy-tales and was therefore familiar with the thought of monsters which dwell in the forests but in the story are slain, in case now he were to go out into the real world with a prodigious sword at his side and an equally prodigious courage in his breast, nothing stranger could befall him than what befell that youth in established Christendom. Though he were to encounter a monster stranger than any he had heard about or read about, that would not be the strangest thing, it would not amount to anything in comparison with the strange thing which actually happened to him, that he never could anywhere catch a glimpse of anything resembling a monster. So then there came to him a kindly elderly man and said: 'My young friend, thou art in error, thou art not in the world of fairy-tales, but in the civilized and polite world where there are no such monsters, where thou dost live amongst cultured and well brought up people, and where moreover the police attend to public security, the clergy to morality, and where the gas-lights make the night as safe as the day. Put up thy sword, therefore, into its sheath, and learn what now, when the age of monsters is long past, man's task is, namely to be an agreeable person, altogether like the rest of us, that in every other man thou mayest recognize thyself, and every other man recognize himself in thee, with the most deceptive degree of likeness that is possible.'

The triumphant Church, as has been said, does no more resemble the militant Church than a quadrangle resembles a circle, and established Christendom resembles it just as little. Nevertheless, the militant Church alone is the truth, the triumphant Church and established Christendom are vain conceits.

'But,' I hear somebody say, 'this thing of the militant Church is surely unreasonable and impossible now. When we are all Christians, what could there be to contend about?' My dear chap, if there was nothing else, we might (for the sake of having something to contend about) contend about the affirmation that we are all Christians, and raise the question how this agrees with the facts. 'How! Wilt thou presume to be a searcher of hearts, judging people in the inward man? When a person says of himself that he is a Christian, thou surely wilt not presume to deny it?' Now, evidently, we have got something to contend about. But does he say that? I thought that in established Christendom the hidden inwardness required that we should keep this hid. 'Yes, indeed, we should keep it hid, just because it is assumed that all are Christians.' How is it that this is assumed when each person severally keeps it hid because it is assumed that we all are that?

The situation is this: when everyone in turn qualifies himself as a Christian *like* 'the others', then, if you will, there is really no one who confesses Christ; on the other hand, it is, if you will, recognized and confessed of everyone that he is a Christian of sorts. Everyone is baptized as an infant; later, but while he is still a child, he is confirmed—presumably in order that as early as possible everything may be arranged about that sort of passport which is so necessary if one is to get through the world without receiving a reproof from the magistrate. And of everyone who as an infant was baptized, as a boy or a girl was confirmed, it is certain that he is a Christian—by consulting the parish register one can ascertain this. But presumably he cannot in later life get to the point of confessing Christ, because in fact he lives in established Christendom, where it is acknowledged and confessed of all (cf. the parish register) that they are Christians. It is true even of parsons in 'established Christendom' that it is not so much they that 'confess Christ', as it is 'confessed of them' that they are Christians. If anyone would say that by their sermons they do actually confess Christ, it might be said in reply that the circumstance that their preaching is their livelihood, together with the fact that they do what they do as civil functionaries, brings it about that the emphasis does not fall upon the *personal* factor in confessing Christ.

In hidden inwardness all are Christians. Who would dare to deny it? He who would undertake to deny that this is true would incur the danger of wanting to play the part of a searcher of hearts. So no one can deny it. In that way it is an established fact that everyone is a Christian in hidden inwardness, a mysterious secret which, so to say, is secured by a lock for which nobody can

find a key: whether all these thousands and thousands really are
Christians no one can know, for all of them, it is said, are that in
hidden inwardness; and the maxim applies not only to the Church
but to everybody, 'that one does not pass judgement upon secret
things', because one cannot judge.[1]

Yet might it not be possible to break this mysterious silence
and get a little light on the subject without presuming to be a
searcher of hearts? 'Why! how can that be done?' In this way,
that somebody for his own part undertakes quite simply to
confess Christ in the midst of Christendom. He does not judge
a single person, far from it; but many will reveal themselves by the
way they judge him. He does not claim to be a more perfect
Christian than the others; no, far from it, he concedes that the
others are no doubt more perfect Christians than he, holding it
hidden as they do out of religious fear of receiving honour and
esteem, whereas he, poor simpleton that he is, is so anxious on his
own account lest a religiousness screwed up so high might turn
out to be humbug, and therefore keeps to the old way of confessing Christ. So he does not denounce any of the others as not
being Christians; ah, far from it, he only denounces himself as
such a poor simpleton—and yet the thoughts of many hearts will
be revealed by the way they judge this poor simpleton, this
imperfect Christian. He merely expresses the fact that he, as he
has been brought up to be, is a member of the militant Church—
and then it will be seen whether this peaceable community,
established Christendom, will not come to his aid, will not aid
him by persecution and suchlike, to the point that it becomes
quite true that he is a member of the militant Church.

'But is this your meaning, that so long as this world endures,
or so long as the Christian Church shall exist in this world, it is
and should be a militant Church?' Yes, quite certainly this is the
meaning, certainly this is what Christ means, and quite certainly
there is also meaning in this meaning. 'How unreasonable,' I
hear someone say, 'for it is surely impossible that we might all
become martyrs. If we are all to become martyrs and be put to
death, who then is there to put us to death? If we are all to
become martyrs and be persecuted, mocked, derided, who then is
there to persecute and mock us?' You have hit the mark—if only

---

[1] *De occultis non judicat ecclesia* is a maxim of the Canon Law in which S. K.
once took comfort in view of his own secret sin.

the assumption is correct which draws as it were the bow-string for this acute critical objection, the assumption, namely, that we are all Christians; in case this assumption is correct, that is, true at a given moment, or in case even it were Christ's meaning that there would come a moment here in this world when literally all would be Christians in truth.

The situation is this. With the everlasting contemplation of world-history and the history of the human race, with the ever-lasting talk about universal history and its significance, &c.,[1] people have become all too nimble in appropriating Christianity without more ado as a part of world-history, they have come to regard it as a matter of course that Christianity is a stage in the development of the human race. They have quite forgotten that Christ's life on earth (and this is what Christianity is—a different thing entirely from the history of Christians, of the lives of Christians, their biographies, their fate, not to speak of the history of heretics and of science) is sacred history, which must not be confounded with the history of the human race or of the world. They have entirely forgotten that the God-Man is essentially heterogeneous from every other individual man and from the race as a whole. They have entirely forgotten that Christianity is essentially related to eternity, that life here on earth (to recall an earlier argument) is the time of probation for every individual in particular among the countless millions who have lived or shall live. Doubtless Christianity expects that it shall be preached to all, but does it follow from this that it ever has had any expectation that it might come to pass that all would accept it and become true Christians? If such were the case, then there must have been (if I may say so) some inadvertence in God's counsel when from all eternity it was decreed that Christ should come to the world, Christ who preached that this life here on earth is a period of probation. One of two things: either it was the thought of divine governance (which by foreknowledge can know what will come to pass, whereas man is guilty for the fact that it does come to pass) that it never will be the case that all, or at least the greater number, become true Christians; or else governance did not look far enough ahead, for if ever this situation were to come about, that all are true Christians, this life is no longer a period of probation. For probation is self-denial, to deny oneself; to be a Christian

[1] This polemic is directed especially against Professor Martensen.

means probation, and being a Christian is to deny oneself. But when actually at a given time all are true Christians, there is no self-denial connected with being a Christian, least of all Christian self-denial. Magister Kierkegaard has shown (in the conclusion of the Second Part of *The Works of Love*) what is to be understood by Christian self-denial, that this exists only where there is 'double danger', that the second danger, the danger of suffering because one denies oneself, is the decisive definition. But this danger must of necessity be lacking if at the time when I live all are true Christians; for then everything all about me will be sheer encouragement and incitement to become a true Christian. And if such were the case, if I lived in such a situation, then as far as concerns me and my life, it would not be true to call this a life of probation in the Christian sense—and Christianity in fact was the inventor of this expression. No, in this case governance has not really understood how to devise a test, it has overlooked a circumstance, overlooked the possibility of its occurrence, a circumstance which might turn upside down the whole purpose it had with Christianity.

If, on the other hand, instead of jumbling together with characteristic human levity world-history and Christianity, one takes Christianity for what it gives itself out to be, if one believes that this life is a time of probation, believes that governance knew perfectly well what it was about, believes that it was and is Christianity's will that it be preached before all, but it was by no means Christianity's expectation that all will accept it—then everything is as it should be, then this life remains for each individual the period of probation, the Christian Church here in this world remains always a militant Church.

Such a conception as that of 'the congregation', about which people in these days especially have been so busy,[1] is really, as applied to this life, an impatient anticipation of eternity. What properly corresponds to the notion of combat is the single individual—at least when the combat is understood in a spiritual and Christian sense, not in the material sense of engaging in a pitched battle, which does not so much depend upon the individual as upon how many thousands are engaged, how many cannon they

[1] The reference is to Grundtvig's movement, to which S. K.'s brother Peter belonged. 'The congregation' (*Menighed*) was used rather sentimentally, like Royce's 'Beloved Community'.

have, &c. The Christian combat is always waged by the individual; for this precisely is spirit, that everyone is an individual
before God, that 'fellowship' is a lower category than 'the single
individual', which everyone can be and should be. And even
though the individuals were numbered by thousands and thus
were fighting in union, yet, Christianly understood, it is each
individual that fights, and in addition to fighting in union, he
fights at the same time within himself and shall as an individual give account on the day of Judgement, when his life as an individual shall be on trial. 'The congregation' therefore belongs
properly to eternity; 'the congregation' is at rest what the 'the
individual' is in unrest. But this life is precisely the time of
testing, the time of unrest, hence 'the congregation' has not its
abiding place in time but only in eternity, where it is the assembly
at rest of all the individuals who stood the test of combat and
probation.

So long as this world lasts and the Christian Church within it,
it is a militant Church, yet it has the promise that the gates of hell
shall not prevail against it. But woe, woe to the Christian Church
if it would triumph in this world, for then it is not the Church
that triumphs, but the world has triumphed. Then the heterogeneity of Christianity and the World is done away with, the
world has won, Christianity lost. Then Christ is no more the
God-Man, but only a distinguished man whose life is homogeneous with the development of the race. Then eternity is done
away with, and the stage for the perfection of all is transferred to
the temporal. Then the way of life is no longer strait, nor the
gate narrow, nor are there few that find it; no, then the way is
broad and the gate wide open—the gates of hell have prevailed,
and many, yea, all find entrance. Christ never desired to conquer
in this world; He came to the world to suffer, *that* is what He
called conquering. But when human impatience and the impudent
forwardness which ascribes to Christ its own thoughts and conceptions, instead of letting its thoughts and conceptions be transformed by Christ—when this got the upper hand, then, in the
old human way, to conquer meant to conquer in this world, and
thus Christianity is done away with. It was not a petty quarrel
Christ had with the world, so that substantially it was His own
fault that He didn't get along better with the world; no, love of
God is hatred of the world. And the day when Christianity and

the world become friends Christianity is done away with. Then there is no more any question of Christ coming again to judge the world; no, then the judgement has been passed upon Him that substantially He was a visionary, an impetuous man; for had He not been so over-impetuous, He would have been able to get along very well with the world, He would not have been put to death, for which there was no need at all, and so He would have become great in the world, as did His disciples in the triumphant Church, who abolished or treated as untruth the saying that the disciple is not above his master—for He was crucified, whereas they became mighty through honour and high esteem, just as in established Christendom His disciples became mighty, not by reason of their Christianity, but by . . . Christianly keeping their Christianity in hidden inwardness and employing their natural gifts and talents to succeed in the world.

Here, however, the same man we earlier introduced as speaker perhaps comes back again to his original contention and says, 'In spite of all you say, I cannot but repeat that it is and remains an impossibility for us all to become martyrs.' I answer: 'Is it then an impossibility for thee to become a martyr?' 'Yes, of course it is if all must be that.' But what hast thou to do with these 'all'? Is it really thy meaning (this meaningless meaning) that at the moment when thou wouldst regulate thy life and affront the test of becoming and being a Christian thou must first ask about the others, or learn to know something about 'all', before thou canst begin? I supposed that the very beginning of the test of becoming and being a Christian was for one to be so introverted that it is as if all the others do not exist for one, so introverted[1] that one is quite literally alone in the whole world, alone before God, alone with the Holy Scripture as guide, alone with the Pattern before one's eyes. The language thou speakest, on the contrary, is in the greatest possible degree the language of extraversion, it quite resembles the way a journalist writes.

This is easy to understand. The very first condition for becoming a Christian is to be absolutely introverted. Being thus infinitely

---

[1] *Indadvendt* and *udadvendt* are in form so precisely equivalent to the words C. G. Jung has coined and put in universal circulation that I cannot resist the temptation to use them here, though of course they are not to be understood in the technical sense attributed to them in the so-called 'deeper psychology'. The meaning is clearly but more awkwardly rendered by 'turned inward', 'turned outward'.

introverted, the introvert has nothing whatsoever to do with anybody else—this is what it means to be serious, it is a far sterner rule than that of the school where the teacher commands each pupil to keep his eyes to himself and not to look at the others at all. Being thus introverted, the learner then understands, or learns to understand, what the task of becoming and being a Christian really is—every instant that he is extraverted is wasted, and if there are many such instants, all is lost. He may perhaps know everything that is to be known about the task, may have committed it to memory, perhaps also lectured upon it declamatorily before others, and with that have become a parson and been rewarded by the State; but one thing has escaped his attention, the thing which Christianly is decisive, that what he says applies to him, and applies to him in endless introversion, whereas perhaps he has the notion that what he says applies to the congregation, and only the salary and the advancement apply to him.

Thus endless introversion teaches a man to understand to the utmost what the task is (if to the utmost he is introverted), that to be a Christian is to believe in Christ and to suffer for the sake of this faith, in other words, that it is self-denial in the Christian sense. But now, in order to show clearly the foolishness of that objection ('that it is quite impossible for all to be martyrs'), let us make the very absurd assumption that literally all amongst whom this Christian lives are true Christians—in that case he cannot possibly become a martyr. Certainly not. But when will he get to know this? At the very beginning, do you suppose, so that this knowledge becomes an evasion and excuse which keeps him from entering upon the task? Impossible, for he is, as we have seen, endlessly introverted, knows nothing, nor desires to know anything, about the others. So this he will get to know only at the end of his life (using this expression strictly for the instant of death) and not before; for up to this instant he could not know whether this fate might not yet befall him. But at the instant of death this consideration no longer concerns him in the least. In any case he has experienced martyrdom in the possibility. And this, as we remarked, was on the very absurd assumption that literally all, or maybe the great majority of the contemporaries, were true Christians, and that thus the gate of life, in spite of Christ's saying, is not narrow, but either stands absolutely wide open, or at any rate by reconstruction has been considerably enlarged and widened.

'But,' I hear somebody say, 'hast thou then, thou who art speaking here, hast thou the strength to be a martyr? Or hast thou the courage, not to say impudence, to affirm that no one was ever a true Christian who did not become a martyr? Or hast thou always been so strong that thou never hast longed to have someone speak to thee gently and reassuringly? Or art thou one who is anxious and apprehensive yet takes delight (as an apprehensive person is inclined to do) in scaring others?' To this question I owe an answer, and I give it, only hoping that the questioner will not misunderstand me, since I do not by any means fail to appreciate the question.[1] That I feel need of gentle treatment is admitted, but truth compels me to say that I feel this need precisely because I was brought up with severity and for a long, long time have lived under it, yea, every instant that is to come shall still be under it. To 'scare' others has never been my delight; I am conscious that I can talk gently and reassuringly to the suffering, the sick, the sorrowful; I know that this has given me delight. I have never affirmed that every Christian is a martyr, or that no one was a true Christian who did not become a martyr, though it is my opinion that every such person (and as such I account myself) should, just for the sake of being a true Christian, make the humble admission that he had got off easier than they who were true Christians in the strictest sense, and that he should make this admission in order that, if I may so speak, the Christian order of precedence may not be confused, and place No. 1 drop out entirely, so that place No. 2 becomes the first place.[2] And now, finally, I come to what is my principal answer to the question. Christianity is quite literally dethroned in Christendom; but if it is dethroned, then it is also abolished. For a king, e.g., because the land in which he lives has declared itself a republic and made him president, does not cease to exist; but Christianity is abolished so soon as it is cast down from the throne. Christianity is the absolute, has only one mode of being, namely absolute being; if it is not absolute, it is abolished; in relation to Christianity either/or applies absolutely. For a very long time there has

[1] Here and in the three following paragraphs it is evidently S. K. that is speaking in his own person, and very personally.

[2] This is a thought which was developed by S. K. more fully on pp. 246 f.

made itself heard, and very loudly, the impudent talk about 'going farther', that one cannot stop at faith, at simplicity, at obedience, at the 'Thou shalt'. And this has penetrated farther and farther down among the people, who naturally are influenced by the judgement, if I may so speak, of the highest circles. It has penetrated, and only too easily, since unfortunately every man has a natural, a congenital disposition to disobedience. Hence 'reasons' (believing on three grounds) replaced obedience, for people were annoyed at obeying. Hence gentleness replaced severity; for no one ventured to command, and people were loth to be commanded—they that ought to command became cowardly, and they that ought to yield obedience became froward. So it is that Christianity was abolished in Christendom—by gentleness. Without authority, in tattered and outmoded garments, it slinks about in Christendom, and one does not know whether to take off one's hat to it, or whether it ought to bow to us, whether we are in need of its compassion, or whether it is in need of our compassion.

For us, however, there is but one salvation: Christianity. And verily for Christianity there is but one possible salvation: severity. By means of gentleness it cannot be saved—that is to say, it neither can nor will be saved in this way, such a thought is the crime of *lèse majesté* against Christianity; but by severity it must be reinstated in its rights as sovereign. And though I myself were to sink under the weight of the measure I apply, and though I myself were the first to fall under condemnation, or though I were to be the only one—I can do no other. I know well what I am doing; I know also what I, in fear and trembling, pursued by trials of temptation, have suffered by venturing so far out,[1] in loneliness employed day and night with such thoughts, and for so long a time employed with them, in loneliness and with constantly increasing effort, alone although I was living in Christendom, where indeed all are Christians, but where nevertheless I have never heard any discourse or sermon about which, if before God the question was put to me, I could dare to say unconditionally that it was Christian—for even the most Christian sermons I have heard had ever about them a suspicious admixture of reasons, a

---

[1] By this figure, which is constantly used by S. K., he means far out at sea, 'where God can get hold of me', but where there is no prospect of return to the security of dry land.

smack of human whimper and compassion, a dissonant note of
ingratiation. I have no monastery where I might take refuge,
seeking an environment which might in some measure correspond
to my inward preoccupation. I chose the only expedient left in
Christendom—that of appearing to be the most frivolous of all
men, of 'becoming a fool in this world', in order to preserve if
possible in this serious world a little bit of seriousness which I
kept hidden in my inward man, and in order that this inwardness
might grow up quietly in the peace of personal reserve. By this
life I have learnt furthermore what perhaps in this way, through
acquaintance with man's thoughtless frivolity and self-contented
aberration, one can learn even better than in the desert and from
the stillness of the night; by this life in the human swarm, by this
false life, if you will—for it is true that I hid something else in
my most inward parts, but it was the best I hid, I have never,
never deceived in such a way as to make myself out better than
I was—by this life in the human swarm I have learnt with
frightful verity to understand that severity is the only thing that
can help.[1]

This I have employed. But I have no might, neither soldiers
nor any other sort of might; I have no powerful connexions, have
absolutely no power or influence over the fate of others; I am
of all men the most solitary, in a worldly sense the most impotent.
To employ severity may easily inflame men; hence he who would
employ severity is accustomed to assure himself first of force to
compel. In such wise I neither can nor will employ severity; for
I would not rule, I would only serve the truth, which is the same
as to say, Christianity.

Severity is the only thing that can help a man. Hence a child,
in comparison with grown-ups, is capable of so much, is far hardier,
because there is still some severity in the upbringing of children;
and what was not a child capable of when severity was greater!
Hence the Romans always conquered in battle. Why? Because
severity helped them, helped them to fear that which was worse
than death, and therefore to conquer. And so it was also with
Christianity. Once there was a time when with divine authority
it exercised dominion over men, when it addressed itself to every
single individual briefly, laconically, imperatively, with 'Thou
shalt', when it dismayed every individual by a severity which never

[1] It must be confessed that this sounds very much like 'hidden inwardness'.

before was known, by the punishment of eternity. This severity helped; in fear and trembling before the inevitable hereafter the Christians were capable of disdaining all this life's dangers and sufferings, regarding them as mere child's play and a half-hour's foolery. Yea, this severity helped; it made truth of the saying that to be a Christian is to be akin to the divinity. This was the militant Church; Satan was able to do nothing against it except to afford the heroes of faith the longed-for opportunity of being irradiated with the splendour of martyrdom, the opportunity needed for the glory of the hidden man to become transparent—for the Christian glory is an inward man, which must be held up before the light in order to be fairly seen. Then said Satan to himself, 'In this way I am making no conquest'; and he changed his tactics. Little by little he got the Church to imagine that it had conquered, now it ought to take rest after conflict and enjoy its triumph. And that looked seductive enough; for in the period when the Church was in conflict a man would naturally hesitate to join it, so that its growth was not yet great. But after it had conquered—then indeed it won adherents by the million. What could one want more? For if there might be any misgiving about a triumphant Church, it could only be lest it gradually shrink in size, diminish in numbers. But exactly the opposite was the case. Yes, most certainly; it did not shrink in size, did not decrease in numbers, nay, it increased, this is as true as that a man with the dropsy increases in size; it swelled with unwholesome fat, it was almost nauseous the way it broadened out in fleshy plumpness, hardly recognizable any longer.

Now all had become Christians. But power and authority were lost. People were pampered by hearing the rigmarole of Christian verities perpetually preached—great things! if anybody had a mind to listen to them any longer. Great God! and the scene was laid in Christendom, where all are Christians, and where it was doubtful if anybody had a mind to listen to the Christian verities! But to talk in the now antiquated, almost ludicrous language which Christianity talked when with divine authority it exercised dominion over men and with hitherto unknown severity brought them up with the fear and trembling of the punishment of eternity, a punishment which only Christianity essayed to apply— to talk this language is a thing the preachers of Christianity in

Christendom do not venture to do. 'That will never do in all eternity', one of them says to himself, 'not only should I become ridiculous, not only might they perhaps put me to death; but even if I should venture to do it, I should accomplish nothing, I should merely make people so furious that they would throw off the yoke entirely.' That was a time when good counsel was dear. So then human shrewdness, perhaps with good intentions, began the most deplorable of all undertakings: to betray Christianity by defending it. And then the devil laughed within himself and said, 'Behold, now I can be quite tranquil, now the game is won. They who thus defend Christianity know not what they do, the secret is deeply hidden, they will constantly ascribe failure to the imperfection of the defence hitherto advanced, and therefore they go ahead more and more zealously and become more and more absorbed in the defence. How could it occur to anyone that he who defends is precisely the betrayer, though he does not know it?' So they defended Christianity—righteous God! And the scene of this was laid in Christendom! So it was before the face of Christians that Christianity defended itself, as when a king is forced to defend himself in the face of his subjects.[1] They defended Christianity; there was no talk of authority, nor was it employed, the 'Thou shalt' was never heard, for fear of arousing laughter; they defended Christianity and said, 'Do not disdain Christianity, it is gentle doctrine, it contains all the gentle consolations a man some time in his life may find himself in need of. Good Lord, life does not always smile upon one, we all need a friend, and such a friend is Christ, do not disdain Him, He means so well by you.' And it succeeded; people actually listened attentively to this talk, they actually gave ear to this beggar ... the Lord Jesus Christ—who though He Himself was not a beggar, was nevertheless the one on whose behalf they begged. People found that there was something in it, it tickled the ambitious ear of Christendom that it was pretty much like balloting, putting the thing to a vote, with a 'Right O! On this condition we accept Christianity.' Righteous God! And the scene of this was laid in Christendom, where all are Christians, and where on this condition Christianity is accepted by the Christians!

So things went backward with Christianity; and now we live

[1] The futility, indeed the blasphemy, of defending Christianity with the proofs of apologetic was one of S. K.'s favourite themes.

in established Christendom, where there certainly is no talk of severity, where there lives a coddled race of men, proud and yet cowardly, defiant and yet effeminate, who occasionally hear these gentle consolations preached, but scarcely know whether they will make use of them even when life smiles its prettiest, and in the hour of need, when it is seen that they are really not so gentle after all, they are offended. Righteous God! And the scene of this is laid in Christendom! Righteous God: yes, whoever will see, can see precisely here the righteousness of God—frightful punishment, because the militant Church became the triumphant Church or established Christendom. Thou, verily, when thou seest a man who has become a drunkard, when thou seest him in all his wretchedness, dishonour, and misery, canst perceive the righteous God—so must thou (if thou hast had the good fortune by God's grace to be brought up severely in Christianity) perceive in 'established Christendom' the righteous God.

For only the militant Church is the truth, or the truth is that so long as the Church endures in this world it is the militant Church, which associates itself with Christ in His humiliation, although drawn to Him from on high. On the other hand, it is falsehood, all that talk by which men flatter the race and themselves, about the world advancing. For the world goes neither backward nor forward, it remains essentially the same, like the sea and the air, in short, like an element; for it is and shall continue to be the element which can furnish the proof of the reality of being a Christian, which always means a member of a militant Church. The triumphant Church and established Christendom are falsehood, are the greatest misfortune that can befall the Church; they are its destruction, and at the same time are a punishment, for such a calamity cannot come about undeserved.

VI

O LORD Jesus Christ, Thou didst not come to the world to be served, but also surely not to be admired or in that sense to be worshipped. Thou wast the way and the truth—and it was followers only Thou didst demand. Arouse us therefore if we have dozed away into this delusion, save us from the error of wishing to admire Thee instead of being willing to follow Thee and to resemble Thee.

JOHN 12: 32. AND I, IF I BE LIFTED UP FROM THE EARTH, WILL DRAW ALL UNTO MYSELF

In Christendom one often enough hears sermons, addresses, discourses, about what is required of a follower of Christ, what is involved in being a follower of Christ, what it means to follow Christ, &c. What one hears is, generally speaking, quite right and true, only by listening more closely one detects a deeply concealed unchristian confusion or defect at the bottom of it all. Nowadays Christian sermons have become for the most part 'reflections'.[1] 'During this hour let us reflect'; 'I invite you, my hearers, to reflect upon'; 'the subject of our reflection is', &c. But to reflect (*betragte*) means, in one sense of the word, to come quite close to something which one would look at (*betragte*),

---

[1] This polemic is directed principally against Bishop Mynster, who frequently talked about Christian 'reflections' and in 1833 published a volume of sermons entitled, *Reflections on the Christian Doctrine of Faith*. We have seen (in a note to p. xxv) that in a colloquy with S. K. he referred to these very chapters we are now reading as 'reflections'—and S. K. registered in his Journal this designation without taking any exception to it. But evidently it was with the intent of avoiding this word that he adopted a rather unusual word as the title of the seven chapters of this last part of *Training in Christianity*. He called them 'Developments of Christian Themes' (*Christlige Udviklinger*), to indicate that they were reasoned arguments, in contrast with the familiar forms of 'reflection' or 'meditation'. 'Meditations' and 'quiet hours' were no doubt distasteful to S. K. for the reason that they savoured of a vague mysticism which was foreign to his temperament. But we shall see later that he knew how to reprove the more objective tendency to 'reflect' upon Christianity with arguments more cogent than those that he adduces in this paragraph, which take advantage of the fact that the Danish language covers with one word (as I have felt compelled to indicate in the text) so many different meanings as 'to look at', 'to regard', 'to consider', and 'to reflect'.

whereas in another sense it implies an attitude of remoteness, of infinite remoteness so far as the personality is concerned. When a painting is pointed out to one and he is asked to regard it (*betragte*), or when in a shop one looks at (*betragte*) a piece of cloth, for example, he steps up quite close to the object, in the latter instance he even takes it in his hands and feels it, in short, he gets as close to the object as possible. But in another sense, by this very movement he goes quite out of himself, gets away from himself, forgets himself, and there is nothing to remind him that it is he that is looking at (*betragte*) the picture or the cloth, and not the picture or the cloth that is looking at (*betragte*) him. That is to say, by reflection (*Betragtning*) I enter into the object (I become objective), but I go out of or away from myself (I cease to be subjective). So it is that the sermon, by its favourite way of regarding (*Betragtning*) Christianity, which is that of 'the reflection' (*Betragtning*) or the 'reflections' (*Betragtningerne*), has done away with that which in a Christian sense is the most important thing in the sermon, namely, the 'thou and I', the speaker and the person addressed, the fact that he who speaks is himself in movement, is a striver, and that so likewise is the person spoken to, whom one encourages, incites, exhorts, admonishes, all with a view to an effort, a life, the speaker constantly aiming, not to get away from himself, but to return to himself, and to help the hearer, not to get away from himself, but to return to himself. In our time the sermon has not only itself quite forgotten, but has contributed to consign to oblivion the fact that Christian truth cannot properly be the object of 'reflection' (*Betragtning*). For Christian truth, if I may say so, has itself eyes to see with, yea, is all eye; but it would be very disquieting, rather quite impossible, to look at (*betragte*) a painting or a piece of cloth, if when I was about to look (*betragte*) I discovered that the painting or the cloth was looking at me—and precisely such is the case with Christian truth, it is that which is looking at (*betragter*) me to see whether I do what it says I should do. This, you see, is the reason why Christian truth does not allow itself to be presented for reflection (*Betragtningen*) or expressed eloquently as a reflection (*Betragtning*); it has itself, if I may say so, ears to hear with, yea, it is as it were all ears, it listens attentively while the speaker talks; one cannot talk about it as about an absentee or as a thing present only objectively, for since it is from God and God is in it, it is present in a very special sense while one is speaking about it, and not as an object, rather it is the speaker that is the object of its regard, in speaking he has conjured up a spirit which examines him.

Hence it is a venturesome thing to preach; for when I mount to that sacred place [the pulpit]—whether the church be crowded or as good as empty—I have, though I myself may not be aware of it, one hearer in addition to those that are visible to me, namely, God in heaven, whom I cannot see it is true, but who verily can see me. This hearer listens attentively to discover whether what I say is true, and He looks also to discern (as well He can, for He is invisible, and in that way it is impossible to be on one's guard against Him)—so He looks to see whether my life expresses what I say. And although I possess no authority to impose an obligation upon any other person, yet what I have said in the course of the sermon puts me under obligation—and God has heard it. Verily, it is a venturesome thing to preach! Doubtless most people have a notion that it requires courage to step out upon the stage like an actor and venture to encounter the danger of having all eyes fixed upon one. And yet this danger is in a sense, like everything else on the stage, an illusion; for personally the actor is aloof from it all, his part is to deceive, to disguise himself, to represent another, and to transmit accurately the words of another. The preacher of Christian truth, on the other hand, steps out in a place where, even if all eyes are not fixed upon him, the eye of omniscience is; his part is to be himself, and that in an environment, God's house, which, being all eye and ear, requires of him only this, that he be himself, be true. 'That he be true'— this means that he himself is what he preaches, or at least strives to be that, or at the very least is sober enough to admit that he is not. Alas, and how many who in mounting to this sacred place to preach Christianity are keen enough of hearing to detect the repugnance and scorn which this sacred place feels for him at hearing him preach with enthusiasm, in moving tones, with tears, the opposite of that which his life expresses.

So venturesome a thing it is to be the 'I' which preaches, to be the speaker, an 'I' who by preaching and in the act of preaching puts himself absolutely under obligation, lays his life bare so that if it were possible one might look directly into his soul—to be such an 'I', that was a venturesome thing. Therefore little by little the parson found out how to draw his eye back into himself, indicating thereby that nobody had any business to look at him. In fact it was not (so he thought) about himself he was speaking, it was about the thing at issue; and this was admired as an extraordinary advance in wisdom that the speaker ceased to be an 'I' and became if possible a thing. Anyhow, in this way it became far easier to be a parson—the speaker no longer preached, he employed these moments to introduce some reflections. Some reflections! You can perceive that in the speaker: his glance is drawn back into the eye, he resembles not so much a man as one of those figures carved in stone which has no eyes. Thereby he creates a yawning gulf between the hearer and himself, almost as wide as that between the actor and the spectator. And what he preaches are 'reflections', whereby again he creates a yawning gulf between himself and what he says, as wide as that between the actor and the poet or playwright—personally he is as as much aloof as possible while he 'employs these moments to propose reflections'.

So it is that the 'I', who was the speaker, dropped out; the speaker is not an 'I', he is the thing at issue, the reflection. And as the 'I' fell out, so also the 'thou' was done away with, thou the hearer, the fact that thou who sittest there art the person to whom the discourse is addressed. Indeed, it has almost gone so far that to talk in this personal fashion to other people is regarded as 'a personality'. By personalities ('resorting to personalities', 'taking the liberty to employ personalities') one understands unseemly and rude behaviour—and so it will not do for the speaker, 'I', to talk personally, and to persons, the hearer, 'thou'. And if this will not do, then the sermon is done away with. But so it is in fact—they merely suggest reflections. And 'reflections' do not come too close either to the speaker or to the hearer; the 'reflection' is a very safe assurance against the danger of employing personalities—the speech is not about me, the speaker, it is hardly I that speak, it is a reflection, and it is not to thee, the hearer, it is spoken, it is a reflection; whether I do what I say, is none of thy business, it scarcely is my business, for surely I owe to myself the same consideration I show to every other man, not to indulge in personalities; whether thou, the hearer, dost do what is said is not my business, scarcely is it thine: it is a reflection, and at the most the question is whether the reflection contents thee.

This fundamental change in the character of the sermon, by which Christianity was done away with, is also (among other things) an expression of the fundamental change which came about with the triumphant Church and established Christendom, that as a rule Christ obtained admirers, not followers.

By giving an account of this distinction, *the distinction between an admirer and a follower*, this 'exposition' will seek to throw light upon Christianity, with constant reference again to the sacred text, 'From on high He will draw all unto Himself'. For here again it is the relationship to exaltation or the relationship to lowliness which decides. If Christ exists for us only as on high, if everything about His humiliation is forgotten, or if He had never existed in lowliness, then (in this case) not even He Himself, if He were consistent with Himself, could require anything but admirers, worshipping admirers; for exaltation and admirers, divine exaltation and worshipping admirers, correspond perfectly. Indeed, with respect to exaltation it would on our part even be impertinent, presumptuous, an infatuation, perhaps madness, to wish to be followers instead of declining with becoming modesty to aspire to what possibly is not granted to us because it is granted to another, instead of being becomingly content with admiration and admiring worship. On the other hand, what corresponds to humiliation is a follower.

Now it is well enough known that Christ constantly uses the expression 'follower'; He never says anything about wanting admirers, admiring worshippers, adherents; and when he uses the expression 'disciples', He always so explains it that we can perceive that followers are meant, that they are not adherents of a doctrine but followers of a life, a life which had no adventitious marks of loftiness which would make it presumptuous on our part, or mere madness, to wish to resemble it. It is also well known (as in another place I have reiterated again and again) that it is the humiliated Christ that speaks, that every word we have from Christ is from Him in His humiliation. Now we may surely assume that Christ knew perfectly well why He selected this expression ('follower') which alone and absolutely is in the deepest and most inward agreement with what He constantly said about Himself or declared Himself to be, namely, the way, the truth, and the life, implying that He had not merely a doctrine to deliver, so that he might be content with hearers who accepted it—although in life they treated it as nothing, or 'let five be an even number'. And we may surely assume also that He knew perfectly well why His whole life on earth, from beginning to end, was calculated only to procure 'followers', and calculated to make 'admirers' impossible.

Christ came to the world for purpose of saving the world, and at the same time (as was implied in His first purpose) to be 'the pattern', to leave behind Him footsteps for those who would attach themselves to Him, who thus might become followers, for 'follower' corresponds to 'footsteps'. Just for this reason He let Himself be born in lowly station, and thereafter lived in poverty, despised and humiliated. Indeed, no man ever lived in such humiliation as He. Even the poorest man, on comparing his own life with His, must come to the conclusion that, humanly speaking, his own life was preferable in comparison with the conditions of His life. Why then was this, why this lowliness and humiliation? It was because He who in truth is to be 'the pattern' and is concerned only with followers must in one sense be located *behind* men, to drive them on, whereas in another sense He stands *before* them, beckoning them on. This is the relationship of loftiness and lowliness in 'the pattern'. Loftiness must not be of the direct sort, but it must be of the spiritual sort, and so precisely the negation of worldly and earthly loftiness. Lowliness must be of the direct sort; for the direct (plainly apparent) lowliness, when one has to pass through it, is precisely the way, but at the same time for the worldly and earthly mind it is a detour which ensures that loftiness shall not be taken in vain. 'The pattern' is therefore located infinitely near to man in lowliness, and yet infinitely far away in loftiness, even more remote indeed than if it were simply put at a distance on high; for the fact that a man in order to reach it, to determine his character in likeness to it, must go through lowliness and humiliation, that there is absolutely no other way, constitutes a still greater remoteness, really an infinite remoteness. And so in one sense 'the Pattern' is *behind*, more deeply down-trodden than ever any other man was, and in another sense *before*, infinitely exalted. But 'the Pattern' must be behind in order to catch and encompass all. If there were one single man who truly could underbid or duck under by showing that that in lowliness and humiliation he was still more humbly placed, then the pattern is no longer *the* Pattern, it is but an imperfect pattern, that is, a pattern only for a great multitude of men. *Absolutely* the Pattern must be behind, behind all, and it must be *behind* in order to drive forward those who are to be fashioned in its likeness.

The human race, in fact, and each individual in the race, whether consciously or unconsciously, possesses a deep craftiness in dealing with what is imposed as a pattern, a craftiness which is of the evil one. If he who is to be regarded as the pattern is in possession of earthly, worldly, temporal advantages, what then? Why, then the pattern is in the wrong position, faced the wrong way, and so the race, together with every individual in the race, takes this as a pretext for a right-about-face, the pattern is pushed in front of the ranks as a theme for poetic admiration, whereas instead the pattern should be stationed behind, should come up behind men as a claim upon them. When the pattern has thus become an object of admiration, people shirk 'the claims'; they say, 'Yes, he can do it of course, since he is in possession of all these advantages and favourable conditions; if only we were in his place we could become just as perfect as he is. As it is we can do no more than admire him, and it is to our honour and credit that we do this, and do not indulge in envy. But anything other than admiration is beyond us; for he has qualifications which we have not and which he cannot give us, how unreasonable it is therefore to require of us the same thing he requires of himself.'

Now Christ is 'the Pattern'. If He had come to the world in worldly or temporal loftiness of station, the greatest possible untruth would have been occasioned. Instead of being 'the claim' upon the whole race and upon every individual in the race, He would have been a universal excuse and pretext for evasion to the whole race and to every individual in the race. In this case, He certainly would not have been put to death—for this also contributed to enflame the contemporaries against Him, that (if I may say so) they could not get Him turned in the direction they would, that He 'defiantly and obstinately' *would* be the humiliated One, and (what embittered men's selfish effeminacy most of all) that He would only have 'followers'—no in this case He would have become an object of admiration, and the confusion would have become so prodigious that we can hardly imagine it. He Himself had said that He was the truth, and then, according to this assumption, people admired Him, and so it might seem as if they also loved the truth, and it was made almost impossible to get at the facts. For in the situation of contemporaneousness the confusion would have been exactly as great as in established Christendom, where people admire and worship in admiration, and admire and worship Christ with the strongest expressions, whereas their lives express exactly the opposite of Christ's life as it was lived by Him who just for the sake of being 'the Pattern' was born and lived in lowliness and humiliation. But the admirer has an excellent cover; 'For', he will say, 'more surely cannot be required of me than that with the strongest expressions—and if there are expressions still stronger in the language, I am ready to use them—I acknowledge and confess that I worship Christ admiringly as the truth. More, surely, cannot be required of me—can you mention anything higher?'

We see therefore why Christ was born and lived in humiliation; no man, absolutely no man contemporary with him lived in such humiliation, there never has lived a man so humiliated, and therefore it was absolutely impossible for any man to shirk the claims made upon him with the excuse or evasion that 'the Pattern' was in possession of earthly and worldly advantages which he had not. To admire Christ in that sense is the false invention of a later age with the help of 'exaltation'. In His actual life there was absolutely nothing to admire in that sense, unless one would admire poverty, wretchedness, the suffering of contempt, &c. He did not even escape the last degradation, that of being pitied, of being a pitiable object of commiseration. No, there verily was not the least thing to admire.

And in the situation of contemporaneousness there was not the least occasion to admire; for Christ had only the same conditions to offer to the man who would join Him, and on those conditions there was never any admirer who would take part. The same conditions: to become just as poor, as despised, as much scorned and mocked, and if possible even a little more, considering that as an aggravation one was an adherent of a .person so despised, whom every sensible man shunned.

What, then, is the distinction between 'an admirer' and 'a follower'? A follower is or strives *to be* what he admires; an admirer holds himself personally aloof, consciously or unconsciously, he does not discern that the object of his admiration makes a claim upon him to be or to strive to be the thing he admires.

To avoid, however, any misunderstanding, I call attention to the fact (which also is easily understood) that there are situations in which the attitude of admiration is the right one. For when that which is the object of my admiration does not properly imply and cannot imply any claim upon me to resemble it, then indeed it is quite right that I should confine myself to admiration. Thus I can admire beauty, wealth, extraordinary talents, distinguished achievements, success, &c.; for in all this there is implied no claim upon me, but it all has to do with a difference between man and man which no man can bestow upon himself but which has to be bestowed upon him. That is to say, admiration is true wherever it is true that through circumstances beyond my control I am prevented from being able to resemble the object of my admiration, even if I heartily wished it. 'Even if I heartily wished it'—but no, when such is the situation, I decidedly ought not to wish it. If I get it into my head that I could so heartily wish to resemble or to be the object of my admiration, then something else easily comes to pass, namely, that my admiration is transformed into envy. Hence in this situation I must distinctly refrain from wishing for my part to be the object of my admiration; for, as the Scripture says, thou shalt not covet, what is denied to thee thou shalt not covet, if it is bestowed upon another, thou shalt rejoice that it is granted to him, and if this gift is of such a nature that it can properly be the object of admiration, thou shalt admire it.

It is quite different with respect to the universal human, or that which every man, absolutely every man, is capable of, which is not dependent upon any conditions except such as are within the capacity of every man, that is to say, the moral actions which every man is required to perform, and therefore also is surely able to perform. Here admiration is entirely out of place, and commonly it is fraudulent and disingenuous, seeking evasion and excuse. If I know a man whom I respect for his unselfishness, devotedness, magnanimity, &c., I ought not to admire him, I ought to resemble him; I ought not to deceive myself and imagine that to admire him was something meritorious on my part; on the contrary, I ought to understand that this is merely a device of indolence and effeminacy, I ought to resemble him, and at once begin the effort to resemble him.

What does this mean? It means that the admirer stands personally aloof from himself, he forgets himself, forgets that what he admires in the other is denied to him (here of course we are speaking only of the situation where admiration is in place), and just this is the fine quality in admiration, that one forgets oneself in admiring. In the other case (i.e. where admiration is not in place) the first thing I do is to think about myself, to think simply and solely about myself. Upon becoming aware of the other, this unselfish, magnanimous man, I at once begin to say to myself, 'Art thou then such as he?' I forget him completely in my absorption with myself. Since unfortunately I discover that I am not such as he, I have so much to do in and with myself that now—yes, now I have entirely forgotten him. Yet, no, it is not that I have forgotten him, but for me he has become a claim upon my life, he is like a prick in my soul which projects me forward, like an arrow which wounds me. In the one case I vanish more and more, losing myself in the object of my admiration, which becomes greater and greater, the admired object swallows me. In the second case, the other man vanishes more and more, in that he is taken up into me, or in that I take him into me, as one takes a medicine, that I swallow him—but, be it observed, since he is 'a claim', this all is for the purpose of giving him out again as a reflection—and it is I that become greater and greater by coming more and more to resemble him.

It is surely easy enough to see that in relation to Christ the wish to admire, or (what comes to the same thing) to worship in admiration, is a falsehood, a fraud, a sin. Since, however, this form of conscious or unconscious self-deceit is so very common in the world or in Christendom, and since Christ's life as the Pattern is precisely calculated to put an end to this game of self-deception, for which reason it is particularly deplorable that precisely in Christendom this self-deception has become very general through the misuse of Christ's exaltation, therefore it is surely quite necessary to throw light by means of the Pattern upon a subject which, either of set purpose and intent, or merely by thoughtlessness, has been rendered obscure.

So then, to take for a moment an example on a lower plane,[1]

---

[1] There can be no doubt that this whole paragraph is coloured by S. K.'s bitter experience when in the interest of right and decency he attacked the *Corsair*—and found himself left in the lurch by all the superior men who privately expressed to him their sympathy but did nothing to support him in the fight or to defend him from 'the attacks of vulgarity'

when a man fights enthusiastically for the truth and the right,
with every sacrifice, entirely disinterestedly—well, of course there
is in this world a vileness, a paltriness, which just for this reason
opposes him with all its might, about which, however, I have
nothing to say here—but if this is so, it is true also that there are,
if not many, at least a few who cannot withhold their admiration
for such an enthusiast; they are glad to affirm it to him with the
strongest expressions, it is in fact a fond satisfaction to them to
let him understand that his whole effort has their approval and
admiration; they make no concealment of their indignation at
the vileness and paltriness which are opposing him. But so far
and no farther. If it can be said with justice that they make no
concealment of their indignation at the unrighteous opposition
he suffers, this must be understood with a certain restriction,
namely, that in giving utterance to their indignation they shield
themselves a tiny bit against the danger of coming themselves
into conflict with the vile power. They choose therefore a certain
apartness for the utterance of their indignation, a place and an
environment where one may express oneself without danger, the
cosy security of the parlour, for example, where in company with
the admired one and a few intimate friends upon whose silence
one can absolutely rely, one can, without any even the least un-
pleasant consequences for one's own person, raise one's voice and
thunder, pounding the table heroically to express embitterment at
the paltriness of the world, a place where, 'not for pleasure alone',
yet not exactly in seriousness, one can appear in the role of the
hero or the strong character. But in case he, the man they admire,
were in any way to put it up to them whether they should not now
decide to do as he did, instead of playing at warfare in the parlour
—then everything is changed, they cautiously withdraw from
the admired man, they even become angry with him. And this is
not all, for if he merely declines to accept their admiration because
he understands that there is fraud and falsehood in it, then they
become angry with him. For with respect to moral qualities, to
want to admire instead of imitating, is not the invention of bad
men; no, it is the flabby invention of what one may call the better
sort of men, but weak men for all that, in their effort to hold
themselves personally aloof. It is only through imagination they
are related to the man they admire, to them he is like an actor on
the stage except that, this being real life, the effect he produces

is somewhat stronger. But for their own persons they demand the same privilege they demand in the theatre: to sit safely and tranquilly, without any real relationship to the danger, reckoning it, however, to their personal credit that they admire the man, thinking thereby presumably that they have a claim to share (on fairly easy and cheap terms, and at the same time with something like voluptuousness) in the merit he deserves from the part of truth and righteousness. If then he is willing to accept their admiration, they are only too ready, for then his life is an occasion for jubiliation—that is to say, jubilation with a proper admixture of caution, lest one come personally into touch with danger. But that his life ought to be a claim upon them they will not understand; and if they observe that he himself understands that this should be so, then it is about over with their admiration; they become offended in him on account of his odd character, so that they cannot attain the repose requisite for admiration, they notice that to converse with him amounts pretty nearly to an examination, because, though he says nothing, his life silently examines theirs.

Upon this sunken rock many a moral effort well begun has foundered. In such a case a person has so far prevailed upon himself as to will the good, but to his disaster he ran up against human admiration. This perhaps in the first instance seemed to him a very pretty thing, something quite laudable—he did not understand at once how much fraud and falsehood there is in it. When subsequently he became conscious of this, and learned also how easily admiration, being in itelf so frail and false a thing, can display itself as something quite different—for all this he did not venture to break with it. Admiration appropriated him for its reunions and festivities—and he was lost for the truth.

We will now turn our attention to the Pattern, in order to perceive more and more clearly how His life was calculated to require followers and to make admirers impossible. As has been said, He was not in possession of any the least earthly advantage which truly could become the admiration of anybody else or suggest to any one the excuse or evasion that He, the Pattern, 'of course was able to, since He is in possession of these advantages'. Besides, His life was 'the Truth', which constitutes precisely the relationship in which admiration is untruth.

'But all the same, was he not an object of admiration?' Yes, undoubtedly; for it is impossible at once and, at the very instant

of beginning, to avert the danger called admiration, which is
requisite in one sense in order to get people enlisted. But when
'the truth', true to itself in being the truth, little by little, more
and more definitely, unfolds itself as the truth, the moment comes
when no admirer can hold out with it, a moment when it shakes
admirers from it as the storm shakes the worm-eaten fruit from
the tree. And it is Christ's life precisely which has made it
evident, terribly evident, what a dreadful falsehood it is to admire
the truth instead of following it, a thought which in the pros-
perous days of Christendom, when peace and security favour this
misunderstanding, ought if possible to be brought to remembrance every Sunday. For when no danger is present, when there
is a dead calm, when everything is favourable to Christianity, it is
only too easy to mistake an admirer for a follower, and this may
pass quite unobserved, the admirer may die in the illusion that the
relationship he assumed was the true one. Attention therefore to
contemporaneousness!

How is it possible for anyone with the least understanding of
human nature to doubt that *Judas* was an admirer of Christ?
And at the beginning of His life Christ had many, many admirers.
Admiration was eager to spread its web for Him also, hoping to
appropriate Him. But as a plant unfolds itself by inward
necessity, so was His life the unfolding of truth. He made no
clamour, was not embittered, did not judge, but by being Himself
the truth He compelled with the might of eternity everything
round about Him to become revealed in the truth, or to become
revealed for what in truth it is. And when the time came to make
the reckoning, it resulted finally that among the one-time admiring contemporaries there were found barely twelve followers,
of whom one was only an admirer, or, as he is generally called,
a traitor, namely, Judas, who precisely because he was an admirer
quite naturally became a traitor. For this is just as easy to
anticipate as the movements of the stars, that he who in relation
to the truth is merely an admirer will at the approach of danger
become a traitor. 'The admirer' is only effeminately or selfishly
in love with greatness; if trouble comes or danger, he draws back;
and if this is not possible, he becomes a traitor, as a way of liberat-
ing himself from the one-time object of his admiration. And so it
is likewise when 'the admirer' has beheld and expected in something and from **something**, or in somebody and from somebody,

great things, everything, and then discovers that there is nothing in it, indeed that it is the very person in question who squanders the opportunity (as was the case with Christ, who 'willed His own destruction'), then the admirer becomes impatient, he becomes a betrayer. Admiration (when it is in the wrong place or in the situation where only 'following' is the truth) is an ardour just as equivocal as sensual love, which can be transformed in the twinkling of an eye into its very opposite, into hate, jealousy, &c.

Sacred history has handed down to us the story of still another admirer—it was *Nicodemus*. In established Christendom a sermon is preached every year on Nicodemus[1]—by all these thousands and thousands of parsons therefore. The subject is treated thus. The Parson says: 'Fundamentally, Nicodemus was a weak man; instead of joining Christ openly, he came to Him stealthily by night, for fear of men.' The Parson pleases himself by this discourse, and it finds favour in the eyes of the congregation—and in fact it is exceedingly courteous, for tacitly the suggestion is smuggled in that the Parson and all those present are people of a totally different sort from Nicodemus—they confess Christ quite openly, without any fear of men. Capital! Since the situation is so altered that perhaps the majority are restrained rather by fear of men from openly renouncing Christianity! When they preach like this, what wonder then that Christianity, to speak quite frankly, has become sheer nonsense, what wonder then (to recall a word of Luther's in one of his sermons)[2]—what wonder then that 'lightning' (the fire of God's wrath) 'most often strikes churches!' What wonder!—or rather, how wonderful! that it does not strike a church every Sunday to punish such a way of preaching, which in fact is nothing but a sort of debauchery, inasmuch as the speaker lyingly ascribes to himself and his hearers what is not in the least true of them.

Everybody who has any knowledge of men, and is not restrained from being honest by regard for money—or by fear of men—must concede unconditionally that in each generation a Nicodemus is a great rarity. When danger seriously threatens—and one is a superior person, and the danger precisely is insult,

---

[1] In the Danish Church it is the Gospel for Trinity Sunday, as it is in the Anglican Church.

[2] Luther's *Kirkenpostille*, Sermon for St. Stephen's Day, Erlanger ed., vii, p. 213.

mockery, ejection from society—verily there are to be found in
every generation—among superior persons, who indeed in such
a case have much to lose—there are to be found very, very few,
perhaps only a single individual, with feeling enough for the
truth to go out at night to communicate with it. Nicodemus was
an admirer; the actual danger was too much for him; personally
he desired to keep aloof. Yet, on the other hand, the truth concerned him so much that he sought to get into relationship with
it. Secretly by night—for he was treading forbidden paths—he
stole to the despised truth; it had already cost him an effort to
make this venture of seeking the society of the despised person.
For dark as the night was, and carefully as he hid himself in his
cloak, it was nevertheless possible that some one might have seen
and recognized him, it was possible that he might have run into
some one who promptly would have denounced him; and, finally,
what assurance had he that the man whom he visited might not
make such a use of it as would be injurious to Nicodemus' good
name and fame? In this respect, however, he could now feel
secure, and hence our thought is led back to Christ. There is,
however—not as though I or the average man might be justified
in saying this about Nicodemus, as though we were better than
he, for, as has been said, it is rather Nicodemus who might judge
us—there is, however, something contemptible in being an
admirer of this sort, and at bottom it is really an insult when one
regards a man as being in possession of the truth and sees that he
is mocked and persecuted precisely on this account, then to approach him in this way—it is an insult, it excites one to wrath.
But in Christ there was no excitement, He had only to command
every turmoil of excitement, and it was still. And so it is precisely
in this instance; there broods over the conversation with Nicodemus the same sacred stillness as in every case where Christ takes
part.

One sees here what an admirer is, for Nicodemus never became
a follower. It is as if Nicodemus might have said to Christ, 'In
case we come to an understanding, I will accept thy teaching in
eternity—but not here in this world, no, that I cannot do.
Couldest thou not make of me an exception? might it not suffice
if I come to thee from time to time by night? But by day—oh,
yes, I acknowledge it, I feel how humiliating it is for me, how
shameful it is, and also how insulting it really is to thee—but by

day I do not recognize thee, by day I shall say, I know not this man!' You see here in what a web of falsehood an admirer entangles himself—and do not forget that in established Christendom there is no real danger which might make it perfectly evident whether one might not be only an admirer. Nicodemus was no doubt willing to asseverate and protest in the strongest words and phrases that he espoused the truth of the doctrine—it perhaps escaped his notice that there is a limit, however, to this ascending scale of asseveration and protest, that it shifts to its opposite, the asseveration becoming a refutation of the more and more zealous protester; it perhaps escaped his notice that the more strongly a man protests while his life remains thus unchanged, the more he merely make a fool of himself, denounces himself as being either a fool or a deceiver. For when a man says of a doctrine, 'There is perhaps something in it', and his life is not changed thereby, the thing is quite reasonable and consistent. But when a man is so thoroughly convinced as he protests he is, and ready withal, if the slightest doubt is expressed of his conviction, to protest in still stronger terms—that this conviction should have no influence upon his life is a highly suspicious circumstance, and in a way a ludicrous self-contradiction. If Christ had permitted the publication of a cheaper edition of what it is to be a follower, letting it mean an admirer who protests by all that is high and holy that he is convinced, then Nicodemus might have been eligible; and so also (though here the danger is rather a different one, not so definitely that involved in confessing Christ, but rather the danger of self-denial involved in being a Christian), so also that rich young man might have been eligible, notwithstanding he would not give all his goods to the poor and follow Christ; and so also that man might be eligible who merely wanted first to bury his father; and so one is almost persuaded that King Agrippa who was 'almost persuaded' might also have been eligible. In a mere strife of words there is no essential difference between an admirer and a follower, except perhaps that the follower has not quite so rich a vocabulary, nor is so much inclined to protest. The thing is very deceptive. The admirer can say challengingly to the follower, 'Is it not thy conviction that this doctrine is the truth? and canst thou say more than I do when I protest by all that is holy that it is my most sincere conviction?' And yet there is an infinite difference between an admirer and a follower, for a follower is, or at least strives to be, what he admires.

Only real danger can make this difference clearly evident, and hence it is that by contemporaneousness with Christ it was made clearly evident who was the admirer, who the follower, and how few there were of these last. It may be said that in the generation immediately following the contemporary generation, i.e. in the militant Church, the men who risked everything as Christians in the face of real danger became more numerous. This statement, however, needs to be more closely defined before it is quite true. In the first place, many more were brought into relationship with Christianity than when the little land of Palestine was the stage for it, and so as a matter of course the actual number of followers was greater, even if it was proportionally the same. In the next place, it must be remembered that the test (examination) with respect to adventuring one's life and one's all for this cause had become easier, so that the distinction between an admirer and a follower could not become so decisively evident. For then it had become certain in another way (historically) that Christ was the extraordinary figure (not the God-Man, for that has to do with faith, and historically can neither be proved nor disproved), but when so much is established, so much the easier it is to venture, that is, so much the easier it is to make up one's mind to venture, that is to say, by this easier test it cannot become so absolutely and decisively evident how far one's conviction is absolutely and decisively that of a follower. In contemporaneousness the test was made more rigorous (*examen rigorosum*) by the fact that everything seemed to witness against Christ, to disprove that He was the extraordinary figure, not to say the Son of God, to disprove that what He said of Himself was true; and yet here the follower, in order to be a follower, must venture his life, his all, here where it is so completely demonstrated what the certitude of faith is, here where there is absolutely no other certitude, no help from historical certitude.—And now in established Christendom! In established Christendom (assuming it is true that all are Christians) there is no danger involved in being a Christian; and even if it is not true that all are truly Christians, there is no danger involved in the name of being a Christian. Here therefore an admirer can rise to greater heights of asseveration and protestation than Nicodemus could; he can say, 'It is my conviction that this doctrine is the truth, by all that is holy, this is my conviction, *in case* it were necessary, I am willing to die for it;[1] *in case* all were to fall away, I will yet remain faithful; *in case* it were to become a despicable thing to be a Christian, yet I shall remain faithful; *in case* I had lived as a contemporary of Christ, I would not have come stealthily to Him by night, for fundamentally Nicodemus was a weak man.' This he can say with tears in his eyes, while the listening congregation are dissolved in tears. This is highly deceptive, this '*in case*' makes an incomparable historical effect; it formulates the speech in likeness to that of the men who built the tombs of the Prophets and said, 'In case. . . .' A follower will hardly be able to deliver so ravishing an address. Yet there is an infinite difference between an admirer and a believer.

'But', I hear somebody say (probably the same one who intervened in the foregoing 'exposition'), 'but yet when we are all Christians it surely is impossible that there might be any such definite distinction between an admirer and a follower. The real danger involved in being a Christian, which was the thing that made the distinction evident, is now done away with by the fact that we are all Christians and confess Christ, and so the distinction has been made impossible. Now that we all of us are Christians in a decisive sense, for anyone to want to be a follower in contrast to the rest of us, to want (though certainly in vain) to seek the danger attendant upon confession—that indeed would make about as queer an impression as a youth who was cultivated, or rather had become high-flown, by the reading of romances, and therefore had his head full of ogres, monsters, and enchanted princesses, and in real life set out in quest of the marvellous. My opinion is, that when all are Christians, the individual, unless he has a disordered mind, cannot, however earnestly be would, get any farther than to asseverate his conviction; there can be no longer any question of danger, and so the concept of "a follower", so precisely differentiated from an admirer as you would have it, has passed away.'

A sufficient answer has been given to this objection in the foregoing 'exposition'. But, assuming that there is truth (and not rather mere jugglery) in the assertion that there is now no danger in confessing Christ, the logical consequence would simply

---

[1] Precisely these 'protests' (except the last) S. K. heard in a sermon by Bishop Mynster—and forthwith registered them indignantly in his Journal.

be that the distinction admirer/follower had become unrecognizable in so far as the ground of this distinction lies in the danger connected with confessing Christ, but it would not follow that the distinction admirer/follower has become entirely unrecognizable.

The distinction none the less remains as between being, or at least striving to be, what one admires and holding oneself personally aloof. Let us now forget entirely the danger connected with confessing Christ,[1] and let us think rather of the real danger which inevitably is connected with being a Christian. Does not the Christian doctrine of ethics and duty, Christianity's requirement of dying from the world, of giving up the worldly, of self-denial—does not all this include claims enough, if they were complied with, to constitute the real danger which reveals the difference between 'an admirer' and 'a follower'? Is not this revealed precisely in the fact that the follower lives in these dangers, while the admirer holds himself aloof from them, though both of them alike acknowledge in words the truth of Christianity? So the distinction holds good nevertheless: the admirer is not willing to make any sacrifices, to give up anything worldly, to reconstruct his life, to be what he admires or let his life express it —but in words, verbal expressions, asseverations, he is inexhaustible in affirming how highly he prizes Christianity. The follower, on the other hand, aspires to be what he admires—and so (strange to say!) even though he lives in established Christendom he will encounter the same danger which once was involved in confessing Christ. Again, by means of the 'follower's' life, it will be revealed who is the admirer; for the admirers will become highly embittered against the follower. And even the mere fact that the situation is presented as it is here presented will embitter many—but they must surely belong to the class of admirers.

But it must not be forgotten that established Christendom has made an attempt to do away also with this danger. The danger which once was involved in confessing Christ has passed away since we have all become Christians, and to that extent the distinction admirer follower has passed away. The next danger, which is brought about by taking seriously Christ's requirement of self-denial and the renunciation of worldly things, they have also

---

[1] It is not quite a century since S. K. wrote this, and already there are several countries in 'Christendom' where the mere profession of being a Christian involves real danger.

wanted to do away with by endeavouring falsely to transform the Christian life into hidden inwardness, kept so carefully hidden that it does not become noticeable in one's life. One should be willing to deny oneself in hidden inwardness, in hidden inwardness to renounce the world and all that is of the world, but (for God's sake! shall I say?) one must not let it be observed. In this way, established Christendom becomes a collection of what one might call honorary Christians, in the same sense as one speaks of honorary doctors who get their degree without having to take an examination. In hidden inwardness we all take degrees, or rather we all receive them, each from the other, as a compliment, and are honorary Christians in the same sense (a mocker might say) as one speaks of 'chimney-students'.[1] But in any case the danger passed away, and therewith also the distinction admirer/ follower; and (if I may recall the introduction to this 'exposition') Christianity became 'reflections'.

However, to conceal in a measure this inconvenience of having no distinctions, there was introduced in established Christendom an entirely new distinction by way of defining what it is to be a Christian. Up to a certain point there still is some sense in bestowing the name of Christian upon an admirer, one who solemnly asseverates his Christian conviction, although he is not exactly that when he is contrasted with the 'follower'. But then when the distinction admirer/follower had passed away, and 'admirer' had become place No. 1, that gave occasion for promotion all along the line, and there arose in Christendom a class of Christians so strange and curious that they might be exhibited for money in a side-show. For in the course of time there emerged in established Christendom free-thinkers and other spirits of that ilk, who attacked, insulted, derided Christianity worse than the worst pagan mockers had done. But as these men were nevertheless born in Christendom and were living in Christendom where all are Christians; and as they themselves presumably did not consider it worth the trouble, or perhaps accounted it too great a sacrifice, to renounce the name of Christian; and as Christendom, by reason of its extraordinary extension no doubt, did not possess elasticity enough to shake off from it such Christians as these—

[1] A name given in Copenhagen to students who matriculated without taking an examination, merely on the ground that they had reached maturity—a regulation which was abolished in 1805.

so these men continued to call themselves Christians, and people continued to call them Christians.[1] However, a discrimination of some sort had to be made, and since the discrimination admirer/follower had passed away, a new distinction was introduced: the admirers became the true Christians, and these free-thinkers, &c., became the untrue Christians, 'poor Christians', but yet Christians all the same. Undeniably, even in contrast with the 'admirers', these non-Christians were bad Christians.[2] Here again it is to be seen how Christianity has been abolished in Christendom. The 'follower' is what we must be guided by if we are to speak truly about Christianity, the 'follower' is the true Christian. But now the 'admirer' had become the true Christian, and the deniers of Christianity also became Christians of a sort—not of course true Christians, for the admirers had assumed that place. Double confusion, infinite depth of confusion!

Only the 'followers' are the true Christians. The 'admirers' have in fact a pagan relationship to Christianity, and hence admiration gave rise to a new paganism in the midst of Christendom, namely, Christian art.[3] I do not wish in any way to pass judgement upon any one, but I regard it as my duty to pronounce what I feel. Would it be possible for me, that is to say, could I bring myself to the point, or could I be prompted, to dip my brush, to lift my chisel, in order to depict Christ in colour or to carve His figure? The fact that I am incapable of doing it, that I am not an artist, is here irrelevant, I merely ask whether it would be possible for me to do it if I had the capacity. And I answer, No, it would be for me an absolute impossibility. Indeed, even with this I do not express what I feel, for in such a degree would it be impossible for me that I cannot conceive how it has been possible to anyone. A person says, 'I cannot conceive of the calmness of the murderer who sits sharpening the knife with which he is about to kill another man.' And to me, too, this is inconceivable. But truly it is also inconceivable to me whence the artist derived his calm, or the calmness is inconceivable to me

[1] In this connexion it may suffice to recall the fact that David Strauss, who in that age was the most effective opponent of Christianity, not only retained his membership in the Church, but took pains to have all his children baptized.

[2] In another place S. K. shows how absurd it is to speak of such people as 'poor Christians', when the simple fact is that they are *not* Christians.

[3] This is the passage to which Professor Swenson so speciously appeals in condemnation of putting a picture of Christ in front of this book.

with which an artist has sat year in and year out industriously labouring to paint a portrait of Christ—without chancing to reflect whether Christ desired perhaps to have a portrait made by his master-brush, however idealized it might be. I cannot conceive how the artist preserved his calm, how it is that he did not notice Christ's displeasure and suddenly cast down brush and colours and all, as Judas did the thirty pieces of silver, casting them far, far away from him, because he suddenly understood that Christ required only 'followers', that He who here on earth lived in poverty and wretchedness, not having whereon to lay his head, and who lived thus not accidentally, because of the harshness of fate, desiring for Himself different conditions, but of His own free choice, by virtue of an eternal resolve—that such as He hardly desired or desires that after His death a man should throw away his time, perhaps his eternal blessedness, by painting Him. I cannot conceive it, the brush would have fallen out of my hand the very second I was about to begin, and perhaps I might not have survived it. I cannot comprehend the calm of an artist engaged in such a work, the artistic indifference, a callousness as it were to the religious impression of religion, a capriciousness, a delight in cruelty, as when the tyrant Philaris[1] derived the pleasure of sweet music from the shrieks of the men he tortured, so that with an enhancement of cruelty he made their shrieks signify something quite different to him—this artistic indifference which doubtless his environment expressed by the fact that he was quite as much occupied with the picture of the goddess of sensuality found in his studio, and that only when he had finished this did he proceed to depict the Crucified. Is not this to have unnatural intercourse with the holy? And yet the artist admires himself, and all admire the artist. The religious point of view was entirely superseded; the beholder contemplated the picture in the role of a connoisseur—to determine whether it is a success, whether it is a masterpiece, whether the play of colours is just, and the shadows right, whether blood looks like that, whether the expression of suffering is artistically true—but he found no incentive to become a follower. People admired the artist, and

---

[1] The story of this Greek tyrant, who roasted his enemies in a brazen bull, was artfully employed by S. K. in the first 'Diapsalm' in *Either/Or*, with his own embellishment (which is here assumed), that the instrument of torture was so constructed as to transform the shrieks of the victims into sweet music.

what was real suffering, the real suffering of the Holy One, the artist contrived to turn into money and admiration—just as when an actor takes the part of a beggar, and with that almost transfers to himself the compassion due to real poverty, from which people shrink away hard-heartedly and likely regard as untrue in comparison with the actor's representation. Yes, this is inconceivable, again I say, it is inconceivable; for perhaps it never occurred to the artist that this was sacrilegious—and this is still more inconceivable to me. But just because it is inconceivable to me I refrain from any condemnation, lest I do an injustice; but I regard it as my duty to pronounce what I surely may rightly dare to call a Christian feeling. It is not a proposal to assail the artist or any particular work of art, not that in the least; no, it is a riddle I feel myself bound to propose. For I am convinced in my inmost heart that what I say is Christian; but I dare not say of myself that I am so perfect a Christian that I might venture to give the impression that at every instant I feel equally vividly what I have here said, not that I would assume responsibility for every deduction from it. But what has been said is for me, and I think for Christianity, like a nautical signal which indicated in what direction Christendom actually is steering, whether deeper and deeper into Christianity, or farther and farther away from Christianity.

It has almost come to the point that an admirer of Christianity is a rarity; people on the average are lukewarm, neither cold nor hot, and many are free-thinkers, mockers, 'strong spirits', deniers. But nevertheless the 'admirer' is not in the strictest sense a true Christian; if one cannot say of him that he is lukewarm, since there is heat in him, neither can one say that he is warm. Only the 'follower' is the true Christian.

It has almost come to the point that one must make use of art in the most various ways to get Christendom to display any sympathy for Christianity. But by the help of art, whether it be the art of the sculptor, or of the orator, or of the poet,[1] we get at the very most only 'admirers', who, while incidentally they are admiring the artist, are led by his presentation to admire Christianity. But yet the admirer is in the strictest sense no true Christian, only the follower is such.

It has almost come to the point that if one will not say that

---

[1] It should not be forgotten that for his part S. K. had already renounced the poetic art.

Christianity is profound, and profound again, a thing for profound thinkers—then nobody can be got to listen to a word about Christianity. But if it is true that all this talk about the profundity of Christianity, this talk which flatters the hearers, if it is true that it wins many, it wins to Christianity only admirers; and the admirer, indeed, is in the strictest sense no true Christian, only the follower is such.

It has almost come to the point that, though sermons are often enough preached (or rather 'reflections' are conducted) about what it means to follow Christ, what it is to be a follower of Christ, &c., yet the discourse, if it has any effect, has only the effect of confirming admirers in their admiration of Christianity, and winning for it once in a while a new admirer. But the admirer indeed is in the strictest sense no true Christian, only the follower is that.

VII

John 12: 32. AND I, IF I BE LIFTED UP FROM THE EARTH, WILL
DRAW ALL UNTO MYSELF

YEA, Lord Jesus Christ, whether we be far off or near, far
away from Thee in the human swarm, in business, in earthly
cares, in temporal joys, in merely human highness, or far
from all this, forsaken, unappreciated, in lowliness, and with this
the nearer to Thee, do Thou draw us, draw us entirely to
Thyself.

How the sacred text just now read ought to be understood, we
have shown from various sides—not as though the meaning of it
had become various; no, not that, but by approaching it from
various sides we have sought to reach the one and only meaning
of these words. That this is the right meaning of the words, surely
no one will deny. Yet to confirm this interpretation we shall not
omit to quote him who as the author of this book is not only the
best interpreter of his own words, but who by his sacred authority imposes silence and forbids further interpretation if it does not
lead to the same result. I quote the Apostle John. He says
expressly in the following verse (12: 33), 'This He said' (that is,
Christ), 'signifying what death He should die'. Thus the Apostle
explains the being lifted up from the earth as humiliation, as the
deepest humiliation, as crucifixion. Thus, Christianly understood,
exaltation is in this world humiliation. Then Christ ascended up
on high, but His life and the story of His life is what He left
behind for the followers, to show that the exaltation is humiliation,
or that humiliation is the true exaltation.

Here, then, we will bring these 'expositions' to a close, leaving
it to everyone whether he will read, leaving it to the reader what
use he will make of what he reads, with respect to inward transformation.

But unto Thee, Lord Jesus Christ, will we pray that Thou wilt
draw us entirely unto Thyself. Whether our life shall be passed
calmly in a cottage by the tranquil lake, or we shall be tried by
conflict with life's storms upon the troubled ocean; whether we

shall 'seek for honour by living quietly',[1] or shall struggle in abasement, do Thou draw us, and draw us entirely, unto Thyself. If only Thou wilt draw us, then indeed all is won, even though, humanly speaking, we were to win nothing; and nothing is lost, even though, humanly speaking, we were to lose everything —then this or the other condition of life would be our true life; for thou dost draw none to an unworthy distance from dangers, but neither dost Thou draw any into foolhardy adventure.

We pray for all. The tender infant whom the parents bring to Thee that Thou mayest *draw* him unto Thyself. And if at a later time the parents exert such an influence upon the child that it is led to Thee, bless, we pray Thee, this work of theirs. But if their influence is disturbing to the child, we pray Thee that Thou wilt make good their deficiency, so that this disturbance may not draw the child away from Thee, and that Thou wilt let this also serve to draw the child to Thee. Thou who didst call Thyself 'the way' hast more ways than there are stars in heaven, ways everywhere, ways which lead to 'the way'.—We pray for them that have renewed [at confirmation] the covenant made with Thee [in baptism] which we all have made, which most of us also have renewed, which most of us also have broken—yet not all, for we pray also for them that, in a way different from the infant, stand at the entrance of life, after having renewed their baptismal covenant. We pray that Thou wilt draw them unto Thyself. O Thou that dost not only accept vows and keep promises, but dost aid poor man to keep his vows to Thee, draw them unto Thyself by the 'vow' and if that is broken, do Thou draw them again and again unto Thyself by vows again and again renewed.—We pray for them that have experienced that which in an earthly sense is the most beautiful meaning of this earthly life, for them that in love have found one another. We pray for the lovers, that they may not promise one another more than they can perform, and, even if they could perform it, that they may not promise one another too much in love, lest this love of theirs might become a barrier to hinder Thee from drawing them unto Thyself, but that far rather it may assist to this end. We pray for the husband,

---

[1] So read the older Danish version of 1 Thess. 4: 11. The modern version, '*make it a point of honour* to live quietly, to do your own business and work with your own hands', does more justice to the original than does ours.

that his important undertaking, if he be so situated in life, or his busy activity, or his toilsome labour, may not cause him to be unmindful of Thee, but that in his undertaking, in his activity, in his labour, he may feel himself more and more drawn unto Thee. We pray for the wife, to whom the quieter lot is apportioned, remote from the world's distractions and turmoil, that in the course of her gracious work in the home she may preserve 'collectedness' in the deepest sense, feeling herself more and more drawn unto Thee.—We pray for the aged in the evening of life, that now, when the season of labour is over, thoughts of Thee, which draw unto Thee, may entirely fill their souls. We pray for the aged at the brink of the grave, that Thou wilt draw them unto Thyself.—We pray for all, for him who at this instant first hails the light of day, that the meaning of his life may be that he is drawn unto Thee; and we pray for the dying, for him who has much and many to hold him back, and for him who has nothing and nobody that cares—we pray that it may have been the meaning of his life to be drawn unto Thee.

We pray for the happy and the fortunate who for very joy know not whither they are bent, that Thou wilt draw them unto Thyself and let them learn that it is thither they should go. We pray for the sufferers who in their wretchedness know not whither to turn, that Thou wilt draw them unto Thyself—that both the fortunate ones and the sufferers, however unlike their lot in life, may in one thing be alike, that they know nowhere else to go but to Thee. We pray for them that are in need of conversion, that Thou wilt draw them unto Thee, from the way of perdition into the way of truth. For them that have turned unto Thee and found the way, we pray that they may make progress in the way, drawn by Thee. And since, truth being the way, there are three ways of going wrong: by losing the way, by stumbling in the way, by deviating from the way—we pray that Thou wilt draw the erring unto Thee from the wrong way, support the stumbling, and bring back the bewildered to the way.

Thus we pray for all. Yet no one is able to mention every individual. And who, indeed, can mention even all the various classes of men? So in conclusion we mention only one class, we pray for them that are the ministers of Thy Word, whose work it is, so far as a man is able, to draw men unto Thee. We pray that Thou wilt bless their work, but that at the same time they themselves in this work of theirs may be drawn unto Thee, that by their zeal to draw others unto Thee they themselves may not be held back from Thee. And we pray for the simple Christians, that, being themselves drawn unto Thee, they may not think poorly of themselves, as though it were not granted also unto them to draw others unto Thee, in so far as a man is able.

In so far as a man is able—for Thou alone art able to draw unto Thyself, though Thou canst employ all means and all men to draw all unto Thyself.

AN EDIFYING DISCOURSE

by

S. Kierkegaard

Copenhagen

1850

IN MEMORY

of

the deceased

MICHAEL PEDERSEN KIERKEGAARD

my Father

I dedicate

this little work

PREFACE

See the Preface to *Two Edifying Discourses* of 1843

December 12, 1850

NOTE BY THE TRANSLATOR

Inasmuch as the Preface to which S. K. refers the reader cannot be found in English, I give a translation of it herewith. But the reader needs also to be apprised of the pathos of this reference. The *Two Edifying Discourses* of 1843 were published as the 'accompaniment' of *Either/Or*. They were the first of a long series of 'Discourses' (82 in all) which ended only three months before S. K.'s death. All those which are entitled 'Edifying Discourses', 20 of them, were dedicated to his father's memory, and the prefaces to all were nearly alike. At this moment, with the notion that he was perhaps uttering his last word in print, he publishes this as a gesture of farewell to his father. It should be noticed that the two discourses which follow were a farewell to Regina: 'Dedicated to one unnamed who some day shall be named.' S. K. lived, in fact, five years longer, and in the heat of his attack upon the Established Church he found leisure of mind to publish what proved indeed to be the last 'Discourse', which was dedicated to his father in substantially the terms he had first used: 'In Memory of my deceased Father, Michael Pedersen Kierkegaard, one time hosier in this city. August, 1855.' The Preface of 1843 is as follows:

PREFACE

Notwithstanding this little book (which is entitled 'Discourses', not sermons, because the author of them has no authority to *preach*, and 'Edifying Discourses', not discourses for edification, because the speaker makes no claim to be a *teacher*) desires only to be what it is, a superfluity, and desires only to remain in obscurity, as in obscurity it was brought to birth, yet I have not taken leave of it without an almost romantic hope. Forasmuch as on being published it started, figuratively speaking, upon a pilgrimage, I let my eye follow it a little while. I saw then how it fared forth along lonely paths or alone upon the highway. After one and another little misunderstanding, when it was deceived by a fleeting likeness, it finally encountered that single individual whom I with joy and gratitude call *my* reader, that single individual whom it seeks, towards whom as it were it stretches out its arms, that single individual who is willing enough to let himself be found, willing enough to encounter it, whether at the instant of encounter it finds him happy and confident or 'weary and pensive.'—On the other hand, forasmuch as on being published it remains, literally speaking, perfectly still, without budging from the spot, I let my eye rest upon it a little while. It stood there like an insignificant little blossom hidden in the immense forest, unsought after either for its splendour, or for its scent, or for its nutriment. But then too I saw or thought I saw how the bird which I call *my* reader suddenly sighted it, plunged down upon the wing, plucked it and took it unto itself. And when I had seen this, I saw no more.

Copenhagen, May 5, 1843.

S. K.

'The Woman that was a Sinner'

Luke 7: 37 ff.

THAT a woman is presented as a teacher, as a pattern of piety, can astonish no one who knows that piety or godliness is in its very nature a womanly quality. If women are to 'keep silent in the Churches' and to that extent are not to teach—well, that means precisely to keep silent before God, and precisely this belongs essentially to true godliness, and this also thou must be able to learn from woman.

From a woman, therefore, thou dost learn then humble faith in relation to the Extraordinary Man, the humble faith which does not incredulously, doubtingly, ask, 'why?' 'wherefore?' 'how is this possible?' but humbly believes like Mary and says, 'Behold, the handmaid of the Lord'. She *says* that, but observe that to say that is really to keep silent. From a woman thou dost learn to hear the Word rightly, from Mary, who, though she 'understood not the saying', yet 'kept it in her heart', so that she did not demand first to understand, but silently treasured the Word in the right place; for that indeed is the right place where the Word, the good seed, is 'kept in an honest and good heart'. From a woman thou dost learn the hushed, profound, God-fearing sorrow which is silent before God, from Mary; for it is true that the sword pierced through her heart, as was prophesied, but she was not in despair, either at the prophecy, or at its coming to pass. From a woman thou dost learn concern for the one thing needful, from Mary the sister of Lazarus, who sat silent at the feet of Christ with her heart's choice, the one thing needful.

So canst thou also learn from a woman the right sort of sorrow for sin, from the woman that was a sinner, from her whose many sins, long, long ago, not only passed into oblivion but were forgotten,[1] but who herself eternally became unforgettable. How, indeed, could it be otherwise but that in this respect one might be able to learn from a woman? For man no doubt in comparison

---

[1] The pathos of this distinction will not be evident to the reader unless it is known that the new sense of freedom S. K. acquired in the Easter experience of 1848 was due to the sudden conviction that God had not only forgiven his sins but '*forgotten*' them.

with woman has many thoughts (if this is to be counted an advantage, especially in the present reference, seeing that in addition to this he has many half-thoughts); and no doubt man is stronger than weak woman, has more expedients, knows much better how to shift for himself: but then again woman has one— one what? Why, just 'one', the fact that *one* is woman's element. One wish, not many wishes—no, only one wish, but that with the whole soul put into it; one thought, not many thoughts—no, only one thought, but that a prodigious power by the power of passion; one sorrow, not many sorrows—no, one sorrow, but so deep in the heart that one sorrow is certainly infinitely more than the many; one sorrow, yes, only one sorrow, but then also so deeply implanted—sorrow over her sin, like this woman. And what after all is seriousness? Let it be granted that man has more seriousness with respect to thought, yet with respect to feeling, passion, decision, with respect to not creating an obstacle to oneself and the decision by thoughts, proposals, resolutions, with respect to not deceiving oneself by coming quite close to decision but without coming to a decision, in these respects woman has more seriousness; but, in fact, decision (especially in a godly sense, and more especially in relation to sorrow for sin) is precisely what seriousness means.

SO THEN LET US DIRECT OUR ATTENTION TO THE WOMAN THAT WAS A SINNER, AND WHAT WE CAN LEARN FROM HER

First, we can learn to become, like her, indifferent to everything else, in absolute sorrow for our sins, yet in such a way that one thing is important to us, and absolutely important: to find forgiveness.

My hearer, One sees only too often in life people who are deeply troubled, people who are troubled now about this and now about that, and sometimes about all sorts of things at once; and troubled people who themselves do not clearly know why they are troubled—but it is rare to see a person who is troubled only about one thing, and still more rare to see a person who is so absolutely troubled about this one thing that all else becomes absolutely indifferent to him.

Yet, although it is not common, it still is to be seen; I have seen, and thou, too, surely hast seen, a man who was unhappy in love, to whom everything became indifferent, permanently or for a long space of time; but this is not sorrow for his sin. The man whose bold plans were all frustrated in an instant by an unlooked-for obstacle, for whom then everything became in-different, permanently or for a long space of time; but this is not sorrow for his sin. The man who combated with the long dura-tion of time, and combated long; he held out, he still held out, even yesterday he was holding out, to-day the vital power of renewal that was within him was lacking, he collapsed, everything became indifferent to him; but this is not sorrow for his sin. The man whose very nature is melancholy—thou hast seen how the melancholy man regards everything indifferently and as a stranger, how in a sense (just as the air may be too light to breathe) every-thing is too light for him because his mind is too heavy; but sorrow for sin it is not. The man who year after year, with a terrible *joie de vivre*, piled crime upon crime, most of whose time was spent in sinning—until he stood there annihilated, and everything became indifferent to him; but truly sorrow for sin there was not —there were sins enough, but sorrow for sin there was not. There is one thing especially which is quite universal, thou canst find it in all and in each, in thyself too, as I find it in me, namely, sin and sins; there is one thing which is rarer, namely, sorrow for one's sin.

Yet I have seen, and thou perhaps also, a man who absolutely sorrowed for only one thing, and that was for his sin. It pursued him everywhere, rather it persecuted him by day, in dreams by night, while he laboured or when in vain he sought rest after labour, in loneliness and when in vain he sought distraction in company; it wounded him from behind when he turned towards the future, and in front when he turned towards the past; it taught him to wish for death and to be afraid of life, and then in turn to wish for life and to be afraid of death, so that without slaying him, it nevertheless took as it were life from him, leaving him as much in dread of himself as of a spectre; it made everything indifferent to him—but lo, this sorrow was despair. There is one thing especially which is quite universal, thou canst find it in all and in each, in thyself too, as I find it in me, namely, sin and sins; there is one thing which is very rare, namely, true sorrow for one's sin; wherefore there is great need for the supplication of the Church at the commencement of divine service on every holy day, 'that we might learn to sorrow for our sins'. Well is it for him in whom is found this true sorrow for his sin, so that the fact that all else is indifferent to him is only the negative expression of the positive fact that one thing is absolutely important to him; so that the fact that all else is absolutely unimportant to him is a mortal sickness which yet is very far from being unto death,[1] but is precisely a sickness unto life, for life is apparent in this, that one thing is absolutely important to him, namely, to find forgiveness. Well it is for him—he is very seldom to be seen. For, my hearer, there is often enough to be seen in the world a man to whom the important has become unimportant, still oftener men to whom every sort of thing has become important; but seldom a man to whom only one thing is important, and still more seldom the man of whom it is true that this one and only thing which to him is absolutely important is also in truth the one and only important thing.

Mark, therefore, the woman that was a sinner, that thou mayest learn of her.

She had become indifferent to all else, she was concerned about nothing but her sin, or every other concern she had was as though it did not exist, because that one concern was absolute. This, if one will, is the blessing connected with having only one sorrow: to be careless and untroubled about everything else. And this is the token whereby the person is known who has only one sorrow.

So it was with this woman. But how different it commonly is in life! When a man who is not without sin and guilt—which indeed no man is—has at the same time other anxieties, so that he is anxious and dejected, he perhaps mistakes this dejection and regards it as concern for his sin, as if only this were required of a man, that he be anxious, whereas in fact the requirement is that he *shall* be anxious about his *sin*, and that he shall *not be* anxious about anything else; but he confounds the two and fails to observe that, if it were his sin he sorrowed for, he would be less sensible of other worries or not sensible of them at all, seizing the opportunity to express true sorrow for his sin by the fact that he bore these other troubles more lightly. Perhaps he so understands the case, yet desires that he might be relieved of his other troubles in order to sorrow only for his sin. Ah, he does not rightly understand what he asks, and that in this way the situation might rather become too stern for him. For when God with stern correction would

---

[1] An allusion to the theme elaborated in *The Sickness unto Death*.

bring down upon a man his sin, He sometimes acts thus: He says, 'I will relieve this man of every other concern, everything shall smile upon him, everything shall conform to his wish, everything he touches shall succeed—but all the less on this account shall he succeed in forgetting, all the more shall he be sensible of that which torments him.' So there is no truth in the excuse often made that because of one's other cares one cannot well find time to sorrow for one's sin. No, it is just the 'other cares' which afford opportunity for expressing true sorrow for sin by bearing the other cares more lightly; and 'other cares' are not an aggravation, but rather an alleviation, in the fact that there is no room for thoughts to stray, but there presents itself at once the task of expressing sorrow for one's sin by bearing the other cares more patiently, more humbly, more easily.

And the sinful woman had become indifferent to everything, to everything temporal, earthly, worldly, to pride, honour, prosperity, the future, kindred, friends, man's judgement; and all other cares, whatever name they may have, she could have borne lightly, almost as nothing, for she was concerned absolutely about only one thing, her sin. This is what she sorrowed for, and not for its consequences, shame, disgrace, humiliation; no, she did not mistake the sickness for the medicine. Oh, how rare is the man who, if on these terms he might receive forgiveness of his sins, would be willing to suffer the penalty of becoming entirely revealed before men, so that they might look right into his soul and behold every secret sin! The very sin for which he condemns himself and for which he prays God's forgiveness is hidden perhaps with miserly pains that no one might get a glimpse of it.

To the sinful woman, on the other hand, everything had become indifferent: the hostility of the environment, the protest of the banquet, the opposition of the Pharisees or their cold derision —the place, indeed, was an impregnable fortress, just so defended as to make her entrance impossible, if everything else had not become indifferent to her. What perhaps no other woman would have dared to do, not even one who was unconscious of being a sinner and could do it without danger, she dared, to whom everything had become indifferent.

And yet, no, it is not quite thus, she dared this because one thing was absolutely important to her: to find forgiveness. And this was to be found within that house—therefore she dared it, this it was that impelled her to move and drove her onward; but the fact that all else had become indifferent to her, that it was which brought it about that she herself hardly observed the opposition. 'That is the courage of despair', thou wilt say. Yes, but verily she is very far from being a despairing person. Was that a despairing man to whom one thing was absolutely important, when that one thing is the absolutely important? She has the strength of despair. That it is which makes her indifferent to everything and stronger than the opposition of the environment, so strong that she does not sink with shame, does not shun derision; but she who has this strength is not a despairer, she is a believer. And so she enters in, indifferent to all else. Yet this does not produce any sensation, cause any noise, this absolute indifference of hers; for she is a believer, and hence she is so quiet, so unobtrusive in her infinite indifference to all, that she attracts no attention by her entrance. To her it was not of the least importance to express her indifference to all; but one thing was of infinite importance to her: to find forgiveness. Yet had not this one thing been important to her to such a degree, she would not have found her way into that Pharisee's house—where she then found forgiveness.

Next, thou canst learn of the sinful woman, what she well understood, that in relation to finding forgiveness she herself could do nothing at all.[1]

If we were to characterize her conduct as a whole from first to last, we must say: she did nothing at all.

She did not wait before going to that house where she would find salvation—she did not wait until she felt herself worthy. No, she would thus have remained a long time at a distance, perhaps never gone thither or entered in; she decides to go at once in her unworthiness, it is just the feeling of unworthiness which impels her, hence the decision is to go at once—thus it is that she herself did nothing, or understood that she herself was able to do nothing. Can this be more strongly expressed than when precisely the feeling of unworthiness is that which determines her?

So she prepares to go—yet not by way of preparing what she

[1] S. K. firmly believed in the Lutheran doctrine of man's impotence to do anything to deserve salvation—but he held it in a Catholic sense, as is evident in *The Works of Love*.

will say, or anything like that; oh, no, she buys an alabaster cruise of ointment. Thus she complies with the scriptural saying: 'When thou fastest, anoint thy head and wash thy face, that thou appear not unto men to fast, but unto thy Father which is in secret.' Then she went festively to the banquet—verily, who would have guessed what her errand was, or what her entrance into that house meant to her! She understands perfectly, however, that she herself is able to do nothing. Instead of abandoning herself to self-torment, perhaps, as though thereby she would be more pleasing to God, and thereby come closer to God—instead of this, she *wastes* (that, in fact, was Judas's opinion), she wastes *frivolously* (that, in fact, is the opinion of the self-tormentor), she made this waste upon something that had to do, in an earthly sense, with a festivity, she takes with her an alabaster cruise of ointment, in festive correspondence with the banquet.

She enters in. She understands perfectly that she herself is able to do nothing. She therefore does not abandon herself in her expressions to the passion of self-accusation, as though this would bring salvation nearer to her, or make her more pleasing to God; she does not exaggerate; verily, no one can lay that to her charge. No, she does nothing at all, she keeps silent, she weeps.

She weeps. Perhaps someone will say, 'So then she did something.' Well, yes, she could not hold back the tears. Yet had the thought occurred to her that these tears even might be regarded as doing something, she would have been able to hold them back.

So she weeps. She has seated herself at Christ's feet, and there she sits weeping. Let us not, however, forget the festive occasion, as she for her part did not forget it, precisely because she perfectly understood that with respect to finding forgiveness she herself was able to do nothing at all; let us not forget the festive occasion—and the ointment she brought with her. She does not forget it, she understands this as properly her work: she anoints Christ's feet with ointment and wipes them with the hairs of her head, she weeps.

Art thou able, in case thou dost not know it, to guess what this tableau signifies? Indeed, since she says nothing, to guess is in a sense impossible; and, indeed, to her the two things are fused or confused as one: this thing of anointing His feet, which agrees with the festivity; and this of weeping, which agrees with something quite different. What it signifies, however, is something that concerns nobody but her, who perfectly understands that she is able to do nothing at all—and Him, of whom she perfectly understands that He is absolutely able to do all.

So she listens to Him as He talks with those present at the banquet. She understands very well that He is speaking about her when He speaks about two debtors, that one owed five hundred pence, and the other fifty, and that it is reasonable, when both are forgiven, that the first shall love more than the other. She understands well enough how the one thing, about the debtor, applies, alas, to her, and how the other thing, about forgiveness, praise God, applies to her also. But at the same time she perfectly understands that she is able to do nothing at all. She therefore does not mix in the conversation, she keeps silent, keeps her eyes to herself or upon the work she is attending to, she anoints His feet and wipes them with the hairs of her head, she weeps. Oh, what a mighty, what a true expression for 'doing nothing'! To be as an absent one, although present, yes, although so present that the talk is about her!

Then she hears Him say, 'Her sins, which are many, are forgiven'—that she hears. He says even more, He goes on to say, '*because* she loved much'. I assume that this last word she did not hear at all; it perhaps might have troubled her that there was a 'because', and as applied to her it might perhaps have alarmed love to hear itself praised thus. Hence I assume that she did not hear it, or perhaps she heard it but heard amiss, so that she thought He said, 'because He loved much', so that what was said had reference to His infinite love, that *because* it was so infinite, therefore her many sins were forgiven her, which she could so perfectly well understand, for it was as if she herself had said it.

So she goes home again—a dumb person in this whole scene. Who could guess what this expedition meant to her, this expedition when she went thither in sin and sorrow, and came hence with forgiveness and joy!

What, then, is it this woman did from whom we are to learn? The answer is: Nothing, she did nothing at all; she practised the high, rare, exceedingly difficult, genuine womanly art of doing nothing at all, or of understanding that with respect to finding forgiveness she herself was able to do nothing. 'How easy!'— yes, were it not that precisely the easiness is the difficulty. Verily he that subdueth himself is greater than he that taketh a city. Greater than he that sets everything in commotion just for the sake of doing something himself, is he who in relation to God and with respect to receiving forgiveness of his sins, can keep quite still, so as in godly fear to let God do all, understanding perfectly that in this respect he himself is able to do nothing at all, that everything a man himself is able to do, though it were the most glorious deed, the most astonishing, is in this respect infinitely nothing, that it is (if, indeed, it is something which, humanly speaking, is really good, and not the pitiful self-deception of the cunning heart) so far from contributing even in the least degree to acquire for him in the remotest way the forgiveness of sins, that it far rather puts him in a new debt, a new debt of gratitude to the infinite grace which in addition to everything else permitted him to succeed in this. No—oh, pitiable aberration, or frightful presumption, that such a thought could occur to a man in the remotest way!—no, with respect to obtaining forgiveness of sins, or *before* God, a man has no power to do anything; how could this be possible, since even in relation to the least thing, a man, humanly speaking, has no power, except *by* God's help?

Finally, we learn from the sinful woman—not indeed directly from her, but by reflecting upon our situation in comparison with hers—that we have a comfort which she had not.

Perhaps some one may be inclined to say, 'Yes, it was an easy thing for her to believe in the forgiveness of her sins, for she heard it pronounced by Christ's own lips; that which throughout so many centuries has been experienced by thousands upon thousands, that which through so many generations has been handed down as an experience from generation to generation, the truth that "one word from Him heals for eternity"—how vividly must she not have felt and sensed it who heard the healing word from His own lips.'

On this point there doubtless prevails a rather general misunderstanding, owing to the fact that people, deceived by their imagination, do not vividly realize the situation, and therefore forget that in one sense it is precisely contemporaneousness with Christ which makes faith peculiarly difficult. Yet how natural this is, for the man who thus believed in spite of all difficulty and danger had indeed an advantage over every one of a subsequent generation, in hearing the word from Christ's own lips, not merely reading it like us, and reading in general terms that in Christ there is forgiveness of sins, but hearing it said to him personally by Christ, so that there cannot possibly be any doubt that it means me, that to me is assured the gracious pardon of my sins, no more doubt of it than there can be doubt that this is actually Christ's word.

But there is another side to the thing. There is a comfort which did not exist so long as Christ lived, and which He therefore could not offer to anyone: the comfort of His death as the atonement, as the pledge that the sins are forgiven. In His lifetime Christ is more especially the Pattern for his contemporaries, notwithstanding that He is the Saviour, and notwithstanding that His life is suffering, so that even in His lifetime he could be said to bear the sins of the world; yet the outstanding fact is that He is the Pattern. And inasmuch as Christianity is not some sort of a doctrine which remains the same whoever the preacher may be, but stands in so close a relationship to the preacher and to the question how far the preacher's life truly expresses the doctrine, that it became only too apparent that, when Christ preaches Christianity and preaches it as the Pattern, nobody can quite keep up with Him, they fall away, even the Apostles.

But then He dies. And His death alters everything infinitely. Not that His death abolished the fact that at the same time He is the Pattern; no, but His death becomes the infinite guarantee with which the striver starts out, the assurance that infinite satisfaction has been made, that to the doubtful and disheartened there is tendered the strongest pledge—impossible to find anything more reliable!—that Christ died to save him, that Christ's death is the atonement and satisfaction. This comfort the sinful woman did not have. She heard from His own lips, it is true, that her sins were forgiven her; but she did not have His death to comfort herself with, as the subsequent generations had. Imagine to thyself that this woman was tempted at a later moment by the doubt whether also her many sins were really forgiven her, she then (inasmuch as she could not again hear Christ saying this to her directly) would find rest in hearing as it were Christ saying to her, 'Believe it nevertheless. Thou hast indeed heard it from My own lips.' On the other hand, the Christian who lives many centuries after Christ, when he is tempted by the doubt whether his sins also are forgiven him, will find comfort in hearing as it were Christ saying to him, 'Believe it, nevertheless, for I have laid down my life to procure the forgiveness of thy sins; so believe it then, a stronger assurance is impossible.' To His contemporaries Christ could only say, 'I will give myself as a sacrifice for the sins of the world, and for thy sins too.' Is this, then, easier to believe than when He had done it, when he had actually given His life? or is the comfort greater when He says that He will do it than when He has done it? No love is greater than this, that one gives one's life for another. But when is it easiest to believe, and when is the comfort of faith greatest? when the lover says, 'I will do it', or when he has done it? No, not till he has done it, not till then is doubt made impossible, as impossible as it possibly can be; and only when Christ is offered as the sacrifice of atonement, not till then, is the comfort at hand which makes the doubt of the forgiveness of sins as impossible—yes, as impossible as it possibly can be; for then it is only for faith that this comfort exists.

INDEX

Since the words listed below are most of them key words which recur many times on consecutive pages, the Index indicates only the page where a particular theme begins or re-begins, without purposing to point to every recurrence of a word.